DOSTOEVSKY'S *CRIME AND PUNISHMENT*

OXFORD STUDIES IN PHILOSOPHY AND LITERATURE

PUBLISHED IN THE SERIES

Ibsen's *Hedda Gabler*: Philosophical Perspectives
Edited by Kristin Gjesdal

Shakespeare's *Hamlet*: Philosophical Perspectives
Edited by Tzachi Zamir

Kafka's *The Trial*: Philosophical Perspectives
Edited by Espen Hammer

The Oedipus Plays of Sophocles: Philosophical Perspectives
Edited by Paul Woodruff

Jane Austen's *Emma*: Philosophical Perspectives
Edited by E. M. Dadlez

Dostoevsky's *Crime and Punishment*: Philosophical Perspectives
Edited by Robert Guay

DOSTOEVSKY'S *CRIME AND PUNISHMENT*

Philosophical Perspectives

Edited by Robert Guay

Oxford University Press is a department of the University of Oxford. It furthers the University's objective of excellence in research, scholarship, and education by publishing worldwide. Oxford is a registered trade mark of Oxford University Press in the UK and certain other countries.

Published in the United States of America by Oxford University Press
198 Madison Avenue, New York, NY 10016, United States of America.

Library of Congress Cataloging-in-Publication Data
Names: Guay, Robert, editor.
Title: Dostoevsky's Crime and punishment : philosophical perspectives / edited by Robert Guay.
Other titles: Dostoevsky's Crime and punishment (Guay)
Description: New York, NY : Oxford University Press, [2019] | Includes bibliographical references and index.
Identifiers: LCCN 2018053850 (print) | LCCN 2018060888 (ebook) | ISBN 9780190464059 (Online content) | ISBN 9780190464035 (updf) | ISBN 9780190464042 (epub) | ISBN 9780190464028 (pbk. : alk. paper) | ISBN 9780190464011 (cloth : alk. paper)
Subjects: LCSH: Dostoyevsky, Fyodor, 1821–1881. Prestuplenie i nakazanie. | Dostoyevsky, Fyodor, 1821–1881—Criticism and interpretation. | Dostoyevsky, Fyodor, 1821–1881—Philosophy. | Russian literature—History and criticism. | Philosophy in literature.
Classification: LCC PG3325.P73 (ebook) | LCC PG3325.P73 D67 2019 (print) | DDC 891.73/3—dc23
LC record available at https://lccn.loc.gov/2018053850

1 3 5 7 9 8 6 4 2

Paperback printed by Sheridan Books, Inc., United States of America
Hardback printed by Bridgeport National Bindery, Inc., United States of America

For Anna

CONTENTS

SERIES EDITOR'S FOREWORD

At least since Plato had Socrates criticize the poets and attempt to displace Homer as the authoritative articulator and transmitter of human experience and values, philosophy and literature have developed as partly competing, partly complementary enterprises. Both literary writers and philosophers have frequently studied and commented on each other's texts and ideas, sometimes with approval, sometimes with disapproval, in their efforts to become clearer about human life and about valuable commitments––moral, artistic, political, epistemic, metaphysical, and religious, as may be. Plato's texts themselves register the complexity and importance of these interactions in being dialogues in which both deductive argumentation and dramatic narration do central work in furthering a complex body of views.

While these relations have been widely recognized, they have also frequently been ignored or misunderstood, as academic disciplines have gone their separate ways within their modern institutional settings. Philosophy has often turned to science or mathematics as providing models of knowledge; in doing so it has often explicitly set itself against cultural entanglements and literary devices, rejecting, at least officially, the importance of plot, figuration, and imagery in favor of supposedly plain speech about the truth. Literary study has moved variously through formalism, structuralism, post-structuralism, and cultural studies, among other movements, as modes of approach to a literary text. In doing so it has understood literary texts as sample instances of images, structures, personal styles, or failures of consciousness, or it has seen the literary text as a largely fungible product, fundamentally shaped by wider pressures and patterns of consumption and expectation that affect and figure in non-literary textual production as well. It has thus set itself against the idea that major literary texts productively and originally address philosophical problems of value and commitment precisely through their form, diction, imagery, and development, even while these works also resist claiming conclusively to solve the problems that occupy them.

These distinct academic traditions have yielded important perspectives and insights. But in the end none of them has been kind to the idea of major literary works as achievements in thinking about values and human life, often in distinctive, open, self-revising, self-critical ways. At the same time readers outside institutional settings, and often enough philosophers and literary scholars too, have turned to major literary texts precisely in order to engage with their productive, materially and medially specific patterns and processes of thinking. These turns to literature have, however, not so far been systematically encouraged within disciplines, and they have generally occurred independently of each other.

The aim of this series is to make manifest the multiple, complex engagements with philosophical ideas and problems that lie at the hearts of major literary texts. In doing so, its volumes aim not only to help philosophers and literary scholars of various kinds to find rich affinities and provocations to further thought and work, they also aim to bridge various gaps between academic disciplines and between those disciplines and the experiences of extra-institutional readers.

Each volume focuses on a single, undisputedly major literary text. Both philosophers with training and experience in literary study and literary scholars with training and experience in philosophy are invited to engage with themes, details, images, and incidents in the focal text, through which philosophical problems are held in view, worried at, and reformulated. Decidedly not a project simply to formulate A's philosophy of X as a finished product, merely illustrated in the text, and decidedly not a project to explain the literary work entirely by reference to external social configurations and forces, the effort is instead to track the work of open thinking in literary forms, as they lie both neighbor to and aslant from philosophy. As Walter Benjamin once wrote, "new centers of reflection are continually forming," as problems of commitment and value of all kinds take on new shapes for human agents in relation to changing historical circumstances, where reflective address remains possible. By considering how such centers of reflection are formed and expressed in and through literary works, as they engage with philosophical problems of agency, knowledge, commitment, and value, these volumes undertake to present both literature and philosophy as, at times, productive forms of reflective, medial work in relation both to each other and to social circumstances and to show how this work is specifically undertaken and developed in distinctive and original ways in exemplary works of literary art.

Richard Eldridge
Swarthmore College

CONTRIBUTORS

Caryl Emerson is A. Watson Armour III University Professor Emeritus of Slavic Languages and Literature at Princeton University. Emerson's scholarly interests focus on nineteenth-century Russian literature (Pushkin, Dostoevsky, Tolstoy), Russian music, Mikhail Bakhtin, Soviet-era theater, and the rediscovered Russian modernist Sigizmund Krzhizhanovsky. Her books include *The First Hundred Years of Mikhail Bakhtin* (1997), *The Cambridge Introduction to Russian Literature* (2008), *The Life of Musorgsky* (1999), *Mikhail Bakhtin: Creation of a Prosaics* (1990, co-authored with Gary Saul Morson), and *Boris Godunov: Transpositions of a Russian Theme* (1986).

Rick Anthony Furtak is Associate Professor of Philosophy at Colorado College. Furtak's philosophical interests include the moral psychology of the emotions, the relations between philosophy and literature, and the tradition of existential thought (especially Søren Kierkegaard and his legacy). He is the author of *Wisdom in Love: Kierkegaard and the Ancient Quest for Emotional Integrity* (2005) and *Rilke's "Sonnets to Orpheus": A New English Version,* *with a Philosophical Introduction* (2007), the editor of *Kierkegaard's "Concluding Unscientific Postscript": A Critical Guide* (2010), the co-editor of *Thoreau's Importance for Philosophy* (2012), and the author of *Knowing Emotions: Truthfulness and Recognition in Affective Experience* (2018).

Susanne Fusso is Marcus L. Taft Professor of Modern Languages and Professor of Russian, East European, and Eurasian Studies at Wesleyan University. Fusso is a specialist in nineteenth-century Russian prose, especially Gogol and Dostoevsky. She is the author of *Designing Dead Souls: An Anatomy of Disorder in Gogol* (1993) and *Discovering Sexuality in Dostoevsky* (2006). Her most recent book is *Editing Turgenev, Dostoevsky, and Tolstoy: Mikhail Katkov and the Great Russian Novel* (2017). Her most recent translation is that of Sergey Gandlevsky's autobiographical novel *Trepanation of the Skull* (2014).

Sebastian Gardner has been Professor of Philosophy at University College, London, since 1998. His books include *Irrationality and the Philosophy of Psychoanalysis* (1993), *Kant and the "Critique of Pure Reason"* (1999), and *Sartre's "Being and Nothingness"* (2009). His main research interests lie in Kant, nineteenth-century German philosophy, and aesthetics; he is currently working on the legacy of Kant's Third Critique.

Robert Guay is Associate Professor of Philosophy at Binghamton University, State University of New York, where he has taught since 2006. He works primarily on nineteenth-century European philosophy, especially as it relates to issues of agency, history, and ethics. His work has appeared in the *Oxford Handbook of Nietzsche* (2013), the *Journal of Nietzsche Studies*, the *Edinburgh Critical History of Nineteenth Century Philosophy*, and other venues. He is currently working on a book on Nietzsche's ethical thought.

Garry L. Hagberg is James H. Ottaway Professor of Aesthetics and Philosophy at Bard College and has also held a chair in the School of Philosophy at the University of East Anglia. He is the author of numerous papers at the intersection of aesthetics and the philosophy of language, and his books include *Meaning and Interpretation: Wittgenstein, Henry James, and Literary Knowledge* (1994) and *Art as Language: Wittgenstein, Meaning, and Aesthetic Theory* (1995); his most recent book is *Describing Ourselves: Wittgenstein and Autobiographical Consciousness* (2008). He is editor of *Art and Ethical Criticism* (2008) and *Fictional Characters, Real Problems: The Search for Ethical Content in Literature* (2016) as well as, most recently, *Wittgenstein on Aesthetic Understanding* (2017). Co-editor of *A Companion to the Philosophy of Literature* (2010) and Editor of the journal *Philosophy and Literature,* Hagberg is presently writing a new book on the contribution literary experience makes to the formation of self and sensibility, *Living in Words: Literature, Autobiographical Language, and the Composition of Selfhood,* and editing a volume, *Stanley Cavell on Aesthetic Understanding.*

Randall Havas is Professor of Philosophy at Willamette University. He is the author of *Nietzsche's Genealogy: Nihilism and the Will to Knowledge* (1995) and a number of articles on the notions of agency, individuality, and community in Nietzsche's thought. He is currently working on the role concepts of authority and force play in Nietzsche's account of the will, as well as on the notion of agency in early Buddhism.

Introduction: *Crime and Punishment* as a Philosophical Novel

ROBERT GUAY

A novel is sometimes an occasion for philosophy. It can situate doubts and decisions, assertions and denials, and ideas and deeds in the same landscape as philosophical thinking, somewhere between reflection and wonder; it can make manifest what is otherwise concealed. With *Crime and Punishment,* furthermore, we perhaps even have a distinctively philosophical novel. But what could this amount to? How could a novel, and this novel in particular, be particularly philosophical? Dostoevsky does present us with a reflective, internally divided standpoint trying to figure out the boundaries of its own authority; this might suffice for an affinity to philosophy. This affinity might be a superficial one of rhetoric or mood, however, or there might be some more substantial way in which the novel and philosophy engage in the same enterprise or inform each other.

The essays in this volume do not take on the task of answering these questions. They have their own agendas in relating philosophical (or anti-philosophical) perspectives on *Crime and Punishment*: they are more concerned with persons and voices that occupy the text, their words, and the issues they confront than with general questions about the relationship between philosophy and literature. At the same time, however, we could read these essays as setting out, in the course of offering their perspectives, a diverse range of models for how philosophy and the novel could be in sympathy with one another. I suggest, that is, that they implicitly make a case that taking philosophical perspectives on novels can at the same time be a way of gaining perspectives on philosophy; the novel has as much to say to philosophy as philosophy does to the novel. This introduction will fill out that suggestion, by identifying how the essays' attention to particular elements of human experience might indicate ways in which philosophy and *Crime and Punishment,* at least, might be mutually informing.

Before discussing the essays, however, I want to note how difficult engagement between philosophy and *Crime and Punishment* might be, in spite of their shared interests. If only because there is a "philosophy of . . ." almost anything, they are bound to have overlapping areas of concern. *Crime and Punishment,* however, does seem to approach philosophy on its own territory on occasion: it offers reasoned inquiries, both first-personal and dialogical, about metaphysical and normative commitments. For example, characters express—albeit in specific contexts rather than on a general level—concerns about the kinds of authority that law, religion, and society furnish or fail to furnish, and what the sources of such authority might be. (Taking on these matters is indeed so natural to philosophy that the essays do not even need to accord them treatment as independent topics of discussion; they can be assimilated into philosophical discussions.) We could also take the novel's psychological characterizations as a descriptive enterprise that shares with philosophy an interest in delineating features and processes of the mind. The novel arguably even has its own characteristic epistemic concerns, taking the form of doubts about its own powers of realistic representation.

These shared interests by themselves do little to establish a connection between *Crime and Punishment* and philosophy, however. Both, after all, share features with other kinds of writing and other domains of experience. Without a better account of how philosophy and the novel might speak to each other, we would be left with crude understandings of how the two could be made to fit together. *Crime and Punishment,* for example, *contains* philosophical discourse of a certain sort. But these bits of discourse are, within the novel, necessarily poor examples of philosophy. They are sometimes secondhand tellings from characters who do not understand the ideas they are recounting, sometimes ideas that are not worth being translated into Russian accurately, and in every case ideas that confound and mislead their speakers and auditors. If the philosophical merit of *Crime and Punishment* depended on containing philosophical theory, then it would be judged on poor arguments that are ineffectual in shaping beliefs and actions. *Crime and Punishment* fares badly as a dramatized thought experiment, or as a set of incidents that philosophy could mine for examples, too. The problem with using *Crime and Punishment* as a philosophical construction material is that it does not make clear what the thought experiments are or when they begin or end, if they ever do. The novel does not present us with clear illustrations of puzzles that philosophy could generalize and resolve.

Through the specificity of their examples, however, the essays in this volume give us a variety of models for thinking about a connection. The first essay, Garry L. Hagberg's "Portrayals of Mind: Raskolnikov, Porfiry, and Psychological Investigation in *Crime and Punishment*," examines Dostoevsky's representation of the nature of mind through a series of discussions: on the nature of mental privacy as it is accorded to Raskolnikov, the language of interpersonal engagement between Raskolnikov and Porfiry, the relationship between self-knowledge and knowledge of others, and the affinities between the novel and the philosophical ideas of Wollheim, Moran, and Murdoch, for example. In these discussions, Hagberg shows that Porfiry's investigation depends on his appreciation for language and his interpretive talents. Porfiry succeeds by virtue of his ability to understand Raskolnikov's linguistic expressions not only for their literal content but for what they reveal about the workings of his mind, and thereby to understand who Raskolnikov is in a way that Raskolnikov himself does not. Much of the drama of the novel, then, can be framed as the investigation of the crime merging into the process of gaining a view of Raskolnikov's mind. And this view of another's mind comes about through discourse in its embodied, social situation.

The philosophical claims that Hagberg finds implicit in the novel, then, concern the social and discursive character of the mind. Even mental privacy, as it appears in Raskolnikov's case, depends on a context of shared outlooks from which unstable, unsettled self-descriptions can be produced. Self-knowledge, in general, becomes available through public interconnectedness: characters rely on each other for their abilities to produce and confirm their conceptions of each other's minds. Mental contents, rather than being available in a self-transparent inner space, take shape through discursive engagement: the characters understand their thoughts and feelings, and what they mean, by talking about them. Language, in this picture, is not a neutral medium of communication but rather "can assume a life of its own." Words, once spoken, depart from the speaker's intentional control and enter into a shifting public process of interpretation.

Of course, mental privacy for Raskolnikov or Porfiry might be fundamentally different than it is for us. So how, if at all, does the novel do the philosophical work of making points about the mind rather than confining its philosophy to the inside of its fictional world? For Hagberg, *Crime and Punishment* does philosophical work by offering two interconnected sets of reminders: one about the nature of mind and the other about the workings of language.

According to the former set of reminders, showing the elusive character of mind reveals, at the same time, that our depictions of mind play a constitutive role in what it is. The mind's capacities and processes are in part a function of how we represent them, and thus the novel, by contributing to the mind's depiction, contributes to our own possibilities for self-representation. The other set of reminders operates, similarly, not by furnishing a priori grounds for an explanatory theory, but by calling our attention to the very specific ways in which language may function. Here the philosophical work is to resist the philosophical temptation to abstraction and overgeneralization, and focus instead on the variety of ways in which language may work within our lives.

Emotional transformation is the central issue in the second chapter, Rick Anthony Furtak's "Love, Suffering, and Gratitude for Existence: Moral and Existential Emotions in *Crime and Punishment*." Furtak presents the main problem of *Crime and Punishment* as Raskolnikov's development of a mature moral perspective. Raskolnikov is thoughtful and prone to compassion and generosity, but it takes him the length of the novel to acknowledge his crime as such and arrive at an empathetic connection to others. Strangely, then, it remains puzzling both how it could have taken him so long to achieve moral growth and how he managed to do so at all. On Furtak's account, what made Raskolnikov's development difficult but possible was that it turned on coming to an affective realization that sometimes ran counter to his rational reflections or consciously endorsed beliefs. Raskolnikov's starting point was a general antipathy to human existence: he wished to avoid vulnerability to grief and suffering by transcending emotional attachments. To move away from this characteristic detachment, he needed to develop his capacity for love and care, but that carried the cost of making himself susceptible to loss. Nevertheless, his acknowledgment of guilt allowed him to resolve his emotional ambivalence toward human existence. He was able to accomplish this by accepting Sonya's love and following her example of "existential trust" in the face of misfortune.

On Furtak's reading, then, *Crime and Punishment* engages philosophically in at least two ways. First, it represents the complexity of affective attitudes in their relationships to conscious reflection, decision-making, and moral growth. To make his case, Furtak uses a number of distinctions: between emotional dispositions and specific, episodic emotional states and between moral emotions and existential emotions, for example. He also takes note of a distinctive category of higher-order emotions and coordinates this conceptual repertory with the roles that emotions play at important junctures in the novel. The novel accordingly offers a richness of emotional characterization that can provide insight into the nature of emotions and their role in a human life. The novel's other main philosophical engagement is with the existential concerns that Raskolnikov raises and Sonya addresses. Even when these concerns are not spelled out in such a general form, the characters' thoughts and decisions turn on their attitudes toward life as a whole, what would make it worth living, what kinds of commitments can be sustained in it, and what kind of standing their deepest commitments might possess. In presenting the simplest concerns, the novel becomes inescapably philosophical by summoning reflection on human existence as a whole.

The novel can carry out philosophical work, then, by remaining at its own level of specificity. In representing the particularities of emotional engagement, *Crime and Punishment* shows how emotions are interconnected within a human life. There is no logical connection between, say, trust, care, love, and, guilt; in principle it is possible to experience each without any experience of the others. But in lives that require emotional commitments for access to distinctively human values, and in which maturity comes about through a gradual process of affective development, emotions are connected in a way that the novel can represent. The novel, furthermore, presents a problematic that might not be accessible in more abstract terms, of what it means to affirm a finite human existence. This question, at once existential and hermeneutic, arises for Raskolnikov and Sonya. It resists theoretical treatment since it involves caring and concern, but the novel manages, at least, to make the topic available for reflection.

My own essay, "Crime and Expression: Dostoevsky on the Nature of Agency," concerns what it means for a person to perform an action, and thus for an event to somehow count as distinctively belonging to that person. I contend that in *Crime and Punishment* various characters manifest familiar, commonsense ways of understanding the relationship between doer and deed: the women, for example, represent the importance of choice, Marmeladov represents the importance of inner motivational states, and Svidrigaylov the importance of control. There are, furthermore, two distinctive features of Dostoevsky's presentation of the characters' attempt at agency. First, every familiar way of establishing an agent's relationship to her own action fails. The characters satisfy their own implicit conditions for genuine agency. Dunya chooses and Marmeladov is moved by his own sentiments, for example, but their public performances are nevertheless failures. The results of their attempts are not anything that they would recognize as their own; they fail, often dramatically, to establish a connection to their own deeds. The other distinctive feature of Dostoevsky's presentation is that Raskolnikov stands above it all. He reflects on others' modes of activity, over time engages in some version of each one, and attempts novel ways of making himself the author of deeds. Yet, for all that, his failures are the most conclusive: he ends up deeply estranged from his own activity and even renders it more difficult for himself to engage in public deeds again. His concerted, reflective attempts at agency are the biggest failures until the end, when, through confession and forgiveness, he takes on a new relationship to his own activity.

I claim, then, that the novel makes a case for an "expressive" view of agency. Actions, on such a view, are not determined according to antecedently available criteria of what counts as the proper kind of origination or performance. An action, rather, takes shape as such only in its expression. Agency is attributed to persons and their deeds in light of the social context of public performances. This context provides the conditions for an action to make sense as such: especially important is that actions count as such only when agents can acknowledge them as their own and the public meaning of the deeds fits with the agents' sense of their own intentions. Dostoevsky, I also argue, offers a kind of philosophical anthropology of how persons arrive at this capacity. In the novel, at least, there is no rational, reflective path to becoming an agent; the path to eventual success requires, instead, guilt, sacrifice, and forgiveness. Crime, in particular, is exemplary of human agency: one distinguishes oneself as an agent through transgression, and then requires some kind of redemption in order to identify with what one has done.

The novel, of course, does not engage with philosophy by setting out a determinate problem and then offering arguments to establish that agency is in fact expressive. It rather starts from the characters' standpoints and the concerns that they have. From within these standpoints, however, the characters face problems of how to make their own wills effective, and this is how *Crime and Punishment* engages philosophically. It shows that there is no single problem of what it means to be an agent or how to be genuinely involved in one's activity; the nature of the problem is itself part of the problem. The novel's contribution here, then, is inventing meaningful possibilities for success and failure. In this way, it shifts the nature of a solution from finding what relationship holds in all and only instances of genuine action to identifying what could potentially satisfy the demands of persons who wish to find themselves in their activity. Its philosophical accomplishment is articulating and thereby altering what it means to recognize oneself in one's deeds.

The fourth chapter, Sebastian Gardner's "Metaphysical Motivation: *Crime and Punishment* in the Light of Schelling," takes up a range of issues that overlap with those in my chapter, but from the perspective of post-Kantian debates about the metaphysical conditions of human freedom. For Gardner, *Crime and Punishment*'s suspenseful concealment and disclosure of Raskolnikov's motivations raise an issue concerning the possibility of autonomous agency. For Raskolnikov, as for the philosopher F. W. J. Schelling, freedom cannot be specified in merely formal terms, as a kind of lawful self-governance; meaningful freedom, rather, demands a substantive choice between good and evil. Raskolnikov's murders are thus best seen as an experiment that seeks to establish the actuality of evil, and thereby to furnish Raskolnikov with metaphysical knowledge of human freedom. The enigmatic character of Raskolnikov's decision-making stems from its metaphysical character: his motivations do not make sense along any ordinary lines, because his actions are not taken up from any familiar, finite standpoint. The novel portrays Raskolnikov's projects as ultimately misguided, however. In attempting to demonstrate the reality of evil, he accorded his own will independence in resolving the matter. The novel shows this assumed independence as a failure; he must gradually come to the realization that his ability to choose goodness requires orienting himself to something that transcends individual will and reflection.

Gardner's reading renders *Crime and Punishment* a fundamentally philosophical enterprise. Raskolnikov's task is to carry out an experiment that, like all experiments, aims at producing knowledge; this knowledge transcends his own individual case to point to the possibility of human freedom in general; and the novel provides an additional vantage point on Raskolnikov's experiment so that we—and perhaps, ultimately, Raskolnikov himself—might properly appreciate its metaphysical significance. Within the novel, freedom requires an effective will that cannot merely be the product of ordinary psychological tendencies or the normal causal determinations of events. There must be a decisive choice, and choice as such is meaningful only against the background of important, substantially opposed alternatives. In order for one to exit from passive determination and choose goodness, this option must stand in contrast to the availability of evil. So the possible pursuit of evil for its own sake is a necessary condition for the possibility of goodness and hence freedom.

For the novel to function philosophically, however, its fictional experiment must be capable of demonstrating something actual about the possibility of human freedom. In Gardner's view, it does this by making impossibilities meaningfully available to us. Through fictional representation, we can encounter Raskolnikov's doomed enterprise on its own terms: whether or not it makes sense as a metaphysical pursuit, the nature of such an attempt comes into view. More generally, *Crime and Punishment* allows us to occupy the practical standpoint from which Raskolnikov tries to become aware of human freedom. Human freedom is opaque to any reflective understanding: to be possible it must transcend the conceptually articulable motivations and influences that ordinarily determine events, for the sake of a substantive choice that has no rational ground. Because freedom is opaque in this way, theoretical representations of it would miss the point. Such representations would subsume freedom into ordinary patterns of psychological motivation. So without a theoretical grasp on freedom, the only way to gain any purchase on it all is to witness it by aesthetic means. The novel's experiment, then, works by giving us access to Raskolnikov and in that way affording us an awareness of something that reflection cannot grasp.

The fifth chapter, Susanne Fusso's "The Family in *Crime and Punishment*: Realism and Utopia," shows how tracing Dostoevsky's conception of the family can inform our understanding of the novel.

The context for *Crime and Punishment*'s conception is the radical critique of the family that one can find in the writings of the "nihilist" generation, especially in Chernyshevsky's novel *What Is to Be Done?* According to this utopian critique, the emancipation of women can bring about a complete transformation of society. Romantic relationships would then be based on truthfulness and love rather than on deceit and money, or made transient in order to rescue individuals from oppressive family life. The consequent transformation of family life would promote privacy and autonomy, which in turn would lead to general moral improvement and radical social change, as individuals would focus on important, socially beneficial projects. Dostoevsky acknowledges the utopian criticism that the traditional family is a coercive trap and alludes in the novel to utopian texts and discussions. But the utopian analysis neglects the suffering of children and the emotional and material comfort of family. Although the traditional family structure is oppressive and irrational, the utopian alternative would also be destructive. This is because the problem with the traditional family is not authority per se, but the dishonest and despotic form that it takes. The suitable realist alternative instead comes with the recognition that in family life, authority has to be balanced with love and obligations; only a non-coercive mutuality makes contentment with one's condition possible. Raskolnikov, accordingly, tries to free himself from the coercion of the family, but is unable to maintain his aloneness. After cutting himself off from his own family, and even, in committing murder, from the human family, he seeks a new family in the Marmeladovs, and only in this voluntary family can he embrace his own life.

The philosophical content of the novel, then, is a kind of antiphilosophy, or at least a rejection of utopian theory-construction. Chernyshevsky's novel promotes a solution to the problems of society; the fiction is employed to advance a program of revolutionary change. But this kind of idealizing theory arrives at its normative demands by neglecting elements of human experience that allow for institutions and relationships to function; by abstracting away from that context, the theory makes prescriptions that could not make anyone's life better. Dostoevsky, of course, does not respond to this by using his novel to promote an alternative social program. But he does portray the limitations of utopian theory in a non-ideal world: part of the novel is concerned with the hopelessness of Raskolnikov's and others' attempts to theorize their way into a better life and better social world. Although theorizing might be dangerous, Dostoevsky does preserve some of the utopian critique. He takes up some of its normative content: the family should be non-coercive and voluntary, based on love rather than merely on biological connection or financial constraints. For Raskolnikov and others, the family that one chooses is what can offer support for emotional health and individual well-being, as long as authority can be balanced with reciprocity and commitment.

Crime and Punishment does not achieve its philosophical (or anti-philosophical) ends, of course, by laying out utopian positions and arguments and then refuting them. Instead it works largely by ridicule, or at least by showing what utopian ideals would look like in any realistic context. The novel shows flawed characters who do not understand the ideas they promote, or who use ideas to excuse unpardonable behavior or serve incidental ends, or who go astray precisely by favoring theory over ordinary sense, or who are too distracted by more pressing concerns to allow for utopian ideals to have any currency in their lives. In the face of limitations and needs, utopian ideals stand little chance of solving problems or directing any meaningful change. What the novel indeed shows, more fundamentally, is that the utopian ideals do not amount to anything within familiar lived experience. *Crime and Punishment* makes the case, indirectly, that the complexities of even fictional experience far exceed what theoretical discourse can accommodate. By setting utopian ideals in relief against the concrete cares of food, washing, sleep, clothing, and companionship, the novel discloses an emptiness to theory-construction that Raskolnikov only slowly comes to realize.

The sixth chapter, Randall Havas's "Raskolnikov Beyond Good and Evil," examines Raskolnikov's motivations with the aim of arguing that a familiar interpretation of them is deficient. According to this familiar interpretation, Raskolnikov aims to step beyond morality so as to both institute and demonstrate his standing as an exceptional person who is thereby free from conventional constraints. Although such a view surfaces among Raskolnikov's passing self-conceptions, the novel shows him to be alienated from the human community; his experience of himself involves working through the details and implications of such a profound alienation rather than trying to establish his own superiority. Havas devotes special attention to the role of Porfiry Petrovich in bringing Raskolnikov to a consciousness of this alienation. Over the course of three conversations, Porfiry undermines Raskolnikov's theoretical account, by which he might have thought himself to be pursuing a rationally purposive project rather than alienating himself further, exposes Raskolnikov's confusions about the demands of individuality, and puts forward the suggestion that Raskolnikov's alienation is religious in character and thus requires confession and repentance in order to remedy it. The conversations move from the nature of the authority of the positive law, which Porfiry himself represents, to the moral demands that Raskolnikov fails to recognize, to religious demands that Porfiry can only point to but that fall outside of his purview. In each conversation, Raskolnikov initially sees the failure of the law to compel his obedience as a failure of its authority, but Porfiry manages to show him that compulsion is not the form that such authority properly takes. Havas elaborates the conflict of interpretations, between stepping beyond morality and overcoming alienation, by analyzing in what sense Raskolnikov's character might be seen as "Nietzschean." Through a series of contrasts he shows that Raskolnikov, unlike Nietzsche, is susceptible to falsely seeing his own identity as dependent on the individual creation of his own original moral outlook rather than as a form of mutuality.

Crime and Punishment, on Havas's reading, thus stakes out philosophical positions on the nature of authority and individuality. For Havas, Raskolnikov's existential troubles stem from his philosophical problems, and in particular his "Platonism" about the nature of authority. Raskolnikov, that is, considers genuine authority—whether moral, legal, or religious—to take the form of self-interpreting rules that somehow apply themselves, without reliance on the interpretive practices of a community or the acknowledgment of their force within a way of life. He does not articulate such a conception; indeed, it might not even make sense. But he looks for some form of authority that is utterly compelling and, failing to find it, first substitutes violence as an alternative and then imagines that he can construct a philosophical theory that establishes his own individuality as indifferent to recognition by others. Raskolnikov attempts to develop a conception of himself according to which his identity is sublimely independent of any social context for its self-evident significance. Indeed, it excludes recognition by others and participation in communal norms as things that would degrade his independence into a form of submission. The novel, however—primarily through Porfiry, but also through Raskolnikov's own failures—shows this self-conception to be unsustainable. Without acknowledging the ordinary ways of carrying on, in terms of which norms make sense, he has no way to substantiate his individuality.

Within the novel, then, Porfiry achieves philosophical ends by frustrating Raskolnikov's attempts to resort to philosophy. Raskolnikov tries to turn his practical problems into intellectual ones that could be solved by developing the right kind of theory. Porfiry, however, obstructs his turn to philosophy by showing him that his theories fail to make sense of particular cases and that he has failed to articulate an outlook that is distinct from that of his community; he has no way of getting outside of the normative picture that he wishes to reject. The novel as a whole also works toward philosophical ends by leading the reader away from Raskolnikov's perspective. According to Havas, *Crime and Punishment* presents Raskolnikov's perspective as a kind of temptation; those who find the novel engaging are likely to sympathize with the idea that standing moral conventions are empty and harmful and that self-realization would require creating an entirely new, self-sufficient vocabulary in terms of which to describe one's life and commitments. The novel shows this as an evasion of responsibility, however: it is an attempt to refuse participation in the social world that one already, inevitably participates in. Raskolnikov's constant evasions and their quick collapses show the reader, much better than a theory of nihilism would, what such a temptation amounts to.

The final chapter, Caryl Emerson's "Bakhtin's Radiant Polyphonic Novel, Raskolnikov's Perverse Dialogic World," takes a different approach than the other essays. Emerson approaches *Crime and Punishment* through a philosophical consideration of Dostoevsky's most influential interpreter, Mikhail Bakhtin, with an eye to reconciling some long-standing tensions. Bakhtin furnished an entire worldview from which to consider Dostoevsky's novels: one that finds in them a plurality of equally weighted voices, without any finalizing authorial intention or other limitation to the open-ended freedom of the characters. And Bakhtin articulated this worldview in terms of a now familiar vocabulary that included, most notably, the terms "dialogical" and "polyphonic." Emerson notes, however, that two sets of challenges have arisen with respect to Bakhtinian readings of Dostoevsky. One is that there seem to be two Bakhtins: a spiritual pan-Christian who is partial to a divine order and a materialist, liberational one who is fascinated by the temporal and carnal.

The other challenge is that Bakhtin's dialogism seems inadequate to the novels themselves. Bakhtin's worldview privileges discourse and ideas over silent events; it treats fictive characters as accessible, independent interlocutors rather than as historically distant cultural artifacts; and it contravenes narrative structure by trying to accord equal importance to every voice. Emerson, however, shows how these challenges can be addressed by properly distinguishing between dialogue and polyphony, and returning the understanding of polyphony to its roots in music.

Emerson brings out this contrast by examining two episodes in the novel: Raskolnikov's internalization of the letter that he receives from his mother in Part One and the moment of rapture between Raskolnikov and Sonya at the end of the Epilogue. The former is a virtuoso example of dialogue, and indeed of "microdialogue." The plurality of voices from the letter are distilled inside of a single consciousness and projected back out onto the world. Dialogue, here, is the medium through which Raskolnikov's openness to others is inverted and fixed into resentment and hate; he interprets the words but distorts their personal connection to him, leaving him isolated and unstable. Others' voices bind him to his own thoughts and his own individualized, impassioned situation. The scene from the Epilogue, by contrast, exemplifies polyphony: dissonant voices preserve their distinctness but resolve into harmonies. Raskolnikov's open possibilities for understanding himself and his relationships to others had tormented him, but in the Epilogue he can embrace his own unfinalizability in the joyful acceptance of another. Polyphony, unlike dialogue, effects reconciliation with what lies outside of itself.

For Emerson, and for Bakhtin, then, *Crime and Punishment* is philosophical through and through. The novel manifests a dialogical picture of personhood, which is accompanied by its particular ethics and metaphysical commitments. A person, in this picture, is a point of view on the world that develops out of its own words and social interactions. In the process of such development, spontaneous creativity emerges out of a worldly, embodied context. Because of this rootedness, and because creative development has no principled limit, persons can never be fully comprehended or completed. The ethics that goes with such a picture is one of recognition of and connectedness to others, as one depends on those others to make one's own thought articulate and reconcile oneself to who one is. This picture, furthermore, is committed to an existential freedom that is sustained by its hope that the passage of time offers the potential to transcend present limitations.

These essays, of course, do much more than suggest various modes of philosophical engagement. Like *Crime and Punishment* itself, they have other interlocutors and other, more specific interests. They share with the novel, however, a depth of interest in human understanding and human experience. So in spite of all the differences between philosophy and fiction, there are these common interests to make a sustained conversation possible.

Chapter 1

Portrayals of Mind

Raskolnikov, Porfiry, and Psychological Investigation in Crime and Punishment

GARRY L. HAGBERG

I. INTRODUCTION

How the mind is to be depicted—that is, how the mind will form an image of itself—has of course been central to philosophy from the outset, and it remains so. And a conceptual model or philosophical picture of the mind, once installed deeply and beneath reflective reconsideration in our cognitive stock, powerfully shapes how we will then picture or imagine (a) the contents of a mind, (b) the individual or (as we spatially describe it) interior knowledge of those contents, and (c) the possibility of another knowing, or coming to know, those contents. Thus Plato's tripartite soul, Aristotle's mind-in-action, Descartes's dualism, Hume's bundle theory, Kant's transcendental unity of apperception, Freud's psychic divisions, Skinner's behaviorism, contemporary enactivism, and numerous other conceptions of the mind or the cognizing self, once taken on board, will determine how we model both self-knowledge and knowledge of others.

Dostoevsky was profoundly engaged with these issues from a literary point of view.

In the second part of this essay, I will set out Dostoevsky's portrait of the mind of Raskolnikov; this is the mind into which the lawyer-detective Porfiry will, with instructive intricacy, imaginatively enter. In the third part, I will look into the language within which Dostoevsky exactingly captures the nature and character of the interpersonal engagement with which one mind comes to know another's mental contents. Then, in the fourth part, I will offer a retrospective of the ground Dostoevsky has covered in terms of the mind and the mind's language, assessing Dostoevsky's profound contributions to our understanding of these issues in connection with three recent philosophical authors.

II. CONCEPTIONS OF MIND

Solipsism, as the extreme form of other-minds skepticism, paints a picture of ultimate seclusion, where that seclusion is metaphysical: on such a picture, the human mind never genuinely or directly reaches beyond its own internal borders. Dostoevsky, from the first page of *Crime and Punishment,* begins to address this picture. He shows that a comprehensible or intelligible conception of mental privacy will in an ineliminable sense be public: we can indeed recede into privacy, but only of a kind that depends for its very intelligibility on a fundamental public interconnectedness. Introducing Raskolnikov, he writes,

> He had cut himself off from everybody and withdrawn so completely into himself that he now shrank from every kind of contact. (1)[1]

Shrinking from contact is a concept that internally depends, as is evident from its very phraseology, on contact; we understand the privacy that any such retreat manifests within a presumed public context. (Here Wittgenstein and Dostoevsky—whom Wittgenstein read in a close and sustained way over many years, including reading him aloud to the village religious authority—have something at a deep conceptual level in common.)[2]

Dostoevsky next gives us an initial glimpse of the content within that retreated psychic enclosure. Raskolnikov says to himself:

> I wonder what men are most afraid of... Any new departure, and especially a *new word*—that is what they fear most of all . . . But I am talking too much. (2)

A word—that is, language—can be a threat, a threatening instrument. It can run out of control; and exemplifying what he is describing, Raskolnikov here quickly perceives his own language as running beyond his own control. This opens a theme on which we will see many variations, and even at this preliminary stage one sees that for the mind Dostoevsky is painting, language is not merely a passive tool picked up or discarded at will, picked up and used precisely and only as one wants. Dostoevsky is now hinting that language can assume a life of its own, and thus can be much more than an inert transducer of one's intentions. And if language can run beyond voluntary control, so can (what we in a picture-driven way too easily think of as) privately or inwardly controlled thought. Raskolnikov, feeling intense fear at the thought of losing control of his actions (and committing the murder he was carrying within him), realizes that he has, in this moment of powerfully imagining that action, lost control of his thought:

> "If I feel so afraid at this moment, what would it be like if I had really brought myself to the point of doing *the thing itself*?" he thought involuntarily, as he came up to the fourth floor. (4)

And then, interestingly, he retreats *from himself*. He has already done this once by stepping back from his own cognition, but now he retreats from, or in a sense attempts to relinquish by internal cognitive force, his own contemplated future action, actually speaking outwardly against his own inner thought. Dostoevsky writes:

> Raskolnikov went out in great confusion. The confusion grew and grew, and on his way downstairs he stopped more than once as if suddenly struck by something or other. When at last he reached the street, he broke out:
>
> "Oh God, how repulsive! Can I possibly, can I possibly . . . no, that's nonsense, that's ridiculous!" he broke off defensively. "How could such a horrible idea enter my mind? What vileness my heart seems capable of! The point is, that it is vile, filthy, horrible, horrible! . . . And for a whole month I have . . ." (7)

The murderous idea that he attempts to declare as alien ("stopped as if suddenly struck"), as coming from a source outside himself ("enter my mind"), he actually knows—against this attempted self-deception—to be his own, to have emanated from within. And with this internally destabilizing yet self-defining thought, he again retreats from the outside world in a manner that again depends on it:

> He walked along the pavement like a drunken man, not seeing the passers by and sometimes bumping into them. He had left that street behind before he succeeded in collecting his wits. He looked round and saw that he was standing outside a public house. (7)

This is a mind in a condition that, momentarily emerging from an abstracted haze, discovers to its surprise where it is. And it simultaneously is a mind that, not being in control of its possessions or in control of what enters it, can discover to its surprise what it contains: "Even at this moment he dimly perceived, however, that there was something morbid in his sudden recovery of spirits" (8). But as we shall see below, this intimates a related larger fact: neither is he in control of what exits his mind. There is a kind of dualism contained within this mental portrait—but it is very unlike Cartesian dualism. What is this difference, precisely?

Dostoevsky portrays this mind as one that is easily recognized as intelligent ("and you're very clever" (26)) and one that conceives of its own primary labor as intellectual ("What sort of work?" "'Thinking', he replied seriously, after a moment's pause" (27)). And while he is in troubled moments separated from his own mind, it is fundamentally his self-styled intellectualism that serves to separate him from others. The privacy he exemplifies is thus relational ("relational privacy" would be an oxymoron on the Cartesian picture): the distinct dualism in play here is both doubled and necessarily situated or contextual; that is, he observes some of his own mental contents from an inner distance, just as he distantly observes others outwardly where that spectatorial gulf yields alienation. And as spectator to himself, he and Porfiry can ultimately stand, if in a special sense, side by side, viewing his mind together.

Raskolnikov views a moving letter from his loving and devoted mother from a distance—as if viewing himself as he reads it in order to inspect his own response (36). And later, while witnessing internally "the whirlwind of thoughts spinning in his brain," he stands back from himself to observe, "it is true that one must go slowly and carefully with a man if one wants to study him thoroughly" (39). That is, he is not united with, or absorbed by, his own mental whirlwind; rather, in this state, he contemplates the requisite patience with which one must come to understand the contents of another human mind—as if he foresees what Porfiry calls his "method." But still more than that: Raskolnikov is a character who, not in control of his own mental contents or of their containment, here describes what his own self-scrutiny would require were he to achieve full self-understanding. Just as we may not be transparent to each other, he sees here that he is not transparent unto himself. And Dostoevsky is dramatically showing, if in his extreme case, that we as complexly minded persons are similarly not transparent unto ourselves.

Raskolnikov is witnessing within his mind the slow growth of something he cannot control: "Long, long ago his present anguish had first stirred within him, and had grown and accumulated," and finally, now, this inner stirring "concentrated itself into the form of a wild, fantastic and terrible question, that tortured his emotions and his reason with its irresistible demands to be answered" (42–43). This unanswered question within is the question of who and what he shall be as a function of his self-will. Dostoevsky is here painting in very bold strokes: everyone at a young age faces this question at least to some degree, but for Raskolnikov it is a (self-deceiving) question of whether he will rise above the commonplace and by transcending morality show himself to be what he (misguidedly) regards as Napoleonic in stature. If, as he reflects, ethical standards of society are mere paper-thin conventions waiting for towering figures to sweep aside the appearance of universal legitimacy and reveal them for what they are, he feels an inverted moral duty to do precisely that. Murder would be the extreme act with the densest significance packed into it. And there is one more aspect powerfully in play here in the textual subterrain: Raskolnikov already commented on the danger of words, of language, and the way in which they can be used as instruments of destruction as well as of instruction. Here, what he is actually contemplating is which words he will employ to create himself, which words he will make fit in yet another doubled way, that is, by (a) choosing the words ("Napoleonic," "above the shepherded masses," etc.) to which he will make his actions conform, and (b) choosing the actions to which those words will then, after the fact, correspond. What Dostoevsky has depicted here is a sort of self-descriptive/self-creative bootstrapping. To murder would answer his question—if, that is, it lifted him to a superhuman place.

So to review: Dostoevsky's mental portrait is of a mind distanced from itself, unsettled into or uprooted from stabilizing self-descriptions, and further destabilized by a ruinous sense of the utter arbitrariness of moral conventions and that morality's attendant language. Everything that we have considered so far describes a person who cannot find himself in his own cognition, in his own words.

Psychic unity lost, stability of self-description across time unavailable, self-defining ownership of his ideas everywhere in question, and the incessant and inwardly threatening "question" above all work together to demand a resolution—which he presumes will come only in the form of resolute self-defining action. Dostoevsky, in showing the desperation of a character unable to achieve the real thing—that is, genuinely and experientially earned, rooted and committed identity—shows how a mind in this state will flailingly grasp for that rooted identity's thin simulacrum. And indeed precisely now is the moment this mind grasps for resolution like a drowning man:

> He had learnt, suddenly and quite unexpectedly, that at seven o'clock the next day Lizaveta, the old woman's sister and only companion, could be out, and that meant that at seven o'clock in the evening the old woman *would be at home alone.*
>
> It was only a few steps farther to his lodging. He went in like a man condemned to death. He did not reason about anything, he was quite incapable of reasoning, but he felt with his whole being that his mind and will were no longer free, and that everything was settled, quite finally. (59)

It is of special significance that the falseness of the self-definition and its actual instability are captured in microcosm by Dostoevsky in what, with Raskolnikov's words not a bit more in control, he has Raskolnikov say in the seconds before he murders the elderly woman with the axe: "He had not intended to say this, but it seemed to come of its own accord" (73). Indeed, he is so lost unto himself that in the act he was "hardly conscious of what he was doing, and almost mechanically" struck the blow (73). And it is only minutes before the profound falseness of the resolution to act is hammering at his mind from the inside: his having now also murdered Lizaveta when she arrived unexpectedly, "The terror that possessed him had been growing greater and greater, especially after this second, unpremeditated murder" (76), and worse, "Disjointed scraps and fragments of ideas floated through his mind, but he could not seize one of them, or dwell upon any, in spite of all his efforts" (83). With these descriptions of mental life—the extreme opposite of newfound, stabilized, mind-and-language integrity and composure—we as readers understand that "He wanted to get away as quickly as possible." (76) But we understand as well that, of course, there is no getting away for him: his mind will come with him.

Dostoevsky, in his continuous development of the picture of this mind, returns time and again to one central element of human selfhood: our relations to our words. Wittgenstein, Austin, and Cavell have investigated this matter with analytical acuity and humane depth. If in a different idiom, Dostoevsky has anticipated and joined this area of linguistic philosophy. So we understand still more of Raskolnikov when Dostoevsky gives us this as Raskolnikov's exchange with the chief clerk (Zametov) of the police office:

> "You're mad!" said Zametov, also for some reason in a whisper, and recoiled suddenly from Raskolnikov. The latter's eyes were glittering, he had grown shockingly pale, and his upper lip

> trembled and twitched. He leaned as near as possible to Zametov and began moving his lips, but no sound came from them; they remained like this for half a minute. He knew what he was doing, but he could not restrain himself. A terrible word trembled on his lips, as the bolt had trembled *then* on the door: now, now, the bolt will give way; now, now, the word will slip out; oh, only to say it!
>
> "And what if it was I who killed the old woman and Lizaveta?" he said suddenly, and—came to his senses.
>
> Zametov looked at him wildly, and went as white as a sheet. He smiled crookedly.
>
> "Can it really be so?" he said, in a barely audible tone. Raskolnikov looked furiously at him.
>
> "Admit that you believed it! Yes! You did, didn't you?"
>
> "Not at all! Now less than ever!" said Zametov hastily.
>
> "You're caught at last! The cock-sparrow is caught! If you believe it now less than ever, that means that you believed it before!" (159)

The glittering eyes, the face gone pale, the upper lip trembling and twitching remind us that speech is embodied, that speech acts are always within a sense-determining circumstance, within a personal and social history, within an evolving language-game, and that gesture, facial expressivity, and tone of voice are not separable from them or only contingently added to them after the fact. They are *of* the verbal-human expression and not mere presentational decorations of it (and one might suggest that the philosophy of language forgets what Dostoevsky is showing about linguistic expressivity in this novel to its peril). We see that saying something very close to a person is significantly different than saying it from a usual distance. We recognize a severed or troubled relation between a person and his words when his lips move with no sound forthcoming—divided against himself, he is both holding something back and forcing something out. And thirty seconds of this shows the extremity of this mental condition—duration functions as a contributor to meaning and to understanding. This mind makes the connection between the bolt on the door and the "bolt" of his lips about to speak; both trembling, the former gave way and murder immediately ensued. The latter will momentarily give way and a rhetorically densely pressured confession (now grasping for this version of self-stabilization—"oh, only to say it!") will immediately ensue. Finding words that sit on the border between holding back and forcing out, he half-confesses in the form of a hypothetical question ("What if . . . ?"). And it is this utterance that brings him, at least momentarily, to his senses—knowing its danger, he nevertheless feels it as half relief. Zametov's wild look at him, the blood now as quickly draining from his face, and his smiling crookedly together establish both the background and the expressive-performative aspects of his words—which Zametov delivers as a question in response to a question with its near-inaudibility saturating its significance: "Can it really be so?" But the exchange closes with clear seeing as to how language is actually functioning here in comprehending the mind and the present sensibility of the would-be transcendent murderer: throughout these exchanges, Raskolnikov scrutinizes meaning and argues, not from what is explicitly said, but from implication. And Porfiry's work over many years has prepared him, and has him very well rehearsed, for the role of Socratic midwife for the delivery of Raskolnikov's maximally pressured mental content. Living inside a world of implication, later, Porfiry will cleverly say, "He must have a very serious reason for getting so angry over a word" (239).

III. INTERSUBJECTIVE KNOWLEDGE

One can imagine the alarm the murderer suddenly feels when, being taken to meet Porfiry, Raskolnikov's friend Razumikhin says,

"He will be very, very, very pleased to meet you. I have told him a lot about you at different times . . . I was talking about you only yesterday. Come on! . . . So you knew the old woman?" (232). A frantic mind inside this web will naturally and urgently think as a bundle of cognition: (a) Pleased for what reason? (b) What exactly does that mean, given that Porfiry is an investigator? And (c) what exactly have you said to him about me, that is, what implications have you put in play, and how will I negotiate them and maintain control over them when I will shortly be learning of them, or trying to deduce them, at the very moment Porfiry speaks? Or perhaps (d) it will be he, a seasoned investigator, who is maintaining control? And (e) what are you doing putting these thoughts concerning Porfiry the investigator meeting me together with my having known the old woman who was murdered?

But on their entering Porfiry's passageway together, we wonder if Razumikhin is deliberately speaking in doubled meaning, performing one speech act inside another. Razumikhin says:

> "He's a little awkward. I don't mean that he's not well-bred; when I say he is awkward I mean it in another respect. He is an intelligent fellow, very intelligent, he's nobody's fool, but he is of a rather peculiar turn of mind . . . He is incredulous, sceptical, cynical. He likes to mislead people, or rather to baffle them . . . Well, it's an old and well-tried method . . . He knows his business, knows it very well . . . Last year he investigated and solved a case, another murder, where the scent was practically cold. He is very, very anxious to make your acquaintance!" (235–236)

Is he describing, or warning, or doing both by wrapping the latter inside the former? Or, more subtly, is he performing the verbal equivalent of laying one transparency over another that has the same figure inscribed upon it so that, once stacked and aligned, they appear as one transparency? That is, is he, as a hypothetical, placing the warning indiscernibly inside the description in case his friend Raskolnikov is actually guilty, so that if he is guilty he will see it, and if not, not? This of course is further destabilizing, and it is with Raskolnikov in this interpretively unsure condition that the brilliant Porfiry exudes the daunting sense of a person who sees very much more than he says—or than he says directly.

Dostoevsky captures in high resolution the acuity of mutual observation in their first exchange, this first movement of their encounter. Raskolnikov, trying to conceal himself beneath appearance, repeatedly tries too hard and then inwardly berates himself for it; at one point we find him "trying to seem as embarrassed as possible" (240) about his financial situation, where the "acting" aspect layers over the top of the reality just as Razumikhin's warning or threat layered over his description of Porfiry. And it is not long into this exchange before " 'He knows!' flashed through his brain like lightning" (241). But from this point forward and for some time, Raskolnikov is in truth trapped in uncertainty—it is as if his earlier lack of resolution has chased him into this encounter, and he oscillates between believing and not (or sometimes not quite) believing that Porfiry knows his guilt. And so he asks Porfiry, "How do you come to be so observant?" (242), trying to make this sound like a compliment and a genial inquiry but in truth trying to glean from his answer to this question Porfiry's "method" so as to better determine what Porfiry might and might not know.

Dostoevsky follows all of the preceding with what can only be called an astonishing, virtuoso depiction of a tortured mental state—this is Raskolnikov not speaking outwardly but thinking to himself and so is (in the public sense discussed above) private:

> "What is most significant is that they don't even attempt concealment; there is no standing on ceremony! How did you come to

> talk about me to Nikodim Fomich, if you knew nothing of me? It comes to this, they don't even want to hide that they are after me like a pack of hounds! They spit in my face quite openly!" He was trembling with fury. "Well, go straight to the point, don't play with me like a cat with a mouse! That is really uncivilized, Porfiry Petrovich, and perhaps I won't put up with it any longer . . . I will stand up and blurt out the whole truth in your faces; you shall see how I despise you! . . ." He was breathing with difficulty. "But what if it is all my imagination? What if it is a delusion, what if I am quite mistaken, and it is simply my inexperience that makes me lose my temper and fail to keep up this wretched role I am playing? Perhaps it was all unintentional? All their words are quite ordinary, but there is something in them . . . All of them might be said at any time, but still there is something. Why did he say so directly 'in *her* room'? Why did Zametov add that I talked *cleverly*? Why do they take the tone they do? Yes . . . the tone . . . Razumikhin just sat there; why didn't he notice anything? That innocent booby never does anything. I'm feverish again! . . . Did Porfiry wink at me, or not? What nonsense; why should he wink? Are they trying to work on my nerves, I wonder, or are they just laughing at me? Either it's all a delusion or they know!" (244)

Raskolnikov does not know the contents of Porfiry's mind—he does not know what Porfiry knows. And yet he feels in a real sense the presence of Porfiry, the psychological investigator, inside his own mind; he strongly senses that, of Porfiry's words, "there is something in them" and that the tone means something beyond the reach of the words themselves. And was there actually a wink from the cat to the mouse? Are they laughing inwardly? As the next variation on the theme of desperate but thin or un-rooted resolution, he leaps to this thought: "Oh no! I shall not give myself away! Really, you have no facts yet, all this is only supposition! No, produce some facts!" (244).

There are places in the text, powerfully instructive about language and the multiple ways we use it, where Porfiry and Raskolnikov are both almost entirely in the realm of implication beyond what is being explicitly said ("Raskolnikov smiled again. He had at once grasped what they were driving at, and what they wished to push him into saying" (248–249)); Dostoevsky is portraying a kind of double-consciousness by showing a kind of double-language in action. In philosophy, this is an extreme form of Gricean implicature,[3] but it is here conjoined to the Austinian[4] locutionary act of speaking the sentences that house the illocutionary act of trying to push him into a slip, ideally provoking a (perlocutionary) confession. (I see this as an extreme form of Gricean implicature because the speakers, both "cat" and "mouse," are here thinking of the unspoken implications as the primary thing and the literal sentences as secondary.)

What I will call the second movement of the investigation begins with a question, one that moves the function of the words into the realm of the explicit, that can no longer be suppressed: "'Do you wish to interrogate me officially, with all the formalities?' sharply asked Raskolnikov" (256). It was Wittgenstein who emphasized the connection between aspect-perception, or seeing-as, and meaning in language;[5] for Wittgenstein, the way of seeing, the way of making connections, the way of organizing and interrelating what we say and what we know was powerfully determinative of meaning—that is, sentences do not on Wittgenstein's understanding carry their invariant meanings within themselves.[6] Having been politely ushered out of Porfiry's rooms, and now outside, on being asked by his friend about admitting anything, Raskolnikov says, "Any man with even a scrap of intelligence or experience will be sure to try to admit, as far as possible, all material facts that cannot be avoided; only he will look for other reasons for them, turn them to reveal special and unexpected facets, which will give them a different meaning, and place them in a new light" (259). Raskolnikov believes he can control Porfiry with his knowledge of other reasons and unexpected facets and new light. But in this second movement, we as readers see that Porfiry is (a) a master of this very knowledge and its sophisticated employment, (b) a microscopically discerning observer of Raskolnikov's failed attempts to manipulate his (Porfiry's) thought by these means, and thus (c) able to discern the truth about Raskolnikov both in and through Raskolnikov's attempts to recast admitted facts. He sees reality behind, or in a special sense through, appearance. And Porfiry knows that Raskolnikov's superiority complex blinds him to this.

Thus, when he is back to visit Porfiry again, his attention darts outward and inward in turns:

> "I think you said yesterday that you wished to question me . . . officially . . . about my acquaintance with the . . . murdered woman," began Raskolnikov again. "Why did I put in that *I think?*" flashed through his mind. "And why am I so worried at having put it in?" came in another flash. (320)

Following the planned murder, he was to have been in an exalted state towering above the commonplace as a visionary member of the few among thousands of millions; the true result is that he can barely speak, cannot focus, and cannot be fully present because of a severely distancing, ever more neurotic self-monitoring.

Porfiry, seeing into this all the more deeply as the second movement of their verbal dance progresses, now feigns surprise at Raskolnikov's demand that he ask him straight out whatever questions he has ("Good Lord! What are you talking about? What is there for me to question you about?" (322)). And he delivers this reply, theatrically, with a sudden tone of increased concern for Raskolnikov, reassuring him and begging him not to upset himself. Because it is an intricate move in a highly sophisticated language-game, this—as it is perfectly designed to do—upsets Raskolnikov now still more while forcing him to play along with the appearances they both know to be false, thus fraying his nerves and exhausting him to near the breaking point. And throughout this exchange, Porfiry "had been running on without a break, now throwing off meaningless empty phrases, now slipping in a few enigmatic words" (324), so that Raskolnikov has been forced to remain imprisoned within a whirl of unsettled interpretation while pretending not to be. And also: "He [Porfiry] was almost running about the room with his fat little legs moving faster and faster, his eyes fixed on the ground, and his right hand thrust behind his back, while his left gesticulated ceaselessly, making various gestures that were always extraordinarily out of keeping with his words" (324). *Making various gestures that were always extraordinarily out of keeping with his words*: Dostoevsky has Porfiry embodying, indeed acting out, the doubled conversation here, giving to the now nearly deranged Raskolnikov strong gestural signs in front of his face that communicate the presence of thought that is not contained within, or reducible to, the words Porfiry is uttering.

It was Wittgenstein who wrote that a philosophical problem takes the form "I cannot find my way about."[7] Raskolnikov, trapped in Porfiry's web, has what one can see here as the most extreme philosophical problem: What does all this mean? What does this spoken paragraph, this sentence, this word mean? What are these gestures, and what do they convey? And most extreme of all: What is meaning, and how is its determinate content established? One could say: cannot find his way about. Or: *lost.*

The third movement begins with Porfiry at last explicitly articulating his "method"; he sets it out at length, and it is a study in language pretending to be utterly overt that in truth carries a torrent of submerged meaning. Porfiry says:

> "[T]hese are all special cases, I agree; and the present case is really special! But you ought to bear it in mind, my dear Rodion Romanovich, that the average case, the case for which all the

> legal forms and rules are devised, which they are calculated to deal with, when they are written down in the textbooks, does not exist at all, because every case, every crime, for example, as soon as it really occurs, at once becomes a quite special case, and sometimes it is absolutely unlike anything that has ever happened before. Very comical things of that kind sometimes occur. Now, if I leave one gentleman quite alone, if I don't arrest him or worry him in any way, but if he knows, or at least suspects, every minute of every hour, that I know everything down to the last detail, and am watching him day and night with ceaseless vigilance, if he is always conscious of the weight of suspicion and fear, he is absolutely certain to lose his head. He will come to me of his own accord, and perhaps commit some blunder, which will provide, so to speak, mathematical proof, like two and two make four—and that is very satisfactory. This may happen even with a boorish peasant, all the more with people of our sort, the contemporary intellectuals, with their one-sided development. Because, my dear chap, a very important point is understanding what side of a man's nature has been developed. And the nerves, the nerves, you seem to have forgotten them. Nowadays, they are all sick, and fine-drawn, and irritable! . . . And everybody is so full of spleen! And I tell you, in its way that provides a mine of information! And why should I worry if a man goes freely about town! Let him! Let him be at large for a time; I know that he is my prey, and that he cannot escape me. (325–326)

And then Porfiry adds the line most terrifying to Raskolnikov, words showing the special way in which Porfiry is now undeniably present and in a sense almost mechanically operating inside his mind: "the point isn't that he won't run away because he has nowhere to run to, but that *psychologically* he won't escape" (326). Finally fully exploding, Raskolnikov announces that he will not permit any person to laugh in his face and torment him, first shouting repeatedly, "I will not permit it" (329), then saying it more softly, and finally saying it—having realized that this is an empty repudiation and that he is no more in control of any part of the situation than he has been in control of any part of his mind—as a defeated, hopeless, whisper (330).

And there is one final powerfully telling encounter in the third movement: later, when they meet yet again, Porfiry sits "in dignified silence," precipitating a "new wave of terror" in Raskolnikov (432). It precipitates this terror precisely because, almost through a kind of clairvoyant control, Porfiry in his silence recreates the highly pressured empty space for endless interpretation—the space of psychological torture in which Raskolnikov could not find his way about. This is for him all too like being menacingly shown by a prison guard the space of solitary confinement. The prevention of that confinement can only—he sees all too clearly—be achieved by the one and only act Porfiry has left open: confession. After asking his mother to love him regardless of anything she may hear about him (494), he takes himself, unable to focus or really think other than to disorientedly observe passing visual sensations, to the authorities, where, looking troubled, he is offered a glass of water. "Raskolnikov waved aside the water and spoke quietly and brokenly, but distinctly. *'It was I who killed the old woman and her sister, Lizaveta, with an axe, and robbed them'*" (511). Quietly, brokenly, but distinctly, he finds himself in these words, himself unified with his words, himself speaking directly with cathartic sincerity within his words. And: himself without Porfiry.

IV. PHILOSOPHICAL IMPLICATIONS

What then, in review, has Dostoevsky shown more broadly about our language, and our mental life within language, from the microcosmic world of Raskolnikov and Porfiry? (i) Privacy, as it actually functions as a concept on the rough ground[8] of usage, is, in the way we saw above, invariably public (or: privacy takes place within, and not prior to, the public); (ii) language is not an inert instrument solely for the expression of predetermined intentional content; (iii) mental contents are not always under volitional control, and we can (against a simple picture of the mind's furnishings) be alienated from them; (iv) words have meanings that do not stay in place, will not stay still,[9] in such a way that they subtly grow and add or change inflection over time within a circumscribed language-game; (v) words possess ranges of implications beyond what they explicitly state but which can importantly, and sometimes ineliminably, be included within intentional content; (vi) self-description is not anything like (what an oversimplified philosophical picture would suggest) a direct or simple matter of "reading off" inner content; (vii) real resolution is not of the moment, not a fleeting decision; (viii) human verbal expression inseparably includes facial expressivity, tone, complexion, posture and gait, gesture and gesticulation, and so forth through features that an embodied conception of language would incorporate and that a formal analysis of words alone would exclude; (ix) words can be instruments of harm, of psychological intrusion, and of psychological manipulation, and can thus be rationally both seen as dangerous and feared; and (x) entire and extended conversations can proceed on two (or more) levels, with the surface content giving the appearance of moral innocence or guilelessness while the more important submerged content is deliberately psychologically intrusive or harmful. All of these ten features, taken together, function philosophically as what Wittgenstein called "reminders";[10] they keep in view aspects of our verbal lives where that enhanced or expanded view prevents a reductionist or essentialist model of language from which we will then construct an oversimplified theory of linguistic meaning. Thus what literature does here is not so much to polemically refute a certain philosophy as to prevent what Wittgenstein also called "one-sided diets" of a few uniform and too-schematic examples from which we might then prematurely generalize.

But Dostoevsky has shown more about language and our life within it as well: (xi) what can on an initial or cursory glance seem impossible, implausible, or unlikely to say can make perfect sense, and indeed be expected, once we are made to comprehend in a fuller way the sensibility of the individual speaking and the intricate details of the evolved language-game, so what we think of as the "sayable" is not always determinable in advance or from a distance; (xii) implicit meaning can slowly but inexorably gather and focus psychic pressure until it forces its way into the realm of the explicit; (xiii) there is such a thing as what one might call the "texture" of a consciousness, and to grasp this is part of what it is to truly understand a person; (xiv) against the picture of hermetic introspective unity of a kind that is metaphysically guaranteed, one can become a distanced spectator to oneself very much as another is or can be a spectator to oneself; (xv) one can feign false verbal content as a kind of performative that, in the act of feigning, deliberately conveys true intended content; (xvi) gesture, tone, facial expressivity, and so forth as mentioned above, but where this is deliberately out of keeping with the words being uttered, can be similarly performative and meaning-conveying with content antithetical to what is explicitly being said; (xvii) one can be utterly lost to oneself and one's own language while being in full awareness of that self's mental content; (xviii) it can be possible for one to speak inside another's sentences, and one's inhabiting of them can persist; (xix) one can be so awash in the turbulence of constantly shifting or unsettled verbal interpretation or meaning-indeterminacy that one becomes nearly unable to directly listen or directly speak; and (xx) we can be unified, un-unified, and reunified with our words.

All of these twenty observations, taken together, show more broadly that the nature, the contents, the progression, the erosion, and the change of a consciousness are the kinds of things that a literary artist can depict, where that detailed portrait identifies the actual openings and avenues of human understanding that certain philosophical pictures of the mind would have made seem more inaccessible, and inaccessible in a different and metaphysically isolated way, than such understanding actually is.

But before closing, I want to connect this discussion, if briefly, to some issues as investigated by a few other philosophers and offer three observations. Richard Wollheim distinguished between two conceptions of meaning in the criticism and interpretation of a work of art: on the first, meaning is viewed as "something that is to be discovered" and "on the other it is something that is to be constructed and then imposed by the critic."[11] He writes:

> I shall call the two conceptions of the critical aim that are generated by these two interpretations of meaning or understanding Retrieval and Revision respectively. Where meaning is thought of as something to be discovered, the critical aim is Retrieval: where meaning is something to be constructed and imposed and (presumably) done so afresh from age to age, the critical aim is Revision.
>
> My own instincts go in the direction of Retrieval, and the crucial consideration as far as I can see is that Retrieval is, and Revision isn't, an appropriate response to the central fact about art: that it is an intentional manifestation of mind.

One could say: Porfiry, as the psychological investigator he is, is a connoisseur of Retrieval. And the observation I wish to offer here is: it is straightforwardly easy to say that there is a parallel between the interpretation or understanding of a person and the interpretation or understanding of a work of art. But to show in detail—to fathom and articulate the implications of this parallel—is another matter. Seen one way, this is precisely what Dostoevsky has done: to show how it is that we can with the greatest acuity portray a mind in literature, and to show within the larger context of that portrayal how one mind can come to interpret, to fathom, to understand another.

My second observation arises from a connection to some of the work of Richard Moran, where, having argued "the case for seeing the ability to avow one's belief as the fundamental form of self-knowledge," which he rightly describes as "one that gives proper place to the immediacy of first-person awareness and the authority with which its claims are delivered,"[12] he writes:

> This argument has involved giving a more central place to the person as reflective agent, and criticizing both certain theoretical accounts of self-knowledge and certain ordinary stances toward oneself that presume (or enact) a more "spectatorial" relation between the person and her own thought. The agent belongs here because the difference between being in a position to attribute some belief to oneself and being able to avow it is a matter of the person's commitment of herself, rather than something settled by the evidence about herself.

Dostoevsky has shown us a person who, as an extreme case, is locked in a spectatorial relation to himself, to his own thought. As we saw above, this is an internal form of alienation that is at once distancing both internally and externally—it keeps him from himself and from real or grounded relations with others. And Dostoevsky has shown us an agent, in Moran's sense, acting upon Raskolnikov: Porfiry is not a distanced holder of what Moran criticized as a theoretical account, but rather, in the complex way we have seen, an imaginative, comprehending, and as we now say "centered" investigator who knows who he is, knows how to conduct his inquiry with vigilant self-awareness and microscopic acuity, and knows how to locate the precise entry points into Raskolnikov's mind. And so my second observation: the way to account for Raskolnikov's chronic inability to make a truly life-defining resolution just is his spectatorial relation to himself and what we call his inward mental contents; his inability to avow in this sense precludes any internally related ability to make up his mind, to make a real resolution, to define who he is. And so his dramatic achievement at the end—his confession—constitutes an inward move from the spectatorial position to the agential position.

My third observation arises from Iris Murdoch's early philosophical work in ethics, where we find a strong and clear argument against reductive or formulaic models of morality. She there suggests, having argued that (a) we would do well to remove the presumption that the universalizability of moral judgments is an ideal to which we should always aspire and that (b) the exclusion of private or personal considerations in moral understanding removes too much too quickly, that moral vision or ethical sensibility in truth deserves a central place in our ethical thought that it has been denied. Murdoch writes of ethical agents that what we need to grasp in truly understanding a person is

> their total vision of life, as shown in their mode of speech or silence, their choice of words, their assessment of others, their conception of their own lives, what they think attractive or praiseworthy, what they think funny: in short, the configurations of their thought which show continually in their reactions and conversation.[13]

Speaking of her debate with the moral philosopher R. M. Hare, Justin Broackes captures another essential point (Murdoch's words are in single quotation marks and her quotations are in double quotations): “Murdoch’s most radical challenge to Hare lies in her conception of moral freedom. She will conclude, in brief, that freedom does not consist, as Hare believes, in the freedom to ‘choose’ what to apply moral concepts to (e.g. to call different things ‘good’ from one’s parents, or to reject the evaluative ‘criteria’ of other people); instead it resides in the freedom ‘to “deepen” or “reorganize” “our concepts or, in a process of moral evolution, to ‘change’ those concepts for others.”[14] Her opponents of the time believed that, proceeding from a strict and traditional distinction between values and facts, we are free to choose our values in a way that we cannot do with facts; on this dichotomy the former are seen as a matter of decision, the latter not. Broackes continues his exposition of her thought: “But in what sense is that a freedom that we can have? Can we ‘choose’ our values any more than we can choose our mathematics? We may, perhaps, in some sense ‘choose’ our concepts; we do in a sense, ‘choose’ what to believe when e.g. we decide, or make a balanced judgement on the basis of certain reasons, that it is the case that *p* and not *q*; but it is far from obvious—indeed, Murdoch thinks, far from being true—that we can ‘choose’ our values, in the sense of ensuring, simply by ‘deciding’ to take things of kind *k* as valuable, that such things will indeed be of value in the way we have supposed.”[15]

And so my third observation: what Dostoevsky has shown—and here Murdoch’s language fits perfectly—are two total visions of life, as manifest in Porfiry’s and Raskolnikov’s modes of speech and patterns of silence, in their choice of words, in their assessments of others and indeed of each other, in their conceptions of their own lives, in what they find attractive, praiseworthy, funny, and—with the greatest acuity—in “the configurations of their thought which show continually in their reactions and conversations.” And of vision as inseparable from choice: Dostoevsky shows, over the full course of a long novel, what the vision is that Raskolnikov has of himself and of the world that leads him to the murders. To see the power of Murdoch's fundamental point here, if we subtracted all we know down to the finest detail of Raskolnikov and then focused solely on the isolated fact that he committed the double-murder, we would be left minimally having in mind only that one single fact in a manner devoid of any real understanding (this would be, precisely, choice without vision). And then of the matter of freedom to choose: Raskolnikov believed from the start that he possessed a radical freedom to choose "what to apply moral concepts to," that is, that he could align the most extreme crime with moral transcendence into greatness. This is, as Murdoch understood, a dangerous illusion, and everything that it fails to acknowledge—the evaluative criteria of other people that it rejected as inferior and merely commonplace—undercuts the very stability that Raskolnikov came to so desperately desire after the act. Murdoch, in saying that true freedom consists in our freedom to deepen or reorganize our concepts in a process of moral evolution, exactingly captures in philosophy the content of Raskolnikov's desperate and alienated progress. But she ends that passage concerning the deepening and reorganizing of concepts as moral evolution with the words "to change those concepts for others." This begins to reveal what Porfiry actually is: a visionary moving within the intricate weavings of flawed humanity. He possesses this insight, this deep, sophisticated, layered understanding of the human psyche in all its variations as a person; it is not that he has this kind of perceptual ability because he has been an investigator. Rather, he is an investigator because he possesses, to his core, Murdoch's enhanced vision. He understands everything said within the entire world of the novel about Raskolnikov's mind and soul (just as he is an expert at Wollheim's Retrieval and understands the problem instilled in Raskolnikov's mind by Moran's spectatorial position). What Dostoevsky has shown is a person of vision "changing the concepts" of another, but not by simply telling him to change his concepts. This process takes time, multiple exchanges, the incremental expansion of an increasingly intricate language-game, and, finally, in his confession, the realization that he cannot attach and reattach moral values to physical facts as he likes—he at last comes to realize that this is not the form of his freedom. Reuniting himself with himself within the words of his confession, he at the same time reunites himself with humanity. And he has come to see that resolutions have to be real—thin conceptions of chosen values yield equally thin (attempted but ever-failing) resolutions. Porfiry has allowed him the scope to come to see that he cannot "choose his mathematics," that his decision to link concepts as he likes will not deliver to him the sense of transcendence, the value, that he expected as stipulated by him.

Murdoch wrote, "Love is the perception of individuals. Love is the extremely difficult realization that something other than oneself is real."[16] Porfiry is a person made of the discerning perception of individuals. And because he imaginatively enters into the minds of others and comprehends who and what *they* are, he does not see them as versions of himself or understand them on the model of himself. He does not project an image of himself, of his mind and sensibility, into their separate minds and souls and then weakly and falsely claim to see them for who they are. Rather, he continually achieves nothing less than the extremely difficult realization.

So all of these reflections drawn from Murdoch, taken together, will perhaps explain what I mean when—to encapsulate my third observation—I suggest that another part of Dostoevsky's philosophical achievement is to have shown what it is to give Murdoch's vision the place it deserves in moral understanding. But, in closing, how might one try to encapsulate the achievement of the entire novel? One probably shouldn't. But if forced, one might say: if there is a philosophical problem of other minds, philosophical literature is one of its solutions. Or perhaps better: it is literature that shows us that other-minds skepticism, as a generic problem, is not real.

NOTES

1. Fyodor Dostoevsky, *Crime and Punishment*, trans. Jessie Coulson (Oxford: Oxford University Press, 2008). All references to *Crime and Punishment* will be to this edition and given by page number parenthetically in the text.
2. I discuss some of these connections in Garry L. Hagberg, "Wittgenstein Underground," *Philosophy and Literature* 28:2 (October 2004): 379–392.
3. See H. P. Grice, *Studies in the Way of Words* (Cambridge, MA: Harvard University Press, 1989), esp. "Some Models of Implicature," 138–143, and "Presupposition and Conversational Implicature," 269–282.
4. See J. L. Austin, *How to Do Things with Words*, 2nd ed., ed. J. O. Urmson and Marina Sbisa (Cambridge, MA: Harvard University Press, 1962), and "Performative Utterances," in *Philosophical Papers*, 2nd ed. (Oxford: Oxford University Press, 1970), 233–252.
5. Ludwig Wittgenstein, *Philosophical Investigations*, 4th ed., ed. P. M. S. Hacker and Joachim Schulte, trans. G. E. M. Anscombe, P. M. S. Hacker, and Joachim Schulte (Malden, MA: Wiley-Blackwell, 2009); see esp. "Philosophy of Psychology: A Fragment" (formerly part II), sec. xi.
6. I offer a discussion of this matter in connection with interpretation in Garry L. Hagberg, "Word and Object: Museums and the Matter of Meaning," *Philosophy*, suppl. vol.: *Philosophy and Museums* (Cambridge: Cambridge University Press, 2016), 261–293.
7. Wittgenstein, *Philosophical Investigations*, sec. 123.
8. I borrow this metaphor from Wittgenstein, *Philosophical Investigations*, sec. 107.
9. This alludes to T. S. Eliot in *Burnt Norton*, sec. v, in *Four Quartets* (New York: Harcourt, Brace, Jovanovich, 1943), 19, where this aspect of words is powerfully captured.
10. Wittgenstein, *Philosophical Investigations*, sec. 127.
11. Richard Wollheim, "Art, Interpretation, and Perception," in *The Mind and Its Depths* (Cambridge, MA: Harvard University Press, 1993), 133–134.
12. Richard Moran, *Authority and Estrangement: An Essay on Self-Knowledge* (Cambridge, MA: Harvard University Press, 2001), 150.
13. Iris Murdoch, "Vision and Choice in Morality," *Proceedings of the Aristotelian Society*, suppl. vol. 30 (1956): 39. This passage is quoted and very helpfully

discussed in Justin Broackes, ed., *Iris Murdoch, Philosopher: A Collection of Essays* (Oxford: Oxford University Press, 2012), 25.

14. Broackes, *Iris Murdoch, Philosopher*, 27. As he indicates, these words and phrases come from Murdoch's "Vision and Choice in Morality," 55.
15. Broackes, *Iris Murdoch, Philosopher*, 30.
16. Iris Murdoch, "The Sublime and the Good," *Chicago Review* 13:3 (Autumn 1959): 51.

Chapter 2

Love, Suffering, and Gratitude for Existence

Moral and Existential Emotions in Crime and Punishment

RICK ANTHONY FURTAK

I.

Readers of *Crime and Punishment* may wonder why some of Raskolnikov's emotional responses seem to be nearly inhuman. Typically, for a person who loves and cares about others (as most of us do), the separation from a loved one is an occasion for sadness. Nor is this just a factual observation about what tends to occur. Rather, the emotion makes sense: when I value someone's company, it's good for him to be close and therefore bad for him to be far away or out of touch. It's even worse, then, if the separation will be for an indeterminately long time. Appropriately enough, literary expressions of how sad it is to witness the departure of a beloved other are copious and at their best can be powerfully moving.[1] Such is the situation when Raskolnikov takes leave of his sister Dunya as he goes away to confess his crime to the authorities and accept his criminal sentence: they know that it is likely to be a long time until they see each other again. As Dunya watches her brother walk away, she wants simply to watch him until he disappears from view around a street corner in St. Petersburg. Yet Raskolnikov's unfriendly reply to her is an expression of annoyance and a cross gesture:

> She walked away, but when she had gone fifty yards she turned round again and looked at him. He was still in sight. When he reached the corner he too turned round; their eyes met for the last time; when he saw that she was watching him he impatiently, even irritably, waved her on, and himself turned sharp [a]round the corner.[2]

To his credit, Raskolnikov immediately feels ashamed of his hurtful gesture, showing that he does care about his sister; yet he also appears to be vexed and irritated by the burden of Dunya's love for *him*—as he has shown before in relation to her, toward his mother, and also toward Sonya. What makes him capable of shame is that he cares about Dunya. Yet at the same time, he resents the fact *that* he cares. His shame prompts him to exclaim to himself, "If only I were alone and nobody loved me, and if I had never loved anyone! *All this would never have happened!*" (500). What he expresses here is nothing less than a wish to be utterly disconnected from the human community—never to have been loved or to have loved anyone. He wishes for a counterfactual state of affairs in which he is emotionally remote from others.

In feeling ashamed, Raskolnikov has an emotion that arises and makes sense within the world.[3] In becoming annoyed or irritated, and in feeling resentful that he loves anyone or that anyone loves him, Raskolnikov shows a longing to escape from that world altogether. Dostoevsky's character is not only someone who lives and struggles;

he is someone who struggles above all with the question of *whether* or not to exist and to be emotionally involved. The alternative, which often seems to him more attractive, is never to have been born—or, barring that, at least never to have loved or to have been loved. What is affectively at issue for Raskolnikov throughout *Crime and Punishment* is this tension between his general antipathy to human existence (especially his own) and his capacity to love and care—at times, seemingly in spite of himself. This explains the internal conflict that persuades many readers to agree with an observation made by his friend Razumikhin when he says of Raskolnikov that "it is as if he had two separate personalities, each dominating him alternately" (206). What I will examine in the following pages is the transformation of Raskolnikov's characteristic emotions—toward his crime and toward his entire life in the world—from the beginning to the end of Dostoevsky's novel. Specifically, I argue that Raskolnikov's growing capacity to feel guilt and remorse over a specific deed enables him to resolve his emotional ambivalence toward the limits of finite being. By committing a crime and consequently suffering he is led, although by no means unequivocally, to change his affective attitude toward the world and to accept the many intricate ways in which he is situated in the human world, a realm in which people, things, and relations matter to us and appear meaningful.[4] Sonya plays a critical role in enabling this change, through her selfless love for Raskolnikov and her compassion toward him, but also because she maintains an emotional outlook of gratitude and trust—even when faced with tragic misfortune. In order to begin his process of atonement, he must not only accept Sonya's love but *also* follow Sonya's example: by loving and affirming the world, including his own life, despite all of its (and his) defects and concrete limitations. Only then does Raskolnikov wholeheartedly begin a morally accountable existence; by taking on the burden of profound guilt and remorse, he also becomes able to hope.

II.

Yet for much of the novel, Raskolnikov hovers tentatively above finite existence rather than being immersed in it. He feels the type of emotional ambivalence which is displayed toward his sister in the passage quoted above. At first, we encounter Raskolnikov as someone who has for some time been "in an almost morbid state of irritability and tension," withdrawn to the degree that he has "ceased to concern himself with everyday affairs," and—except when feeling loathing and contempt—drifted along in a state of complete "unconsciousness of his surroundings" (1–2). His fierce bitterness and his revulsion (or revolt) instantly bring to mind another Dostoevsky narrator, that of *Notes from Underground*.[5] Simultaneously, the pathologically abstract freedom in which he is trapped may *also* remind us of the main character in a story such as "Dream of a Ridiculous Man," who confesses that "it *would not matter* to me whether the world existed or whether there was nothing at all anywhere."[6] Raskolnikov's demonstrable feelings of contempt toward others and toward his surroundings in general might justify the conclusion that he suffers from "angelism," defined as a contingent being's refusal to submit to the limits of his or her factical situation.[7] Plausibly enough, Razumikhin and Dunya find themselves discussing whether Raskolnikov's alienation can be attributed to an impaired or suppressed—or, as it appears to her, at this point, nonexistent—ability to love (207). In other words, is Raskolnikov unable or unwilling to become emotionally engaged in the world? And their question is reasonable, because Raskolnikov has of late "resolutely withdrawn from all human contacts, like a tortoise retreating into its shell," as the narrator states (25), spelling this out as follows:

> It should be noted that Raskolnikov had had scarcely any friends at the university. He held himself aloof, never went to see anyone and did not welcome visitors. Very soon . . . he found himself

> left severely alone. He took no part in the usual assemblies, discussions, or amusements . . . He was very poor and superciliously proud and reserved. It seemed to some of his fellow students that he looked down on them all as children, as if he had outdistanced them in knowledge, development, and ideas, and that he considered their interests and convictions beneath him. (48–49)

When Dunya and Pulkheria Alexandrovna arrive and are told by Raskolnikov not to torment or torture him by their presence (188), it is clear that his mood and outlook have not improved since he withdrew from the university. He has felt desperate and has acted accordingly.

However, well before they arrive and before the conversation about Raskolnikov's ability to love takes place in Part Three, Chapter 2, , we have been made aware that this is not the whole story about Raskolnikov. In Part One, Chapter 3, we already find out that he is *also* a loving, emotionally concerned person. Raskolnikov reads a lengthy letter from his mother that he has just received (28–37) and which informs him that his sister is about to resign herself to a marriage of convenience for his sake, due to the family's financial need; and by the end of it his emotional state is unmistakable:

> Almost all the time that Raskolnikov was reading this letter his face was wet with tears, but when he came to the end it was pale and convulsively distorted and a bitter angry smile played over his lips. He put his head down on his thin, crumpled pillow and lay there for a long time, thinking. His heart was beating fiercely and his thoughts were wildly agitated. (37)

As for what mixture of emotions he is experiencing, that is harder to say—his tears reveal his sadness and compassion for the plight of

Dunya and his mother, but why the "bitter angry smile"? We find the answer as Raskolnikov is sorting through his emotions moments later, when he says to himself, "I will not have your sacrifice, Dunechka, I will not have it, mama! It shall not be . . . I will not accept it!" (42). Pridefully and spitefully, he takes a joyless pleasure in refusing their aid: at this early point in *Crime and Punishment,* he feels what he will describe later as the longing to have loved no one and for nobody to have loved him. What kind of "freedom" is it that Raskolnikov is longing for?

He makes scattered remarks, for instance to Sonya, advocating "Freedom and power, but above all, power!" (317). In light of his emotional coldness toward her during the conversation in which he makes this exclamation, it may be that his implicit reasoning is that emotional vulnerability is what binds a person, making him unfree and all too human, condemning him to the misery which is pervasive in Raskolnikov's world. The powerful freedom he longs for may consist in transcending emotional attachments in the manner of a Stoic—such as Seneca, who writes that overcoming passions is the mark of "the lofty mind," one which "is always calm, at rest in a tranquil haven."[8] This ideal of *apatheia,* or peace of mind, holds perennial appeal, because it offers us the promise of overcoming suffering and sailing unmoved through the ups and downs of life. Yet the deliberately cultivated tranquility of the Stoic sage who can encounter any situation without the risk of being emotionally affected is attained at a price: as Seneca himself admits, it requires isolating oneself emotionally from others and closing off one's capacity to love.[9] Insofar as this is the kind of freedom that Raskolnikov seeks, he is similar to other Dostoevsky characters such as the narrator of *Notes from Underground*—a man who is "in revolt against reality itself" and may even "long not to exist," as Rowan Williams points out.[10] Here is how another of Dostoevsky's narrators describes this condition: "You hear and see people living—living in reality, you see that for them life is not something forbidden, their life does not fly asunder like dreams . . . I often drift like a shadow, morose and sad, without need or purpose, through the streets and alleyways of Petersburg."[11] That lamentation, by a person to whom human existence seems strangely unreal, is *especially* dreary due to the realization that not everyone experiences the world in this way—that he, the speaker, is missing a sense of the world's reality and value, that one's life and the lives of others are meaningful.

Some varieties of free will are *not* worth wanting,[12] and the emotional void experienced by a person "free" from love and other emotions sounds in Dostoevsky's account like a sort of freedom that nobody ought to wish for. In fact, if not loving others is equated with being in hell, as it is by Zosima in *The Brothers Karamazov*, then Raskolnikov is spiritually in the worst possible condition insofar as he has this kind of freedom.[13] As Nel Noddings has noted, "I am totally free to reject the impulse to care, but I enslave myself to a particularly unhappy [fate] when I make this choice. As I chop away at the chains that bind me to loved others, asserting my freedom, I move into a wilderness of strangers and loneliness . . . When I am alone, either because I have detached myself or because circumstances have wrenched me free, I seek first and most naturally to reestablish my relatedness. My very individuality is defined in a set of relations."[14] What this implies is that by liberating him- or herself from love and care, a person risks losing his or her sense of identity.

III.

Here, it should be helpful to make a distinction between our emotional dispositions of love or concern, on the one hand, and the specific emotions that we are experiencing at any moment, on the other. This can be conceived of as the distinction between *dispositions toward* and *episodes of* emotion, if we permit ourselves to borrow a couple of terms from Richard Wollheim.[15] Our dispositional affective states are the ones that serve as conditions for the episodic emotions that arise in particular situations, because they *dispose us toward* emotional responses. Once we love or care about someone, we are liable to have a variety of distinct emotions about that person, in response to events in the world that pertain to him or her. For instance, if you love a child, then you are liable to experience relief and gratitude when he or she arrives home safely despite the icy conditions. When we get frightened for someone's safety, we must already love or care about that person.[16] Thus, if love did not lead us to care for the people, places, and things of this world, we would not be disposed to respond to one state of affairs with fear, to another with jealousy, and so on. Embarrassment, to use another example, is an emotion that arises in response to a concrete situation in light of certain morally relevant facts, such as that I care about my reputation in the eyes of those who are present. Whether or not I have appropriately perceived the situation as embarrassing, and to a suitable degree, becomes a legitimate question once it is granted that I am already concerned about this.

It is by virtue of our loves and cares that we find ourselves in the midst of a network of concern, extending out into the world and defining our ethical identity. Our affective states of love and concern, in other words, establish in us dispositions *toward* being affected by a variety of particular emotions.[17] Martha Nussbaum explains that "once one has formed attachments," one has "background" (or dispositional) states that set the stage for "episodic or situational" emotions.[18] Due to Raskolnikov's underlying love for his mother and his sister, he is liable to be affected by whatever may affect *them* for better or worse. Love is therefore a condition of vulnerability; as a Stoic such as Seneca would be quick to remind us, our peace of mind is at stake in relation to what we care about. This emotional vulnerability, the avoidance of which is a main goal in Stoic ethics, is what

Raskolnikov laments when he exclaims, "Oh, if only I were alone and nobody loved me, and if I had never loved anyone!" (500). Here, he expresses what might be called a "higher-order" emotion of resentful annoyance or revulsion toward his love for his sister and toward the shame he feels because of it.[19] What this means is simply that the object of his emotion *is* another of his own emotional states. Without employing these terms in a strictly technical manner, we can interpret *moral* emotions as those that arise within the context of a human life, by contrast with which *existential* emotions are those directed toward one's entire life in the world.

IV.

In these terms, we can say that when Raskolnikov feels shame at having become annoyed and irritated by Dunya's understandable wish to watch him walk away (500), he is showing that he does indeed love and care about her. Yet the negative emotions he experiences in response to Dunya's concern, and his yearning to escape from being loved altogether, demonstrate that his attitude toward being emotionally involved in the world—that is, toward loving and being loved—is deeply ambivalent. To understand the importance of moral emotions such as shame, guilt, and remorse in *Crime and Punishment,* we must appreciate the crucial role played by existential passions—such as the emotional attitudes toward all of human life (or the characteristic ways of loving) which are embodied by Raskolnikov and by Sonya respectively. It is due to Sonya that *his* affective outlook ultimately becomes transformed. His eventual guilt and remorse are not only about the murders he has committed; these emotions *also* reveal Raskolnikov's willingness to accept the ways in which he is implicated in a finite, historically situated existence.

Raskolnikov shows his potential to care for others, to take at least a faint interest in their lives, as early as Part One, Chapter 2, when he is moved to enter the pub because he longs for human contact: although he "had lately avoided all social contacts," he now "suddenly felt drawn to people" (8). By acting on this affective impulse, he momentarily accepts whatever might follow from "an immersion in the matter and interrelation that is the finite world."[20] This positively valenced existential passion of longing for some interaction with another human being leads him to meet Marmeladov, and by doing so he has "opened himself up to the impact of other people on his emotional life."[21] Quickly, however, Raskolnikov is overcome by a flood of negative emotions and shifts back into a stance of defensive alienation:

> In spite of his recent momentary wish for contact, of whatever kind, with other people, no sooner was a word actually spoken to him than he experienced the old unpleasant feeling of exasperated dislike for any person who violated, or even seemed desirous of disturbing, his privacy. (10)

He feels bitter and resentful about his impulse to care, and also toward Marmeladov—who happens by chance to be the human being whom Raskolnikov encounters in the pub. Just as he generally scorns and rejects his family's love, Raskolnikov disapproves of his own desire to open himself to whatever may follow from this random meeting, wishing that he had not compromised the morbid isolation which (as I noted above) is a mode of freedom defined most of all by emotional detachment.

However, Raskolnikov does not remain entirely detached, from his family members or even from the pathetic Marmeladov—and thus begins the dialectic between emotional involvement and disengagement, between love and "amoral emotional distancing," as

Malcolm Jones puts it,[22] which continues throughout *Crime and Punishment.* As I stated earlier, Dostoevsky's character struggles above all with the question of *whether* or not to live and to be emotionally engaged in the world: in Hamlet's terms, to be or not to be. This tension between Raskolnikov's repugnance toward all of existence and his capacity to love and care *nevertheless* is evident if we compare his mood after that first encounter with Marmeladov—when he mutters with contempt that human beings "can get used to anything" (25)—with the kindness and genuinely felt concern he exhibits toward Marmeladov and his family after the poor man is trampled and shortly dies in Part Two, Chapter 7. Although Raskolnikov hasn't seen Marmeladov apart from their one meeting days before, he becomes as vehemently moved by the sight of the injured man he recognizes as if this were "his own father" (170) and acts accordingly. Once Raskolnikov has summoned what help can be offered, then given all his money to the suddenly grieving family and received an outpouring of gratitude as he parts from them, he feels renewed: "Life is! Was I not living just now?" (182). Although he might sound rather too proud of himself, this need not deter us from recognizing a sincere note of hope in his voice. And the observation he makes at this instant is not wrong. What has taken place here is a momentary overture to the profound change that Raskolnikov will eventually *begin* to undergo, by the end of the novel—moreover, it should make us refrain from viewing his inner conflict in simplistic terms of reason versus feeling, the former being imagined as specious and the latter as trustworthy. Although Raskolnikov exemplifies a form of intellectualism toward which the author of *Crime and Punishment* is distrustful for good reason, he also has plenty of untrustworthy feelings, and the main problem with his rational intellect is the use he makes of it. As this scene shows, Raskolnikov *is* able to reflect theoretically on the good that can ensue from allowing himself to care—he does not merely theorize in ways that undermine his moral capacities, such as when trying to vindicate a violent act or wishing that he had never loved or cared about anyone.

We see, then, that Raskolnikov's capacity to open himself to the lives of others, and to become morally and emotionally engaged in the human world, is shown as early as Parts One and Two of the novel. As we have also seen, he tends to withhold any higher-order endorsement *of* this capacity, and his existential emotions toward it are generally negating rather than affirmative, at least through the end of Part Six. So, although Wollheim is right that a significant shift in Raskolnikov's emotional orientation occurs as he begins "to turn his attention from the motivation of the critic to the content of the criticism," it is not clear that this happens "gradually" as a "process of change" takes place in Dostoevsky's character throughout the novel.[23] Some moments that do more apparently fit Wollheim's analysis are those in which, after being shaken when a mysterious accuser confronts him, Raskolnikov protests that he murdered no human being but only a principle (261–264); and, upon stopping by the police station voluntarily, he becomes enraged at the informal inquiries of Porfiry Petrovich (329–335). What happens in Raskolnikov is a fitful and prolonged emotional struggle until he can take responsibility for his actions and begin the "new life" (527) that is foreshadowed at the end of the novel. Until his late repentance, he keeps fighting back emotionally against any gradual change that might be taking place in him—denouncing his primary victim as a "foul, noxious louse" (498), telling Sonya that it was in a sense *himself* and not "that old creature" whom he killed (402),[24] and still thinking about his crime as a mere blunder, regrettable only because he was found out (520–521). Yet Raskolnikov's anger and irritation in each of these protests are a defense against the self-implicating moral emotions of guilt and remorse that are at least dimly felt within him[25] and which will become overwhelming after he wholeheartedly acknowledges his transgression.

Indeed, even when he is protesting to the contrary, and in his own mind fending off blame for the murders, Raskolnikov is emotionally half-aware of something untrue in his attempts to justify himself: he has a "feeling" that his self-justifying beliefs are "profoundly false," and although this sense does not make him renounce them entirely—not quite yet—his outlook has been undergoing a fundamental alteration, one whose effects will dawn on him soon (521). The affective and personal crisis in which the change washes over Raskolnikov occurs all of a sudden,[26] but what is precipitated at that instant does not come out of nowhere. His conscious intellect, and the views which he overtly endorses, have been lagging behind an affective realization that has already taken hold of him at a gut level and will at last overcome him and be willingly acknowledged in the Epilogue's final pages (524–527).

V.

It is hardly necessary to point out that Sonya plays a crucial role in enabling this transformation. This is not only by virtue of her love for Raskolnikov and her compassion toward him, but also because she embodies an emotional attitude of gratitude and trust in the face of tragic misfortune. I shall have more to say about the latter. First, regarding Sonya's love for and trust in Raskolnikov, when she visits to express thanks for his concern and to extend an invitation to her father's funeral banquet, her heart melts at the sight of his living conditions, in light of which his generosity has evidently been extreme (228–229). That she has already begun to love him, and not simply as one instance of suffering humanity, is indicated by the narrator plainly enough: "Never, never had she felt anything like this.

A whole new world rose indistinct and unexplored before her eyes" (233). The description echoes that of Razumikhin, after he has met and started to fall in love with Dunya. He also is depicted as having felt "something out of the ordinary" and as having just "received an impression of a kind that he had never known before" (201).

Regarding his mother's love and Dunya's, but to an even greater extent in Sonya's case, Raskolnikov is fiercely ambivalent about being loved. He repeatedly gets vexed and angry at the women who love him, as if their love were an intrusion from which he recoils or a kind of offense to him; one is tempted to conclude that he feels threatened by their love, but this is not quite accurate, since what he feels does not seem to be explicit or concealed fear. Toward Sonya, his irritation or annoyance is more emphatic than that toward his sister and mother, as if her love in particular seems like an encroachment on his freedom that he wishes to push away forcibly—although not *only* to push away. So after being kind to her when she first visits him (229–230), he becomes cruel to Sonya beginning with his initial visit to *her* apartment (309–310). His cruelty is another instance of how Raskolnikov tends to resist affirming his own love and care: he despises himself for becoming concerned and takes it out on the people to whom he has become emotionally attached. This cruelty also illustrates his reluctance to accept being loved *by* others. Although he begins to acknowledge Sonya's love for him and not *simply* to refuse it, even after he has allowed her into his world to the point of being influenced to act on her advice that he make a confession to the criminal authorities, he will not permit her to come along with him to the police. Speaking to himself, he says, "Do I love her? No, surely I don't . . . I drove her away just now like a dog" (503–504). In fact, even after she has followed him to Siberia, he at first seems to be annoyed by "all [her] concern for him" and frequently "irritated by her presence and monosyllabic or even rude to her" (519). Yet he is protesting too much by adopting this defensive stance and denying other emotions that he wants to disown—including his guilt and remorse over the murders as well as his own dawning love for Sonya. Wollheim gets this just right when he remarks upon Raskolnikov's "inability to tolerate . . . the graver hurt that he glimpses will come" when he stops attempting "to ward off guilt" by feeling "hostile emotions" toward his family and Sonya.[27] It is a significant affective achievement when Raskolnikov admits to himself that, "whatever else" he has done, he has made the women who love him unhappy and that he is at least "responsible for that" (499). That this weighs on him is a sign that he is making moral progress. Still, even when he becomes reconciled to the fact that his mother and sister care about him, Raskolnikov still wonders about Sonya: Why does *she* care so much (see 503)?

When Raskolnikov simultaneously accepts Sonya's love and his own love for her, he also accepts that he is culpable for what he has done, as she has helped him to understand—in part, by rejecting his attempts to rationalize his actions (400–402). He has quietly and gradually started coming back to life,[28] and back *into* an emotional engagement with the world, ever since he first opened himself to feeling love and compassion for Sonya's family. He bravely speaks up for her at her father's funeral banquet (385) and shortly afterward is stunned by "how much love she had for him"—for Raskolnikov himself, that is—even as he perceives that it is "strangely painful and burdensome to be so loved" (404). When he abandons his "artificially bold" manner of speaking to Sonya and decides that he must go ahead and confess to her, his defensive emotions are promptly seen as illusions which disappear:

> He lifted his head and gazed at her, meeting her eyes fixed on him with a look of anxiety and anguished care. There was love in that look; his hatred vanished like a shadow. It had not been real; he had taken one feeling for another. (391–392)

This is when he begins, tentatively, to accept *his* developing love for *her*, as he recognizes and welcomes her love for him. His acceptance of Sonya's love will ultimately bind him to the world and enable him to seek redemption. Still, to participate in a world of temporality, chance, and intersubjective concern, Raskolnikov must accept and even be grateful for the decisive role played in his life by contingent events such as his accidental encounter with Marmeladov and what this leads him to: namely, developing an interest in the predicament of Sonya and her family. To believe in the significance of what transpires in time within an individual existence, in "the continuance of a meaningful history" that is,[29] is to endorse an attitude of reverent, trusting affirmation that brings him nearer to Sonya's own views.

He is shocked that Sonya can show affection for him, even be concerned for *his* suffering, after his confession (394–395) and despite the fact that the innocently murdered Lizaveta was Sonya's friend. He is also astonished when at Katerina Ivanovna's funeral she "grasp[s] both his hands and lean[s] her head on his shoulder," without "the slightest repugnance" and also "no trace of loathing for him" (422). Neither her own profound grief and loss nor Raskolnikov's previous cruelty toward her have kept her from loving him—not principally in the form of pitying him,[30] but of caring about his life and well-being—nor have they prevented her from regarding human existence with gratitude and trust. What amazes him most about Sonya is how she can keep on living, why she has not committed suicide. He doesn't "get it," one might say, when he speaks with her about her family's miserable situation in Part Four, Chapter 4; and he still isn't yet able to understand this when he confesses his crime to her in Part Five, Chapter 4. What Sonya forces him to see, due to the compelling power of the outlook she exemplifies, is that life-denial is not the only available standpoint to choose, even for a person faced with "acute personal suffering,"[31] whose life is wretched in so many ways: there simply are other alternatives.

When Raskolnikov first goes to visit Sonya, "the question remained for him: how could she have stayed in her present situation for so long without going mad?" even if—as he disdainfully assumes—it is "beyond her strength to throw herself into the water" (310). During this conversation, he does not comprehend Sonya's reply after he asks why she does not plunge herself into the cold river and end her dreadful existence.

> "But what will become of [her siblings]?" asked Sonya faintly, gazing at him with anguish, but also without any apparent surprise at the suggestion. Raskolnikov looked at her strangely. He had read it all in her look. She must indeed have had that idea herself. Perhaps many times in her despair she had seriously thought of putting an end to everything, seriously enough not to be surprised now when he suggested it [. . .] But what, he wondered, what could have prevented her until now from resolving to end it all? (309)

Sonya holds a secret which, at this stage in the narrative, remains concealed from Raskolnikov. The question that puzzles him, about how Sonya can love a deeply flawed human being such as himself, is connected to his question about how she can accept her tragic predicament, regardless of whether or not it is clearly worthy of being affirmed or embraced. These are not unrelated facts. It appears to Raskolnikov utterly gratuitous that Sonya can love him as she does *and* that she can go on living for the sake of her loved ones. What he must eventually come to appreciate is that what sustains her *is* gratuitous, yet not therefore naive. Sonya does not assume that her faith in God brings any guarantee of happiness or well-being to herself or her family. Yet she appreciates that to love a person is to affirm his existence, wanting him to be well and to be good, believing in the reality and meaning of his life as an end in itself.

Sonya is a counterexample to Nietzsche's statement that Christian faith makes "life-affirmation" seem evil or misguided.[32] Although she herself and her siblings confirm Schopenhauer's observation that we human beings tend to "pass [our] existence in anxiety and want," suffering "terrible afflictions" and "miseries," she nonetheless accepts her finite life as a precious gift, not an illusion to be transcended but something real to be embraced.[33] Her beliefs bear a strong resemblance to those endorsed by Alyosha in *The Brothers Karamazov* when he states that one must love and affirm life without demanding any assurance that this love "makes sense" or is warranted and that, from this love, some sense or meaning might follow.[34] Her faith, in other words, is a kind of existential trust that sustains her wholehearted participation in the finite realm of her cares and concerns. That is why, when she is asked by Raskolnikov what it is that God *does* for her, her reply is that God "does everything" (311). She inhabits a religious perspective from which even tragic frustration and disappointment can be traced to a God of love, the ground of all significance in human life, in whom (or in which) she continues to trust despite obvious reasons for doubt or despair.

VI.

This is relevant to what might be the most significant decision that Raskolnikov makes in the entire novel, at a critical turning point: as Sonya and Dunya have been worrying about whether he might do something desperate, he decides *not* to commit suicide. His exchange with Dunya, shortly after making this decision, is worth citing in detail:

> Warily he raised his eyes to her.
>
> "Where were you all night?"

> "I don't remember very well; you see, sister, I wanted to reach a definite decision and I found myself walking near the Neva many times; I do remember that. I should have liked to end things there, but . . . I decided against it." [. . .]
>
> "Thank God! We were so afraid of that very thing, Sonya Semënovna and I. So you still believe in life; thank God, thank God!"
>
> Raskolnikov smiled bitterly. [. . .]
>
> "And you don't think, sister, that I was simply afraid of the water?" he asked, with an ugly smile, looking into her face.
>
> "Oh, stop, Rodya!" exclaimed Dunya bitterly. (497)

Does he "still believe in life," is he grateful to be alive? Raskolnikov would not go *that* far. And yet his decision not to drown himself shows that Dunya is right about the direction in which her brother's outlook is moving. He sounds resentful, and his acceptance of life is made begrudgingly, but it *is* made, all the same. Raskolnikov's decision not to emulate Svidrigaylov, who has shot himself that same day (491), is ample evidence of this. He is indeed being brought back to life, even if he seems to be dragged "kicking and screaming," so to speak, and in spite of himself. By giving his assent to human existence, he recognizes that he must come to terms with the meaning of what has happened in his life and also of what he has done. Raskolnikov jokes about how perhaps he was only afraid of the water, but he did (however reluctantly) make a choice in favor of life-affirmation rather than nihilism.

Sonya has, through her example, shown him how to do this. Existential emotions toward one's entire life in the world need not be negating, and it is possible for Raskolnikov to redefine his predominant attitude toward life by ceasing to wish that he had never existed—that he had never been loved and had never loved anyone. Rather than hover tentatively above finite existence and cursing himself when he is involved in moral life among others, he must come to accept the concrete terms of his emotional immersion in the world. His eventual remorse and guilt for his actions—emotions about what damage he has done, and the damage this has done to him in return (see 394–395, 513)—manifest Raskolnikov's willingness to accept this involvement.[35] Nihilism, defined either as a lack of meaning and purpose *or* as the wish not to have lived,[36] can *perhaps* be overcome by the kind of active, unconditional love which is epitomized by Sonya.

Moreover, this form of love also leads to responsible participation in the human world. In order to follow Sonya's example, though, Raskolnikov has to love and embrace an inescapably tragic existence, embracing the world and his own life within it, notwithstanding all of its failings and imperfections. He must identify *with*, rather than disown, his emotional capacities and what he has come to love and care about. Only when he is able to do all of this will Raskolnikov begin a morally accountable life among others. It is by shouldering the burden of profound guilt and remorse that he becomes able to love unreservedly, to hope, and to believe in the promise of renewal.

> How it happened he himself did not know, but suddenly he seemed to be seized and cast at her feet. He clasped her knees and wept . . . At once, in that instant, [Sonya] understood, . . . and she no longer doubted that he loved her, loved her for ever . . . He was restored to life and he knew it and felt to the full all his renewed being . . . He remembered how ceaselessly he had tormented her and harrowed her heart . . . [yet] he knew with what infinite love he would now expiate all her sufferings. (526)

What is implied by this powerful emotional transformation is that Raskolnikov will cease to experience being loved as an unwelcome intrusion and that his anger and annoyance toward those who love him will be replaced by entirely different characteristic emotions. This, our narrator predicts, will become true of Raskolnikov *if* he lives in accordance with what he has felt in this moment. The Epilogue draws to a close as a new mode of existence begins for him, though he does not yet foresee "that the new life would not be his for nothing, that it must be dearly bought, and paid for with great and heroic struggles yet to come" (527). At the end of *Crime and Punishment*, what has occurred in Raskolnikov is presented not as an accomplished fact, but as a conversion to an affective stance that he has continually been drawn toward but has until now resisted. And what overwhelms him is a felt realization, or revelation, which has been latently developing for some time. As we are told by Dostoevsky's narrator, the rest of Raskolnikov's life will be another story altogether.

"It is in my gratitude for life that I may come to love the world," another philosopher says, adding that "if such a change does come, it is not because [one] sees any *reason* for it." Rather, it "is a matter of being able to thank God for the world—no matter what the world is like."[37] By virtue of precisely such a shift in perspective, Raskolnikov is delivered back into a meaningful existence. To see things from a loving perspective—to accept and be grateful for what happens and how it might lead us to suffer—is to accept a radical vulnerability. This is, however, the price one must pay in order to inhabit a significant world. For Sonya, affirmation of life is not a conclusion drawn from outwardly favorable circumstances; rather, it has the status of an axiomatic premise which shapes all of her interpretations. She maintains an emotional comportment of trust and gratitude, through which she perceives and responds to every state of affairs that she faces. Her trust in God is not a reasoned conclusion justified by what God "does" for her: as she knows all too well, the tragic consequences that may follow from trusting in a God of love can make it difficult for a person to "believe in life" as Dunya hopes that her brother still might. Yet as Raskolnikov at last comes to see, and as Dostoevsky appears to suggest, existential gratitude for one's entire existence need not be contingent on the apparent quality of the gift. What it *should* be, on the contrary, is a wholehearted acceptance of a finite life of love and suffering. Provided that this acceptance does not involve the illusion of having overcome the tragic nature of human existence, it must be predicated upon a gratuitous, unconditional affirmation. Raskolnikov ends up in a state exactly contrary to his former emotional longing never to have loved or to have been loved.

NOTES

1. See, e.g., the words of Imogen in Shakespeare's *Cymbeline* when she is responding to the banishment of her beloved. Wishing that she could have watched him go until he appeared to be just a speck on the horizon, Imogen says:
   I would have broke mine eyestrings, cracked them but
   To look upon him till the diminution
   Of space had pointed him sharp as my needle;
   Nay, followed him till he had melted from
   The smallness of a gnat to air, and then
   Have turned mine eye and wept. (*Cymbeline* I.3.17–22)
2. Fyodor Dostoevsky, *Crime and Punishment*, trans. Jessie Coulson (New York: Oxford University Press, 2008), 500. Subsequent citations of this edition will provide page numbers in parentheses within the main text.
3. To clarify this term: "When I say 'world,' I mean the part of existence that answers our call (even if only by way of a barely audible echo), and whose call we ourselves hear . . . A person who finds himself outside the world is not sensitive to the world's suffering." Milan Kundera, *Immortality*, trans. Peter Kussi (New York: Harper Perennial Classics, 1999), 254.
4. On "the human world," see Anthony O'Hear, *The Element of Fire: Science, Art and the Human World* (London: Routledge, 1988), 16–19.
5. Fyodor Dostoevsky, *Notes from Underground*, trans. Richard Pevear and Larissa Volokhonsky (New York: Vintage, 1993).
6. Fyodor Dostoevsky, "The Dream of a Ridiculous Man," in *A Gentle Creature and Other Stories*, trans. Alan Myers (Oxford: Oxford University Press, 1995), 108.
7. As defined by Jacques Maritain, in *The Dream of Descartes*, trans. Mabelle Andison (New York: Philosophical Library, 1944), 28–41. See also Rowan Williams, *Dostoevsky: Language, Faith, and Fiction* (Waco, TX: Baylor University Press, 2011), 75. He employs the term to similar effect, but with reference to Ivan in *The Brothers Karamazov* (and without crediting Maritain for the coinage).

8. Seneca, *De Ira*, in *Dialogi*, ed. L. D. Reynolds (New York: Oxford University Press, 1977): III.vi.1; my translation.
9. See, e.g., Seneca, *Ad Lucilium Epistulae Morales*, 2 vols., ed. L. D. Reynolds (New York: Oxford University Press, 1965), epistles 23 and 116.
10. Williams, *Dostoevsky: Language, Faith, and Fiction*, 167–168. An excellent analysis of the perverse liberty exemplified by the narrator of *Notes from Underground* is given by Frithjof Bergmann in *On Being Free* (Notre Dame, IN: University of Notre Dame Press, 1977), 16–22, 35–44: "The Undergroundman . . . is free only when he flouts not only reason but everything else . . . His true complaint is not that he cannot act [but] that none of his actions are quite his; he never feels that it is he who performs them."
11. Dostoevsky, "White Nights," in *A Gentle Creature and Other Stories*, Trans. Alan Meyers (New York: Oxford University Press, 1995), 26.
12. See, e.g., Daniel C. Dennett, *Elbow Room: The Varieties of Free Will Worth Wanting* (Cambridge, MA: MIT Press, 1984).
13. Fyodor Dostoevsky, *The Brothers Karamazov*, trans. Richard Pevear and Larissa Volokhonsky (New York: Farrar, Straus and Giroux, 1990), book 6, chap. 3. See also the discussion by James P. Scanlan, *Dostoevsky the Thinker* (Ithaca, NY: Cornell University Press, 2002), 110–117.
14. Nel Noddings, *Caring: A Feminine Approach to Ethics and Moral Education* (Berkeley: University of California Press, 1984), 51.
15. Richard Wollheim, *On the Emotions* (New Haven, CT: Yale University Press, 1999), 9–12.
16. Robert C. Roberts indicates the fundamental priority of concern by characterizing emotional responses as "concern-based" construals; see his "What an Emotion Is: A Sketch," *Philosophical Review* 97 (1988): 183–209, esp. 184–187. See also Roberts, *Emotions* (Cambridge: Cambridge University Press, 2003).
17. On this distinction see, e.g., Rick Anthony Furtak, *Wisdom in Love* (Notre Dame, IN: University of Notre Dame Press, 2005), 8–11.
18. Martha Nussbaum, *Upheavals of Thought: The Intelligence of Emotions* (Cambridge: Cambridge University Press, 2001), 69–71.
19. See, e.g., Harry G. Frankfurt, *The Importance of What We Care About: Philosophical Essays* (Cambridge: Cambridge University Press, 1988).
20. Williams, *Dostoevsky: Language, Faith, and Fiction*, 226.
21. Malcolm V. Jones, *Dostoyevsky after Bakhtin* (Cambridge: Cambridge University Press, 1990), 84. Cf. Katherine Jane Briggs, *How Dostoevsky Portrays Women in His Novels: A Feminist Analysis* (Lewiston, NY: Edwin Mellen Press, 2009), 83. She also takes note of the significance of how Raskolnikov begins to show "care and concern for [Marmeladov] and his family" in this scene and soon afterward.
22. Jones, *Dostoyevsky after Bakhtin*, 81.

23. Wollheim, *On the Emotions*, 190–191.
24. He repeatedly miscalculates by counting his murders as one, instead of two.
25. As Wollheim suggests they are; see *On the Emotions*, 192.
26. This has led many readers to complain that the Epilogue ends too jarringly; such complaints are noted, and partially refuted, in David Matual's essay "In Defense of the Epilogue of *Crime and Punishment*," in *Fyodor Dostoevsky's Crime and Punishment*, ed. Harold Bloom (Philadelphia: Chelsea House, 2004), 105–114.
27. Wollheim, *On the Emotions*, 192–193. See also Jones, *Dostoyevsky after Bakhtin*, 83–94, on Raskolnikov's emotional confusion at this stage in the narrative.
28. Cf. Jones, *Dostoyevsky after Bakhtin*, 84.
29. Williams, *Dostoevsky: Language, Faith, and Fiction*, 80–81.
30. It is inaccurate to claim, as Freud does in a letter to Theodor Reik, that "loving out of pity" is all that Dostoevsky "really knew" or all that Sonya represents. See Sigmund Freud, *Writings on Art and Literature*, ed. Neil Hurtz (Stanford, CA: Stanford University Press, 1997), 254.
31. See the discussion of Sonya as "a woman struggling to reconcile her belief in God with acute personal suffering," someone who has endured intellectual doubt and faced the threat of nihilism, by Elizabeth Blake in "Sonja, Silent No More: A Response to the Woman Question in Dostoevsky's *Crime and Punishment*," *Slavic and East European Journal* 50 (2006): 252–271, esp. 260–263. See also Williams, *Dostoevsky: Language, Faith, and Fiction*, 152–153, and Briggs, *How Dostoevsky Portrays Women*, 78–79.
32. Friedrich Nietzsche, *The Antichrist*, trans. Anthony M. Ludovici (Amherst, NY: Prometheus Books, 2000), 24.
33. I cite Arthur Schopenhauer, *The World as Will and Representation*, vol. 2, trans. E. F. J. Payne (New York: Dover, 1966), chaps 28 and 45, respectively, "Characterization of the Will-to-Live" and "On the Affirmation of the Will-to-Live."
34. See Dostoevsky, *The Brothers Karamazov*, book 5, chap. 3.
35. The text here ("Nihilism amounts . . .) belongs in note 36, and the text in note 36 belongs here. Nihilism amounts to the sense that "the aim is lacking" or that the question "why?" finds no answer, according to Friedrich Nietzsche in *The Will to Power*, trans. Walter Kaufmann and R. J. Hollingdale (New York: Vintage Books, 1968), §2. On nihilism as "the view that it is better not to be," see Bernard M. Reginster, *The Affirmation of Life: Nietzsche on Overcoming Nihilism* (Cambridge, MA: Harvard University Press, 2006), 52.
36. On how "in guilt the focus is typically on the self," whereas "in remorse the focus is more typically on the deed and its repair," see Roberts, *Emotions*, 222–225.
37. Rush Rhees, "Gratitude and Ingratitude for Existence," in *Rush Rhees on Religion and Philosophy*, ed. D. Z. Phillips (Cambridge: Cambridge University Press, 1997), 162–164.

Chapter 3

Crime and Expression

Dostoevsky on the Nature of Agency

ROBERT GUAY

I. AGENCY AS A PROBLEM

The *title* of *Crime and Punishment* sets out a determinate structure of events, one that puts antecedent and consequent into a temporal and logical order that spans the entire narrative. The *novel,* however, puts that structure into question. The double-murder certainly counts as a crime, but the event turns out to be so arbitrary that it renders the category of "crime" problematic. The murders seem to occur as something in between an intentional action and a natural calamity. Although Raskolnikov did plan intensively, the commission of the crime depended on so many accidents that it could hardly be considered the realization of a plan, and Raskolnikov could barely bring himself to do anything at all, let alone carry out a complex scheme. The crime, in any case, was disconnected from any resolution or specific motive. Raskolnikov articulates so many explanations to himself and then to Sonya that this surfeit of explanation makes his motives all the more inscrutable. The novel further problematizes its apparent forensic structure, at least in its initial presentation, by dissociating the agent from the deed. The false confession does this publicly, and Raskolnikov takes up multiple, inconsistent strategies for doing so privately. On one hand, he trivializes the deed, insisting that it is more like the scratching of an itch or the swatting of an insect than something that should count as meaningfully performed by him. On the other hand, he tries to call into question his potential guilt by conceiving of the possibility of stepping beyond crime itself.

The novel needs to gradually restore the determinate structure that its title suggests, reconnecting motivation, agent, and deed. The task of doing so, however, requires an extended consideration of agency in which the crime plays an organizing role. Since the story involves a crime, it entails raising questions about an agent who is responsible and can be held accountable. But the narrative is not about the crime, which passes by inauspiciously at the beginning; instead, I suggest, it represents the crime as exemplary of an agent's problematic relationship to his own deed, which is an issue that we see depicted not only in Raskolnikov's case but also with the other characters. What I claim, then, is that the drama of the novel as a whole makes the crime comprehensible not by tracing it back to some prior historical or psychological event, but by locating Raskolnikov's deed in relation to himself and to others. The novel dramatizes a number of persons making different kinds of attempts to establish a relationship to their own activity. In doing so, it exhibits deficiencies in ordinary forms of behaving by showing how they fall short of bringing about an adequate self-relation. By contrast, the crime, although a failure nested in failures, turns out to be confirmed as a success by the end, both in establishing Raskolnikov in a new life and also more philosophically in terms of giving Raskolnikov a relationship to his own activity. Understanding his own failure in light of the shortcomings in everyone else's attempts at agency is what ultimately allows Raskolnikov to make sense of himself and what he does.

My argument in this chapter, then, is that the narrative of *Crime and Punishment* somewhat inadvertently functions as an extended commentary on the nature of agency. Each of Dostoevsky's characters, including Raskolnikov at various points in time, represents a plausible approach to understanding the ways in which an agent relates to his deeds. For example, the relationship between agent and deed is presented in terms of choice (the female characters), inner motivational states (Marmeladov), control (Svidrigaylov), accountability (Porfiry Petrovich), reflective deliberation (Luzhin), and moral reasoning (Dunya). Dostoevsky dramatizes these relations as ending in sometimes spectacular failures, with the result that narrative events become difficult to characterize in intentional terms. Raskolnikov, oddly, switches among all these forms of relationship, but does not arrive at a satisfactory connection to his actions until he is able to recognize himself in his deeds.

The drama of *Crime and Punishment* thus makes a case for treating agency as expressive, and so a matter of realizing in the world deeds that are rationally responsive and adequate to one's own understanding of them. Raskolnikov's agency does not require having a particularly clear, self-conscious, rational antecedent stance toward the deed, but having the ability to make the deed *his own*, even—maybe especially—in the case where he does not want to. I conclude the chapter by discussing what might be called Dostoevsky's philosophical anthropology of agency: the view that, given human nature and prevalent social conditions, being able to recognize oneself in one's actions requires, on one hand, the commission of a violation and, on the other hand, someone in a relationship of both subordination and affection. Crime functions distinctively by forcing an acknowledgment that one does want to make, but also requires the conferral of human forgiveness for its unmerited redemption.

II. RELATING TO ONE'S DEEDS

Raskolnikov begins the novel by introducing a problem of agency as his own: "It was clear that now the time had come, not to languish in passive suffering, arguing that his problems were insoluble, but to act, to act at once and with speed" (43).[1] The urgency of the problem for Raskolnikov, however, left unclear what it might mean for him to act. My aim in this section is to clarify some of the ways that the novel raises a general philosophical problem, or complex of problems, about agency. The problem in its basic form is how to identify the distinguishing features of action as such, which mark them off from other kinds of events. Things can happen to persons, of course, without their active involvement; and some persons' behaviors—itches and breaths and so on—may fail to qualify as being done by them. In the category of action, however, would fall behaviors in whose performance an agent takes an active, purposeful role of a particular kind. So the philosophical question is what relationship to the action an agent must have and what cognitive and conative capacities it implies. This question does not arise in such a general way in the novel, however, because it is not merely an abstract problem. Varieties of the problem arise, sometimes with considerable urgency, *inside* the novel, from within the standpoints of the characters. They want to know what their own activity is: how much if any effective control they have, what ends they might be acting on, what aims or motives would count as their own, and in general, to what extent they are active in the events of their lives. This is true of *all* of *Crime and Punishment*'s characters, but Raskolnikov plays an exemplary role here in two respects. One is that he is unusually reflective about this complex of issues. He devotes almost all his energies to formulating them, which oddly turns out to leave him less clear-sighted about what they entail. The other respect in which Raskolnikov plays an exemplary role is that he has extreme preconceptions of these issues, so much so that his theoretical views bleed into his attempts at agency.

There are many ways to think about how someone might relate to her own behavior so as to be *acting* and not merely being moved as another thing in the world. One might think of action in terms of the role that someone plays in its production or guidance, by locating its source somewhere suitably "within" the agent, in light of the independence or authenticity that the agent manifests, or in terms of what the agent can be held accountable or responsible for. With all of these conceptualizations, one can of course ask what they amount to, whether they identify feasible conditions, and whether they are truly necessary in acting. One could also identify common threats to agency and then conceive of agency as the absence of these threats. Physiological maladies, the stresses of immiseration, unconscious social influences, habit, temptation, boredom, upbringing, mental illness, and possibly even "ideas floating in the air"[2] can each threaten to undermine the sense in which an event might qualify as an action belonging to an agent. There is a stark presentation of this in an early exchange between Nastasya and Raskolnikov:

> "[W]hy do you do nothing now?"
> "I am doing . . ." began Raskolnikov grimly and reluctantly.
> "What?" [. . .]
> "Thinking," he replied seriously, after a moment's pause. (27)

Raskolnikov wants to be active; he wants to see himself as doing something. And thinking might conceivably qualify as a sustained, goal-directed activity initiated by an agent. But here, at least for Nastasya, this is ridiculous: Raskolnikov is lying exhausted and half-delirious on a sofa, not accomplishing anything and not capable of changing his situation; his "thinking" is not apparently something he has resolved upon or that fits into his broader purposes. For Raskolnikov, the philosophical problem takes the form of how he might literally get out of bed, or how to do something rather than nothing. He raises the possibility that lying there would qualify as acting, but in his situation it seems like an empty possibility.

The childishness of Raskolnikov's initial presentation of this complex of issues—that lying on a sofa can count as an active fulfillment of his vocation—shows, I think, how the novel addresses the philosophical issues. This first presentation is so risible that it appears more as a problem than an offered solution. Dostoevsky does not address philosophical problems about agency by dramatizing theories. Philosophical problems arise in the novel because they are matters of genuine concern for the characters. They do not care about formulating philosophical problems as such, of course, but the problems can nevertheless be important, even urgent to them in different ways. And because they are concerned with problems as they face them, and not as abstract formulations, the nature of the problems is itself part of the problem. There is no single question of the nature of agency or the agent's relation to his deed that could in principle be answered. The very terms in which this complex of issues could be articulated are themselves contested. For the characters, they are tied up with practical questions about the possibilities of choice and what roles one might play. The characters have concerns about agency because they are looking for a kind of self-knowledge that consists in being aware of what they are doing: knowing what their actual motives are, the basis for these motives, and whether they are confused or self-deceived about their own ends.[3] They all face, on one hand, a "plenitude of motivations"[4] that could explain what happens and, on the other hand, an inability to determine what in particular is happening, even in their own case. Raskolnikov expresses this most plainly: "I remember everything, down to the smallest detail, and yet if you were to ask me why I did something, or went somewhere, or said something, I don't think I could give a clear explanation" (217). The philosophical problems are inevitably inchoate. And indeed, for most of the characters, an answer would more likely take the form of a satisfactory public achievement than that of a philosophical proof. Nevertheless, they are philosophical problems the characters face about their own agency, and even though none of them know quite what they are doing, they still make an attempt to figure that out.

The characters face problems of agency in a diversity of ways. Sometimes the problems are so basic that whether agency is possible at all is in question. Marmeladov, for example, suffers from a weakness of will so intense that he cannot sustain any self-control. Although he values his family and social standing, he cannot demonstrate this in any fashion and is left shifting between views of his own failings: that he is morally defective, that he is a victim of his own weakness, that his consciousness of his own depravity makes him all the more culpable, and so on. More commonly, there are characters who act strategically. They have immediate, superficial ends, such as marrying Luzhin, offering Raskolnikov something to translate, conversing with Raskolnikov, or going to St. Petersburg. But one has to interpret the pursuits of these ends as somewhat indirect attempts to secure something more important. The characters never say or think as much, however, and it is far from clear what ends they seek or what their motives are. Since it is unlikely that they are rational strategic masterminds who conceal, even from the narrator, the true nature of their activities, they seem unsure about what they are doing and are thus in the same epistemic position that we are: trying to figure out what they are doing by considering their words and behaviors, and attributing causal influences and ultimate concerns on that basis. And for some characters, the challenge to agency is finding an end with value and emotional weight sufficient to sustain an action. For Svidrigaylov, for example, nothing might count as *doing* because there is no pursuit that he can identify with and thus no way to bring himself to action.

Raskolnikov is in the same position and shares the same concerns as the other characters, but he stands out in two ways. One is that, perhaps because the problems for him are particularly acute, he is the most reflective about them. He seems to devote every waking moment and some of his dreams to contemplating problems of agency, both in general terms and in the particulars of his own case. He also stands out by holding extreme, pathological versions of familiar views. His reflections indeed seem to have played a role here: Raskolnikov starts from shared assumptions about agency, tries to articulate them to himself, and in doing so ends up adopting them in extreme and curiously uncritical forms. So he arrives at a pathological sense of the requirements for the possibility of agency while he is farthest from being able to satisfy them.

There are three main conventional beliefs about agency that Raskolnikov adopts and transforms. One is that he treats agency as an intellectual problem to be solved by arriving at a correct and well-reasoned answer. All the others—except possibly Luzhin and Lebezyatnikov—try to resolve questions about their relationship to their own activity by doing something with more or less self-awareness and purposefulness and then trying to assess what they have done. For Raskolnikov, by contrast, the intellectual problem needs to be solved before he can act: "I preferred to lie and think. I spent all my time thinking" (400). Of course, that by itself did not produce a coherent solution, so he oscillated toward an opposite position, to move impulsively and thoughtlessly: "I endured all the torment of this endless debating, Sonya, and I longed to kill without casuistry . . ." (401). But even here, he takes an intellectual position based on intellectual failure; it is more like a homicidal skepticism than a naive practicality. The second conventional belief is that agency is something individualistic and non-mutual. In speaking about his crime, Raskolnikov claims, "By that stupidity I only meant to put myself in an independent position" (498). "Independence" here is both condition and goal: for his agency to be realized he must be capable of acting apart from and uninfluenced by anyone or anything. He accordingly characterizes action in terms of purely inner qualities that somehow manifest themselves externally, such as resoluteness (3), courage (401), and daring (400). And if agency requires complete independence that stems from inside, then sociality can appear only as something imposed by strength of will. One's inner qualities are made effective by force without any reciprocity at all: "And I know now, Sonya, that the man of strong and powerful mind and spirit is their master! The man who dares much is right in their eyes. The man who tramples on the greatest number of things is their law-giver, and whoever is most audacious is most certainly right" (400). The third conventional belief is that agency requires a new temporality, a departure from the ongoing succession of events. Action cannot be a result of the past, but something completely original, a new beginning. So Raskolnikov claims, implausibly, that he had a thought "that nobody ever had before me" (401). He "wanted to forget everything and start again" (401) because agency, on his own conception, required a completely new beginning.

Much of the drama of the novel then entails Raskolnikov going beyond these pathological views by working out their actual consequences and connecting his projects to the lived activity of others. That he starts from defective beliefs makes his attempts at agency much worse than they would otherwise be, but the crime also makes his redemption possible. Raskolnikov works through a range of more familiar approaches to establishing a relationship to one's activity, along with his crime, and this process allows him to arrive at a better standpoint.

III. CONVENTIONAL POSSIBILITIES

In this section I show how each of various characters represents a conventional understanding of the way an agent relates to his or her deeds. This is not to say that they articulate such conceptions; they are not generally interested in theorizing their own agency. Nevertheless, they view their own endeavors in light of implicit qualifications for their actions to be their own. We can see these implicit understandings, in part, from how they frame their deliberations on what they should do and what it would mean to be successful in carrying out their ends. We can also see how they represent conventional understandings in part from how their attempts at agency come to grief: they have distinctive ways of failing to make sense of their own activity and even failing to sustain activity at all. Raskolnikov stands in a special position with respect to these attempts; he lacks a distinctive way of trying to relate to his deeds. Instead, he alternately adopts extreme forms of all the conventional understandings, reflects explicitly on them, attempts to structure his activity in light of them, and fails all the more spectacularly to establish a relation to his own deeds. The crime, which he is forced both by external pressures and his own conscience to acknowledge but which he cannot fit with his self-understanding, leaves him oscillating among the conventional options until all of these break down.

Choice

One basic way we can understand the relationship between agents and their deeds is through the notion of choice: persons are presented with opportunities to choose possible courses of action, and the objects of their choices are what distinctively belong to them.[5] This way of understanding agency is represented, above all, by the women in the novel. For them, agency consists in having multiple options and having the discretion to choose which one seems to be the best. Of course, women have a constrained sphere of choice: for the most part they get to choose whether or not to get married or have sex, or sometimes whom to live with. Thus the letter in Part One turns on the nature of the choice that Dunya has made to marry Luzhin, and embedded in that letter is the choice Pulkheria Alexandrovna has made to live by herself after their marriage (34). Sonya, similarly, is presented by her mother with a choice to prostitute herself: "Oh, Katerina Ivanovna, must I really come to that?" (15). In these cases, furthermore, men confirm the significance of the choices. Razumikhin accedes to a high opinion of Luzhin "because . . . Avodotya Romanovna has chosen him of her own free will" (209). Sonya's choice is confirmed by Lebezyanikov. Even as he recognizes the constraint involved in her actual case, he at the least validates her power of choosing: "In our present society it is not, of course, entirely normal, because it is forced on her, but in future it will be completely normal, because freely chosen" (353).

Only the women find their agency figured entirely as a matter of choice: they have choices presented to them, that is how they may act, and their conduct and character are assessed on that basis. The domain of choice makes sense in relation to the demands of men, who need not be benevolent. Men, by contrast, see their agency in terms of choices only in desperate conditions. The significance of choice comes out in the refrain that Raskolnikov learns from Marmeladov: "Every man must needs have somewhere to turn to" (12). Choice, in that case, is a way of representing the possibility of agency in its absence; having options becomes important when none seem to be available. Raskolnikov, moreover, thinks of making choices as a way of taking control of his activity precisely when he has lost control. For example, when "his mind was firmly made up to go to the police" (168) or when he declares to Sonya, "I have chosen you" (317) to be told who killed Lizaveta. Raskolnikov suffers from the general problems of making sense of one's agency in terms of choice: present choices might foreclose the possibility of future agency, and choices cannot bring about the right relationship between agent and deed when the options are severely constrained—it can be impossible to identify with one's own choices when no good ones are available. Raskolnikov also suffers from unusual problems regarding choice: his choices can be wanton and inconsistent, and he cannot always bring himself to act on them. It turns out, then, that choice is an appealing way of representing agency precisely when there are no genuine options and no good results.

Inner Motivational States

Another way of distinguishing actions as such is by picking out those events that have their source in a special type of mental state that initiates it. Actions then belong to the agent because they arise suitably from "inside" rather than as the byproduct of the agent's interaction with her environment.[6] The inner states that produce action might be desires, motives, volitions, or, as Marmeladov and those around him conceive of them, "sentiments" or "feelings" (*chuvstv*). Marmeladov frequently describes himself in terms of the depth of his feelings (e.g., 14, 19) and characterizes everyone else along similar lines. He links the capacity to act, furthermore, with the sincerity and depth of sentiment, even when such sentiments stand in contrast to actual circumstances and behavior. For example, he excuses his wife's outbursts by saying that "although Katerina Ivanovna is full of generous sentiments, she is a hasty, irritable, sharp-tongued lady" (15). Katarina Ivanovna, in turn, surprisingly claims upon his death, "He was a good-hearted man" (369). Raskolnikov, too, is judged "a man of feeling" (13) by Marmeladov. As Marmeladov sees things, actions are what come from heartfelt feeling and thus reveal the agent's character by showing how she can relate to the world and her own deeds in a genuine way.

Reliance on a connection between heartfelt feeling and action generates problems for Marmeladov's self-conception, however. On one hand, it creates an unsustainable contrast between inner nature and outward behavior that Marmeladov can use to dissociate any particular happening from counting as his deed. Since arbitrary influences can interfere with the effectiveness of sentiment in producing action, any behavior that one does not wish to identify with can always be excluded. On the other hand, reliance on that connection leaves open the possibility of disclaiming any particular feeling as truly one's own and thus discrediting oneself as an agent. One might stand helpless before one's feelings: they are not the sort of thing that one is always responsible for and might not even represent one's character. So this conception of agency turns out to be, for Marmeladov especially, a way of maintaining a category of action for someone who is a failure at it, who wishes to excuse his failings and yet maintain a sense of himself as, at least potentially, active.[7] This conception functions somewhat differently for Raskolnikov, who wishes to think of himself as consistently active but has trouble figuring out what that amounts to. The most consequential actions that he undertakes are those that build his relationship with Sonya. He does not initially see them as consequential, however, and is moved to perform them when he becomes "filled with pity" (226); as a result he is incapable of understanding or identifying with what he is doing. Meanwhile others use their view of him as someone moved by feeling in order to anticipate and manipulate his behavior. For example, his mother explains that she has withheld information from him by saying, "I know your character and your feelings" (28), and Marmeladov explains to him, "the criminal's own nature comes to the rescue of the poor investigator . . ." (328). Taking Raskolnikov's feelings as the basis of his activity makes him a bystander in his own activity.[8]

Control

Actions could perhaps be distinguished by the control that agents have over the performance of their deeds. That is, what distinguishes actions from incidental movements is the guidance or direction provided by the agent over the course of the action, perhaps according to a governing plan or intention.[9] The agent might, furthermore, act with some degree of self-conscious planning that fits into her overall ends and capacities. Svidrigaylov manifests this conception of agency. He does not explicitly reflect on it; taking up such a concern falls outside of his "endless schemes and designs" (444). Nor does the novel take care to represent his involvement in particular deeds. But Svidrigaylov projects a kind of engaged effectiveness in the novel, so that others take him as continuously bringing various schemes to fruition. So Raskolnikov thinks, upon meeting him, "that this was a man who had firmly made up his mind to something, but would keep his own counsel" (271). Svidrigaylov does in fact make numerous arrangements: for example, he quickly establishes himself in St. Petersburg, manages Katerina Ivanovna's affairs after her death, and even becomes engaged. What was striking about Svidrigaylov, however, was that even when his ultimate motives were obscure, he had so much composure and control in his performance of himself that he seemed to be carrying out plans. And he dismisses any factor other than control in his self-presentation as an agent. For example, he depicts his emotions as less his own than what he is subjected to, asking in respect to them, "Am I myself a victim?" (269).

Despite Svidrigaylov's planning and control, he denies agency in his own self-description, however. In a conversation with Raskolnikov, he says, "I make it a rule to condemn nobody, since I never do anything myself (*ya sam beloruchka*) and don't intend to" (472; cf. 450, 272). Svidrigaylov identifies himself as a non-agent, or literally a *beloruchka*, someone with white hands. He actively plans, exerts influence, but never gets his hands dirty; as an aristocrat, he can expect others to bear the burdens of carrying out his aims while he remains insulated from any real engagement or repercussions.[10] Whatever control he exerts, in his own self-image he lacks the substantive involvement, in some way that matters to him, to actually be doing something.[11] He always seemed to be planning and very likely he was, but his planning ultimately amounted to nothing. For Raskolnikov, similarly, the conception of agency as control turns out to be vacuous. This is the conception that Raskolnikov starts with. He begins with the thought ". . . a man holds the fate of the world in his two hands, and yet, simply because he is afraid, he just lets things drift" (1–2). He conceives of the challenge of committing a murder as that of sustaining a plan against the forces of emotion and inertia; he rehearses his plan and even considers planning part of the deed, in that it counts as something heroic rather than as a crime only if he manages to carry it out rationally. He also insists on control in his attempts to manipulate Zametov and Porfiry Petrovich, and in his insistence that he will not "allow" Dunya to make sacrifices for him. And yet his attempts at control turn out to be even emptier than Svidrigaylov's. For Raskolnikov, even the pretense of control is lacking. In getting the axe he remarks, "It was not my planning, but the devil that accomplished that!" (69). Soon thereafter he finds himself governed by instinct (78) and the unconscious swinging of his hands (73); control turns out to be a form of obedience (265). Despite his best efforts, control does not even help him distinguish his actions from mere bodily movements.

Accountability

Our understanding of agency might also appeal to what someone is or could be held accountable for.[12] That is, the idea of someone who takes responsibility for the outcomes of her deeds might be an ineliminable part of our understanding of what an agent and an action are. There are many ways to construe the notion of accountability, but it often involves, on one hand, some kind of closeness to an event such that one is connected to its further repercussions and, on the other hand, a responsiveness to others that could take the form of observing the requirements of a social status, meeting the obligations or responsibilities that derive from a particular role, or acknowledgment of others' expectations, for example. In *Crime and Punishment* Porfiry Petrovich exemplifies this way of thinking about agency, and his version centers around his reliability in meeting the demands of his vocation. Not only is he effective in fulfilling his professional ends, he inhabits his vocation fully, almost literally since his apartment is in the police station and he seems to leave only on official business. Other kinds of considerations and influences do not move him; even if he were not so successful, he would still be above reproach for the way he conducts his investigations. So he does not speak much about accountability: we do not see what it would mean for him to be accountable for failures, and he does not bother to explain his own pursuits in terms of what he will be accountable for. Instead, he has adopted his professional ends so fully as personal ones that no question arises of whether he is accountable for the activity that makes up his professional life.

In Porfiry Petrovich's self-presentation, however, he remains fundamentally passive: he waits for criminals to reveal themselves. As he says to Raskolnikov, "I was relying on your character, Rodion Romanovich, on your character above all!" (431). In his interactions with Raskolnikov, in particular, he declares his interest, makes invitations, and engages in conversations, but seldom asserts anything or even asks pointed questions until the case has, for him, been solved; when he does make an assertion or carry out a task, furthermore, it remains unclear whether he is genuinely committed to the activity or whether the performance is merely part of a process for generating an effect. This makes what he is doing and what of his activity is really his own into something deeply ambiguous. His own personality does little to clear things up. He reports to Raskolnikov, "I am a man who has developed as far as he is capable, that is all. A man, perhaps, of feeling and sympathy, of some knowledge perhaps, but no longer capable of further development" (441; cf. 323, 432). He alludes to a past that no longer matters while he devotes his energies to his job; this leaves indeterminate whether he is doing something himself or merely filling a more or less impersonal role. Whereas Porfiry remains baffling, Raskolnikov vacillates on the place of accountability in his view of himself as an agent. At moments he wants to be recognized, initially for his potential greatness but then, reluctantly, for his crime: "I shall go in, fall on my knees, and tell the whole story" (89). More often, however, he gives up on the idea of accountability for his actions. Even if accountability might, in principle, apply, he wants his murders either to transcend all accountability to others or to be judged so trivial and accidental that they are beneath judgment. For Raskolnikov, accountability is an appealing but inapplicable way of making sense of his agency.

Reflective Deliberation

Another way of thinking about agency is in terms of reflective deliberation. Agents, on this conception, have a distinctive capacity to reflect on their ends and the means to satisfy them, and then to determine a course of action based on their considered judgment. Actions then count as such because they result from the deliverances of this distinctive capacity.[13] This may be the least prominent way of thinking about agency in the novel, but it nevertheless has important representatives. Luzhin is the one who is most committed to such a conception: not only does he engage almost continuously in practical reflection, he also reflects on the soundness of proceeding in that way, seeks out legitimation for doing so, and recommends it to others. Thus he is described by the Raskolnikovs as "practical," "prudent," and "intelligent" (225), and he treats anything he learns strategically, as the material for plotting out his future advantage: "all this information gave Peter Petrovich a certain idea . . ." (347). Lebezyatnikov represents a more theoretical version of this conception as, for him, questions of participation in everyday customs and habits need to be considered in light of "the most fashionable current idea" (349). Dunya is closest to the philosophical version of this conception according to which only moral reasoning counts as distinctively one's own. Her mother thus refers to her "moral freedom" (40) and discusses "the letter which Dunya found herself obliged to write" (31). Writing the letter to Svidrigaylov did not suit her inclinations or immediate advantage, but she judged herself to be constrained by moral considerations and adopted a course of action in line with them.

Luzhin and Lebezyatnikov understand their agency as tied to their powers of deliberation, and they manage to be two of the worst or at least the most unlikeable characters in a novel that contains a murderer and a rapist. This does not by itself show that there is anything wrong with the conception of agency; they could be agents who happen to have unfortunate personalities. But what the novel shows is that either reflection does not lead to action or it leads to defective behavior. Lebezyatnikov is voluble but, despite his familiarity with the latest theories, will never restructure society, establish communes, or do anything else of significance. Luzhin consciously instrumentalizes all of his interactions, including his intimate relationships, which he sees as occasions for power and manipulation. This is not only repugnant, but feckless: it leaves him unable to pursue his own ends since this is a bad way of conducting intimate relationships. Insofar as these two think of themselves as reflective deliberators, they misunderstand themselves and their ends. Dunya is not odious, but she suffers from both flaws. Her moral reflection conceals her actual motivations, since her relationship to Svidrigaylov is more complicated than anyone seems to acknowledge and has the unfortunate outcome of engagement to Luzhin; as her brother tells her, referring to the philosopher of moral freedom, "the Schiller in you is always getting into a muddle" (465). Raskolnikov, who spends so much time lapsed "into profound thought" (2), also manages to suffer from both flaws, sometimes almost simultaneously. Reflection leads him to the conclusion that he should kill: "his casuistry has the cutting edge of a razor, and he could no longer find any conscious objection in his own mind" (67). But when it comes time to act, his rational faculties abandon him: "He did not reason about anything, he was quite incapable of reasoning, but he felt with his whole being that his mind and will were no longer free" (59).

All the characters in the novel fail as agents. In a diversity of ways, they fail to sustain relationships to their own deeds, in part because of how they conceive of the form that those relationships should take. Raskolnikov is the biggest, most comprehensive failure: reflection leads him to adopt, at times, all the others' conceptions and to experience every shortcoming all the more dramatically. But with his failure so general and conclusive, the novel also gives him the only way out.

IV. CRIME AND EXPRESSION

Raskolnikov adopted various ways of thinking about agency, and they hindered his attempts to be in charge of his actions. Not only did he fail to make sense of himself as an agent, he became more confused about what that might amount to and farther away from achieving it. In showing these failures and those of others, the novel makes a case for treating agency as *expressive*. The novel represents one's conception of oneself as an agent as internal to attempts at agency and finds typical but calamitous failings in the standard conceptions. Only by coming to see agency as expressive can Raskolnikov arrive at a satisfactory connection to his actions.

By an "expressive" view of agency I mean one in which there is nothing prior to and independent of the performance of the action that makes it count as such.[14] Actions are not the external manifestation of something separate and inner, but expressions that have a fully public nature and thus take on meaning in their social, historical context. As public phenomena, actions count as such when the agent can acknowledge them as her own: when they show something about the person, when they fit into her reasons and motivations, and when they are at least somewhat adequate to the agent's understanding of them. Raskolnikov adopts expressivist views early on, but then has to come to terms with his practical and theoretical failures. He begins by looking for a form of expression that is completely non-reciprocal, depending only on his own intellectual originality and strength of will. This would take the form of an act that somehow commands acknowledgment, despite not taking anyone's reasons into account; to others it could appear only as a transgression or something beyond ordinary comprehension.

This is an early explanation of Raskolnikov's view: "Kill her, take her money, on condition that you dedicate yourself with its help to the service of humanity and the common good: don't you think that thousands of good deeds will wipe out one little, insignificant transgression?" (62). This might initially appear to be a form of the end justifying the means. But Raskolnikov is indifferent both to the end and to any form of public justification. His aim is not beneficence, but establishing a distinctive meaning for a distinctive act, or as he later puts it, what "his ideas . . . require . . . for their fulfillment" (249). His aim is a completely independent form of agency.

What he quickly learns, however, is that he is not in charge of the meaning of his public deeds. His actions turn out to mean something very different from what he had anticipated they would: "The only thing I knew how to do was kill! And I could not do that properly either, it seems . . ." (264). He starts by taking agency as something that he imposes on the world, without consideration of others. His spectacular failure eventually forces him to realize, however, that the public meaning of his deeds depends on others' points of view.[15] This view is at first abhorrent to him. His initial recognition of failure is not that his plot did not succeed, but that he does not control his past behavior and that this compels him to make adjustments in light of what others think. Acknowledging others is what pains him: " 'Oh, the devil take it all!' he thought in a sudden access of ungovernable irritation. 'If it's begun, it's begun, and to the devil with her, and with the new life! Oh God, how stupid it all is! . . . How much lying and cringing I did today! . . . I ought to spit on all of them, and on my own behavior! It's all wrong!' " (104). But this is not a rejection of expressivism;[16] rather, it is a reluctant, gradual realization that it is not completed until he can accept a relational version of it. He becomes someone who owns his deed by accepting the public meaning of his deeds.

V. THE PHILOSOPHICAL ANTHROPOLOGY OF HUMAN ACTION

With an expressive view of agency, the context matters. Different lives present different possibilities not only for recognizing oneself in one's deeds, but also for the very significance of distinguishing oneself as an agent. The novel, of course, situates its depictions of agency within a particular human context. At the same time, however, it offers a generalized view of how its context functions. The possibilities of agency are not just those of a specific moment in a fictional St. Petersburg, but ones belonging to something more like a general philosophical anthropology. In the world of the novel, a deed that stands out sufficiently to count as one's own can only take the form of a transgression. And although Raskolnikov initially believes that such a transgression can be redeemed by success, he turns out to be mistaken. Human agency does not depend on success, but on the world being hospitable enough for someone to recognize herself in it. And that, in turn, requires finding a relationship that combines affection and subordination.

The novel presents at least two complementary versions of the necessity of crime.[17] One is that achievement can be recognized only through contrastive force, and thus through abject failure. The other is that the social world is structured in such a way that anything that breaks out of conformity must count as a violation. The former appears, presented by Razumikhin, in an innocuous, epistemic form: "Do you think I am annoyed because they talk nonsense? Rubbish! I like people to talk nonsense. It is man's unique privilege, among all other organisms. By pursuing falsehood you will arrive at the truth!" (193; cf. 195). The latter view is specifically Raskolnikov's, for example here: "In a word, I deduce that all of them, not only the great ones, but also those who diverge ever so slightly from the beaten track, those, that is, who are just barely capable of saying something new, must, by their nature, inevitably be criminals . . ." (249–250). Together these two views lay out background conditions for agency. On one hand, human dignity consists in the capacity for going astray; on the other hand, however society responds to deviance, standing out in some way is necessary to establish one's independence.

Raskolnikov initially believes that criminality can be redeemed into agency by surpassing the very category of crime. He tells Sonya, "The man who tramples on the greatest number of things is their lawgiver, and whoever is most audacious is most certainly right" (400). Since the murders fail to establish "right," however, Raskolnikov needs something parallel: someone who responds to awareness of his criminality with an endorsement of him. Sonya provides this response, through her affection and devotion to him. Raskolnikov, of course, has no right to this affection: it is unearned and undeserved. And yet without it, he would have no way of relating to his deeds except to take them as making him a "louse" (260). The novel, furthermore, shows Sonya's subordination as a requirement for Raskolnikov's agency.[18] Sonya almost immediately devotes her limited energies to Raskolnikov's recuperation, and he would not have been able to function without relying on her. In the world of the novel, agency requires excluding oneself from society so that one can recognize the distinctiveness of one's deed; at the same time, it requires reintegrating oneself into a community that can acknowledge one's activity as meaningful. Since, in committing murders, Raskolnikov had left himself no path back, he required someone else to do the work of creating a place for him where his potential for action could be appreciated.

VI. CONCLUSION

Crime and Punishment presents an expressive view of agency, but does so in a way that is inseparable from views about the human condition. Actions are performances that the agent can, retrospectively, acknowledge as her own; at the same time agency is available only through transgression and the institution of subordinative relationships founded on unwarranted affection. More constructive, rational, or equitable opportunities for agency do not seem to be available.

The novel supports its view of agency, then, by presenting its version of the limits of human experience; the strength or weakness of its case depends in part on the plausibility of that representation. The effectiveness of fictional representation here does not come through making an imagined empirical claim about a relationship that actually exists and that can be used to demarcate intentional action as such from mere movement. The novel works, rather, by representing the distance between holding a conception of agency and the possibilities for agency that it supports. In this way it constitutes a philosophical problem of agency: whether any conception can be adequate to the sense that we might want to make of it and the role it might play, more broadly, in making sense of our lives. Part of the case that the novel makes is not about what is instantiated in the world, but about what would be a satisfactory way of making sense of ourselves as agents, whether or not we manage to succeed at it.[19]

NOTES

1. Fyodor Dostoevsky, *Crime and Punishment*, trans. Jessie Coulson (Oxford: Oxford University Press, 2008). All references to *Crime and Punishment* will be to this edition and given by page number parenthetically in the text.
2. This phrase appears in a letter that Dostoevsky wrote in November 1865. It is cited in Robin Feuer Miller, *Dostoevsky's Unfinished Journey* (New Haven, CT: Yale University Press, 2007), 58.
3. These concerns about agency and self-knowledge are similar to what Michael Holquist has called the "particularly urgent problem of self-identification" that appears in Dostoevsky's work. See his *Dostoevsky and the Novel* (Evanston, IL: Northwestern University Press, 1986), ix.
4. Miller, *Dostoevsky's Unfinished Journey*, 59.
5. For a traditional discussion of the importance of choice in agency, see Aristotle, *Nicomachean Ethics*, trans. Roger Crisp (New York: Cambridge University Press, 2000), 37–48 (book 3).
6. John Locke emphasizes the central importance of particular inner states in the chapter "Of power" (II.xxi) of *An Essay concerning Human Understanding* (New York: Oxford University Press, 1975).
7. One can find something similar to this simultaneous acceptance of and subjection to one's feelings in the concept of a "holy fool." For the holy fool, too, the category of agency breaks down under the strain of maintaining the general category while taking away the possibility of making sense of any particular

deeds. See Harriet Murav, *Holy Foolishness: Dostoevsky's Novels & the Poetics of Cultural Critique* (Stanford, CA, Stanford University Press 1992), 26: "[T]he holy fool is understood as the image of the most fallen man because he has seemingly renounced his reason. The hagiographer understands the madness or foolishness of the saint to be a choice."

8. There is also the uncanny moment in the tavern in which the integrity of the "inner" seems to be violated and he literally becomes a bystander to his own idea, when the student brags to the soldier, "I swear I could kill that damned old woman and rob her, without a single twinge of conscience" (62).
9. For a discussion of the role of agent-guidance in the performance of an action see, for example, Alfred Mele, *The Springs of Action* (New York: Oxford University Press, 1992); for a discussion of the role of planning in rational agency, see Michael Bratman, *Intentions, Plans, and Practical Reason* (Cambridge, MA: Harvard University Press, 1987).
10. Hegel makes a similar point about the "self-certainty" of the "lord" being defective because the "bondsman" is left to perform the "work" that allows for an independent standpoint on the world. See G. W. F. Hegel, *Phenomenology of Spirit*, trans. A. V. Miller (New York: Oxford University Press, 1977), 118–119.
11. One can look at this as a matter not only of corporeal involvement, of physically performing deeds, but also of emotional, interpersonal involvement. For example, see Malcolm V. Jones, *Dostoyevsky after Bakhtin: Readings in Dostoyevsky's Fantastic Realism* (Cambridge: Cambridge University Press, 1990), 93: "No doubt this rejection and Dunya's play a crucial role in determining Svidrigaylov finally on suicide, for even Svidrigaylov needs some confirmation from someone he respects."
12. For a philosophical treatment of agency that makes use of a notion of accountability, see Gary Watson, *Agency and Answerability: Selected Essays* (New York: Oxford University Press 2008). The account of responsibility in P. F. Strawson, *Freedom and Resentment and Other Essays* (New York: Routledge 2008), is also relevant here.
13. Although Kant's conception of agency differs enormously from a conception of reflective deliberation, we can perhaps find the latter's origin in his idea that "the will is nothing other than practical reason." See Immanuel Kant, *Groundwork of the Metaphysics of Morals*, trans. Mary Gregor (New York: Cambridge University Press, 1998), 412.
14. For influential formulations of an expressive view of agency, see Charles Taylor, *Hegel* (New York: Cambridge University Press, 1975); Charles Taylor, "Hegel and the Philosophy of Action," in L. S. Stepelevich and D. Lamb, eds., *Hegel's Philosophy of Action* (Atlantic Highlands, NJ: Humanities Press, 1983); and Charles Taylor, "What Is Human Agency?" in *Human Agency and Language* (New York: Cambridge University Press, 1985). Malcolm Jones connects Dostoevsky to "expressivist emphases" (Jones, *Dostoyevsky after Bakhtin*,

6), but works with a notion of expressivism more closely tied to German Romanticism than the one that I am working with here.

15. Harriet Murav presents a similar point in terms of a Bakhtinian point about unfinalizability. See Murav, *Holy Foolishness*, 11: "Hence, paradoxically, the very discourse that permits freedom and open-endedness delays and even prevents the kind of dialogic meeting of the self with another, which Bakhtin claims is the only true vehicle for self-definition."
16. In *Dostoevsky and the Novel* (Evanston, IL: Northwestern University Press, 1986), Michael Holquist frames this transition in terms of a move from a Hegelian historicism to something completely different (90–97). By contrast, I am framing it in terms of a shift from a "debased Hegelian principle of interpretation" (Holquist, *Dostoevsky and the Novel*, 90) to an appropriately reciprocal form of expressivism.
17. In *Dostoevsky's Dialectics and the Problem of Sin* (Evanston, IL: Northwestern University Press, 2010), Ksana Blank also generalizes this idea into a philosophy of the coincidence of opposites, and pairs agency with "sin": "In Dostoevsky's treatment of these binary pairs, counterparts are contrasted but presented as interdependent. Thus Dostoevsky's religious philosophy is built on the idea that man's way to God may lie through sin and crime" (10).
18. Harriet Murav, in "Reading Women in Dostoevsky," in Sona Stephan Hoisington, ed., *A Plot of Her Own* (Evanston, IL: Northwestern University Press, 1995), makes the case that in Dostoevsky's work in general, the ethical standing of persons depends on the "victimization of the female" (48).
19. I wish to thank Jenn Dum, Richard Eldridge, and Randall Havas for discussions about Dostoevsky and agency, and Sidney Dement and Costica Bradatan for invaluable and detailed feedback and help. Unfortunately, I could not have addressed all of their concerns, even if I had managed to give myself an infinite word count.

Chapter 4

Metaphysical Motivation

Crime and Punishment in the Light of Schelling

SEBASTIAN GARDNER

I. WHY MURDER? RASKOLNIKOV'S *EXPERIMENTUM CRUCIS*

What drives Raskolnikov to commit murder? The answer lies neither in self-interest nor in ideology. Raskolnikov sets no value on his own interest. His worldly attachments are severely attenuated, and his concern to evade discovery is less pragmatic concern for the implications of being convicted than it is terror at the meaning of the act itself. The prospect of financial gain allows him to bring the act under a rationalizing description that relates means and end coherently ("saving Dunya from a degrading marriage") and to which an objective judicial category corresponds, but such conceptualization is a mere enabling condition, logically on a par with his use of the axe. Nor is Raskolnikov engaged in challenging the prevailing morality. No trace of ideological justification is present in his state of mind in the opening chapters. He has entertained favorably various ideas concerning the rights of the higher man, but Dostoevsky gets us to see that their motivational force is faint and their role again ancillary: perhaps they contributed to his initial formation of the idea of the murder, and they provide him post facto with a further cover story, yet another pretext, but they are not his reason for going through with it.[1] Indeed it is not even clear that he ever believed the theory. The common gloss on Raskolnikov as an aspirant *Übermensch* is not tenable.

Nor, to consider a third type of incentive, is Raskolnikov's motivation aesthetic, even in the most extended sense. Nothing about the act itself attracts him. The idea of a perfect murder—the artwork-act relished by the members of de Quincy's Society of Connoisseurs in Murder[2]—is not on his horizon. Nor is Raskolnikov an axiological aesthete, desiring to taste the phenomenology of evildoing or criminality. Nor, fourth, can what he does be explained in diagnostic manner as the abreactive effect of some past trauma or as the manifestation of some aspect of his personality. We learn of the death of his fiancée only as an event in the remote past. Whether or not Raskolnikov can be brought under some technical psycho- or sociopathological category, any such label will supply an answer only insofar as it tells us what he is aiming at, which is what must first be determined. The same goes for the ascription of character traits—vanity, arrogance, self-absorption, contemptuousness, maliciousness are all pinned on him—to Raskolnikov.

In Part Five, Chapter 4, in his self-explanation to Sonya, Raskolnikov works his way through all of the substantive possibilities, and of what he says, which is a great deal, the only accounts of his motive that have the faintest ring of truth are the briefest and simplest—and also the emptiest, most cryptic, and perplexing—encapsulations: "I only wanted to dare, Sonya, that was the only reason!"; "I longed to kill without casuistry, to kill for my own benefit, and for that alone!"; "I simply murdered; I murdered for myself"; "it was not money that I needed, Sonya, when I killed; it was not money, so much as something else"; "something else was pushing me along"; "it was only *to test myself*" (401–402). Everything points, therefore, to Raskolnikov's ignorance of his own motivation at the level at which people are ordinarily considered to know what they are doing. Its nebulous and inchoate quality being so pronounced, we might wonder if there is any truth of the matter. The possibility that Raskolnikov's motivation is ultimately indeterminate, or determinate but wholly unknowable, cannot be ruled out, but it is not the conclusion Dostoevsky is asking his readers to draw: *Crime and Punishment* is, as it is often said, a novel of suspense in which, fundamentally, we seek disclosure of the motivation and meaning of the act with which it begins; the police investigation and everything else that belongs to its plot compose a framework for highlighting and exploring this mystery.

If Raskolnikov is motivated at all and in any sense—which he must be, for he is not the medium of an external agent, any more than his act is a random happening—then (we have a right to suppose) some awareness of what he wants to get out of committing murder, however non-conscious and inarticulate, must be present within him. The fact that his motivation is positively nebulous—he himself is overwhelmed by it—counts against its amounting to nothing but an unfortunate accidental conjunction of partial factors of the various types described above. That Dostoevsky wants us to feel the weight of its imponderability—suggesting motives only in order to reveal their adequacy—not only licenses us to interpret Raskolnikov beyond the bounds of what is explicit in the text, but demands that we do so. We need to adopt, therefore, a perspective on Raskolnikov's motivation that goes beyond his explicit self-understanding, and if no obvious answer is available, then we must look to the unobvious. Let us accordingly re-pose the original question: What kind of motive could be *both* nebulous and indistinct *and* compelling, perhaps compelling *because* of its indistinctness and nebulousness?

If Raskolnikov is motivated, then he has an aim, and if he has an aim, then its attainment must have value in his eyes. Clearly he is not aiming directly at moral goodness, for he does not judge the killing *right*, nor does he consider the death of Alena Ivanovna to be itself a *good* or enough of one to make it necessary that she be killed (and many other ways were known to him in which he could have made the world a better place). Yet somehow or other he must—for the compelling reasons that Plato's Socrates gives in the *Meno*[3]—set value on what he sets out to do: *some* conception of the Good must govern his actions. If, then, in committing murder Raskolnikov has the Good in mind, while the act itself and its worldly results are not instances of it, then the act must be a *means* to what is good. But to *what* good could it possibly be a means?

Here is a suggestion: by committing murder Raskolnikov attempts to achieve *knowledge*. This fits with the fact that Raskolnikov does not seem to be targeting any worldly state of affairs. But if this is to make sense, then it needs to be explained what question could be answered by such an act. What hypothesis could murder put to the test?

Manifestly, in order that its acquisition should justify murder, the knowledge sought must be of the highest importance, and it cannot be of an ordinary communicable kind—Raskolnikov already knows that murder is a type of act of which there are real instances—and it would seem furthermore that it carries no special reference to himself. Raskolnikov's sense of his own identity is extremely etiolated. He knows himself to be abnormal, but nothing of a definite, positive kind marks him out in his eyes, and his primary interest is not in figuring out his own psychology. Unlike many protagonists of nineteenth- and twentieth-century fiction, he is not engaged on a journey of personal self-understanding; his indifference to the modern ideal of individual self-realization parallels his stubborn refusal to conform to Luzhin's model of *homo economicus*.

The knowledge at which Raskolnikov aims must therefore concern him not just as *this particular* individual but as an individual in some *universal* respect, making his inquiry a philosophical one. It must also, of course, if it is needed at all costs and anything may be sacrificed for its sake, not be knowledge whose value lies in its being a means to some further, contingent end: Raskolnikov may not expect murder to yield direct acquaintance with the Form of the Good, but nonetheless it must be knowledge the very having of which counts as good in itself.

Now, it is natural to think that the knowledge in question concerns the existence of God, or the reality of morality, or, to the extent that morality may be thought to implicate God's will, both at once. This cannot be far off the mark. But it is not easy to see how committing murder could be thought to give proof of either. Raskolnikov is not in a state of anticipation, waiting to see what happens after the event: he does not anticipate a thunderbolt descending from the heavens, as a child tests the bounds of parental authority. And that the act is morally wrong, and in some plain sense ought not to be done, is not something that he really doubts. Even if the objectivity of moral properties were what puzzled him, actually executing the murder could hardly help to answer the question. Again it is significant that certain things one might have expected to find are absent from Raskolnikov's reflections: he does not ponder in general terms, in the manner of ethical theory, the question of "what it is" for something to be right or wrong, good or bad. It is as if somehow (in some way that we have yet to grasp) Raskolnikov has got beyond such "standard" philosophical questions and struck a deeper, harder level of perplexity. Again, to consider another obvious option: it does not seem that what Raskolnikov needs to know is whether or not he has a conscience. If that were his concern, he could answer his question at greater economy by examining his feelings about the act in prospect, which are in any case entirely clear: the prospect terrifies him, which is why he has to force himself to murder Alena Ivanovna.[4] What absorbs him in the run up is simply whether he is *able* to perform the act that he has proposed to himself.

Here then is a different suggestion, which if correct would explain the necessity of murder: Raskolnikov seeks proof of the reality of human freedom, and it is only by giving reality to evil—killing the moneylender—that this proof can be provided. If he *can* perform it, then whatever else ensues, he will have the knowledge he seeks, and it will be of infinite value.

How (on earth) would murder establish the reality of freedom? And, at a more basic level, why would it matter so much to Raskolnikov to know that human beings are free? The second question is much easier to answer, for the notion that freedom in its negative sense—freedom qua absence of necessity, freedom of the will—is a sine qua non of the Good, and that freedom in its positive sense is a condition at which all human beings properly aim, are core elements of both our religious and our secular legacies: unless God gave us free will, we are not candidates for either salvation or damnation; unless the development of modernity makes us free, its demands and disenchantments are pointless. Unless we are free, then we are as good as nothing.[5]

To answer the first and much harder question, I propose that we turn to Schelling's celebrated essay of 1809, *Philosophical Investigations into the Essence of Human Freedom*, or *Freiheitsschrift*.[6] The central claim of this radical work is that, just as human freedom should not be identified with "free will" in the sense of empirical openness—the mere possibility that I could have not gone through such and such a sequence of psychological states, and in consequence not moved my body in such and such ways—no more should it be identified with rational agency, in the Kantian sense of possession of the capacity to act out of reason alone, that is, on the basis of sheer recognition of the rightness of an action. The latter conception of freedom Schelling calls "merely formal." In order to be real, Schelling argues, freedom must have weight, must be fixed to a content that *matters,* and this content, whatever it may be, must not *force* us to act but must be *chosen* by us. Real freedom presupposes therefore a choice between intrinsically conflicting *final values.* And because genuine freedom requires that something be *at stake,* the formal conception of freedom defended by Kant, which accords well with secular modernity, is defective. Kant's account entails not that we are free to be good but that we *must* be good, where "being good" signifies nothing more (if we follow Kant's reasoning) than, trivially, the rational necessity of conformity with reason. If the law of reason is pure necessity and our non-conformity with it is something merely negative—if immorality amounts only to an empty nonsense, the mere infantile silliness of doing for no reason something which there can be no reason to do—then the law of reason may as well, as far as freedom is concerned, be a law of nature, a psychological equivalent of the law of gravity. Just as Socrates' argument in the *Meno* dooms us to always aim at the Good, however hard we apparently try to do otherwise, so too does Kant's analysis deny the possibility of a choice to *not* be good, and without such a choice, freedom disappears and the Good reduces to a formal structure which we are merely in the grip of, in the way that physical bodies are subject to the mathematically formulable laws of mechanics.

The principal aim of Schelling's essay is to show what metaphysical conditions need to be met in order for real, non-formal freedom to be possible. Schelling's philosophical inquiry does not concern itself with fictional scenarios, but *Crime and Punishment,* I am suggesting, lies directly on the path that it projects, and in its light Raskolnikov begins to make sense. In order for the Good to be real, man must be capable of goodness for its own sake, and if it is also true, as we have seen Schelling maintains, that the Good must be chosen *over and against* its opposite, then man must equally be capable of evil. And in order for man to have a real capacity for evil, it must be possible for him to not merely fall short in relation to the Good; rather he must be capable of willing evil for its own sake.

Does, however, this idea—human *devilry,* as it might be called—make sense? Manifestly, it falls foul of the argument of the *Meno,* which, if sound, vindicates Kant. Schelling's contention, I have said, is that the *Meno*-Kant view must be rejected, but even if we are not persuaded by Schelling's argument, it does not follow that his account fails to encapsulate Raskolnikov's actual motivation, for certainly one may aim at something that reflective scrutiny reveals to be conceptually impossible. And if it is true, in the present case and any other, that human striving is governed by conceptions which are ultimately nonsensical, then literary fiction is especially well suited to show this fact, insofar as it can present as actual what we would never take ourselves to encounter in real life; it can reveal fictional dimensions of the ways we live or, put differently, the ways in which we strive to give reality to fictions. Whether or not *Crime and Punishment* is a case in point need not (yet) be decided.

To make clearer the way in which the question of the possibility of a pure evil will can become urgent in the way that I am suggesting it has become for Raskolnikov, and how this question may be regarded as implicating an internal relation of life and fiction, it will help to consider another character from literature, also drawn to evil. Iago is not a stock villain in the manner of Richard III, though on occasion he pretends to be, nor is he consumed, like Edmund or Macbeth or (again) Richard III, by bitter hatred or ambition or vengefulness, though again he toys with those guises. We may reasonably ask if Iago—"motiveless" evil—is genuinely possible. Some critics have thought not and interpret him accordingly as a mere plot mechanism, but this is a truncated reading of the play. For one thing, Iago himself raises implicitly the question of his own possibility: he knowingly confabulates the usual banal motives, as if seeking to dismiss the puzzle of his own nature. (Othello, he says, may have cuckolded him, and even if those rumors are false, the suspicion alone is reason enough to seek to destroy him.) For another thing, and much more important: If Iago is a "mere fiction," not a real human possibility, then so too is the entire tragedy and all that it means to us. We cannot pick and choose: If Iago is a plot device and not a truth, then the same goes for the goodness of Desdemona and Emilia, meaning that all along nothing of real value has been in jeopardy and that what we took to be tragedy is in fact a farce, consisting merely of an intertwining of conflicting psychological forces. Now Raskolnikov, we may say, is also asking whether Iago is possible, and with high stakes in view, for if he is not, then we can succeed or fail in achieving goodness only as a stone either falls to the ground or encounters an obstacle in its path, in which case the Good and salvation are null. That Iago is a real possibility must therefore be *shown*, which Raskolnikov proposes to do by murdering Alena Ivanovna.

That Raskolnikov's motivation has a metaphysical character explains its enigmatic blankness from the standpoint of ordinary understanding—it eludes familiar distinctions and categories of motive—and why it has for Raskolnikov both the uncomprehended immediacy of instinct and the inexorability of logic. It is unconscious not for the sorts of reasons uncovered in psychoanalysis but on account of the nebulous character of the Idea at its core.[7] It also explains the peculiarly amoral, as opposed to immoral, quality of Raskolnikov's undertaking, and its first-person boundedness. Raskolnikov's question concerns not his own individual good but the possibility of the Good as such. One cannot answer such a question by pointing to any fact within the world, so the reality of evil cannot be established by mere report. Though not a question about Raskolnikov himself, it arises in and from the perspective of the first person, and since it is not posed in a reflective philosophical form, it cannot be detached from that perspective or referred outside it for its answer—hence, again, the necessity that it be addressed by Raskolnikov's own action.

Raskolnikov's project has the brutal impersonality of philosophical inquiry: his indifference to the personhood of Alena Ivanovna is the consequence of methodological solipsism, not egoism, and in that strange internal way—by virtue of occupying a position logically prior to morality, the genuine reality of which it aims to establish—cannot be considered, in its own terms, a matter for moral judgment.

II. "WHY DON'T I PERFORM MY DUTIES, MY DEAR SIR?" (11): MARMELADOV'S CONFUSIONS

The Schellingian interpretation of Raskolnikov is candidly speculative, and thus far I have attempted to support it chiefly by eliminating other candidates, by indicating its coherence with Raskolnikov's state of mind—his indefinite striving to grasp something which eludes ordinary comprehension but on which everything depends—and by suggesting that anything less substantive will fall short. It may now be asked what more specifically in the text of the novel, if anything, positively supports it. The main evidence comes in two forms, one of which comprises the first major dramatic scene of the novel.[8] The other I treat in the following section.

On entering the tavern in Part One, Chapter 2, Raskolnikov becomes immediately aware of his affinity with one man present, Titular Councilor Marmeladov, who in turn recognizes Raskolnikov as a likely receptive auditor, and within minutes Marmeladov has begun to deliver to Raskolnikov and all within hearing what he has clearly rehearsed many times in his own head: a summary account of his condition, as if modeled on the kind of official report expected of a civil servant. He is drunk, and his monologue is characteristic of a drunkard, but it is not the drink that is doing the talking. The problem, conceptually speaking, which is also responsible for the grotesque comedy of the scene, is that Marmeladov's "account"—which is at once a description, an explanation, a moral evaluation, a self-justification, a self-condemnation, an exoneration of his failure as husband and father, an exhortation and plea for forgiveness, an attempt to inspire respect, and an assertion of his dignity—makes absolutely no sense. His "crime," he says, is poverty, though poverty is no crime; his condition is "beggary," which is not merely a crime but a "vice," on account of which he has been expelled, quite justly, from human society; this treatment is "humiliating," and because it is so he humiliates himself further; his requests for loans are refused because compassion is a sentiment no longer in fashion—indeed it is now "prohibited by science"—but in truth he is "a swine," "an infamous wretch," "a beast by nature," "most disgraceful"; his wife refuses him sympathy and treats him unjustly, but when she pulls him by the hair it is "out of compassion"; he was driven back to drink by a reorganization of the civil service and the ill will of certain persons, and yet it was by his own fault that he lost his post; in drink he is able to discover compassion and to increase his suffering; he deserves no pity but "ought to be crucified," though this crucifixion would be, his citation from Pilate implies ("Behold the man!"), the proof of his innocence; and he has an absolute claim on others, because "there comes a time when it is absolutely essential to turn somewhere" (Part One, Chapter 2, 10–22).

The brilliance of Dostoevsky's depiction lies in the manner in which Marmeladov is kept poised on the brink of intelligibility, without allowing us, or Raskolnikov, to grasp the truth concerning the kind of man he really is. Is Marmeladov simply a victim of internal and external forces? Is he akratic? Is he unable to do what he knows he ought due to constitutional weakness or because he is physiologically enslaved to intoxicants? Or do his problems result from a lack of self-understanding? Dostoevsky knows his Freud, as it were, so perhaps Marmeladov masochistically relishes his own humiliation and takes sadistic satisfaction in the suffering he inflicts on his wife; perhaps there is even an erotic aspect to his forcing his daughter into prostitution. If Marmeladov is in these or other ways self-ignorant, is he therefore at the mercy of forces that motivate him unwittingly? Or should we say that he is self-deceived? In which case, is he the victim of his self-deception, or is he its author and culpable perpetrator? Presumably he must be both. Alternatively, might he simply be, as he is said at one point to appear, in a condition of "something like madness" (9)? Or we might cut matters short in a different way by declaring him *tout court* a vicious personality, which would allow us to condemn him without having to account for him. The exact opposite view is also available. When he describes himself as having the nature of a "beast"—"such is my nature"—he is most naturally understood to be putting himself in the position of a judge passing a guilty verdict on himself qua the accused, but perhaps the truth in what he says is that he, like all human beings, is quite literally an animal and nothing more, and consequently behaves as animals do, that is, in accordance with impulse.

All of these are questions which we as readers, attempting to form a notion of Raskolnikov's reaction to Marmeladov (which Dostoevsky does not spell out), are compelled to raise, and they are also questions that Marmeladov is raising about himself; such at least is the logical implication of what he says. But since he fails to answer them—rather he answers them many times over and in conflicting ways—we cannot be at all sure that he really wants them answered. Indeed we might speculate that his entire confusion concerning his own moral-psychological characterization is self-generated and, far from being an attempt to get to grips with himself, amounts to a strategy for avoiding doing so.

Given this morass, we cannot adopt any coherent attitude toward Marmeladov. He may arouse in us contempt or revulsion, but this does not help us decide whether we should condemn him, forgive him, pity him, or subject him to diagnosis and offer him therapy. All these options are open and all are equally arbitrary. (As if matters were not complicated enough: Katerina Ivanovna avows that he was, despite his weakness, a "good-hearted man" (369), and we are told that at the moment of his death his countenance reveals—to Sonya at any rate—"infinite suffering" (179), which seems to raise him to an altogether different plane.)

Marmeladov has therefore posed the question that Raskolnikov needs answered.[9] He presents in a concentrated and dramatized form various contradictory possibilities concerning the nature of human beings that Raskolnikov undertakes to resolve: Raskolnikov has to, as it were, sort out Marmeladov's conceptual mess and establish that human beings are not the nonsensical non-entities that Marmeladov has made them out to be—which means establishing the possibility of evil.

III. PSYCHOLOGICAL FACT AS COMPULSIVE FICTION

The second kind of evidence for the Schellingian interpretation comes from the sustained attention paid throughout *Crime and Punishment* to the concept and theme of psychology. Dostoevsky wants to make the very notion of the psychological (in some way) questionable and get us to (in some sense) look beyond it. This claim of course needs explanation. Let me first spell out why it is an implication of Schelling's conception of freedom and then indicate the features of the text that show its centrality to the meaning of the work.

If freedom is real, and if its reality requires the possibility of a *pure* will—for either good or evil, aimed at for its own sake—then it must be possible for the will to rise above *psychological fact*, by which is meant, first, all of the facts captured in our ordinary talk of individuals, others and ourselves, as having such and such characteristics, dispositions, desires, convictions, commitments, and so on, with such and such a determinate content deriving from our particular history and situation; and, second, all of the would-be attempts to work up these facts by theoretical means into a body of scientific knowledge.[10] All facts, including those of human psychology, are locked into the fabric of the world and as such compose meaningful patterns, allowing us to make sense of what people do. But they also, in direct consequence, preclude our possession of the kind of absolute unconditioned freedom which Raskolnikov wants evidence of. Thus, if Raskolnikov murdered Alena Ivanovna because he merely happened to have been exposed to certain philosophical ideas concerning the rights of moral aristocrats, happened to need money, happened to be repelled by the parasitic pawnbroker, happened to have a narcissistic personality, happened to suffer from feelings of guilt at disappointing his mother and sister's expectations, happened to suffer from "disorders of thought," and so on[11]—if his act just represents a vector resulting from any one or the conjunction of some or all of these psychological factors—then it really does not matter what he did or does in the future, for he does not exist as a genuine entity: he is an accidental unity, a mere aggregate (nor does his "act of murder" have genuine reality). If all this is so, then it would of course help to explain the confusion surrounding Marmeladov: if a person's self-accounting is premised on the existence of something unreal, then it is unsurprising that it runs into incoherence.

Evidently, what it is to be "above" or "beyond" psychology is not something that can be stated easily in positive terms (perhaps it cannot be done at all—a possibility to which we will return). What can be done instead however, negatively, is to alienate us from the psychological—to interpolate a skeptical distance, however slight, between us and what we take to be "psychological reality." Dostoevsky does this in two ways. First, he repeatedly reverts to the concept of psychology and lends it an appearance of peculiarity and arbitrariness, as if setting it within scare quotes. This does not of course extend so far as to undermine our ordinary ways of making sense of human beings—which would in any case make his entire novelistic practice impossible—but it leaves us uncertain how deeply psychological talk penetrates: the question forces itself on us whether any such set of facts represents "what we really are" and whether there may not be some sense in which the psychological is merely a fiction that we are compelled to form.

Second, Dostoevsky employs a technique of constant transition back and forth between two modes of representation of his characters flatly opposed to one another, such that from the standpoint of each the other appears unreal. On the one hand, Dostoevsky *characterizes* in the familiar nineteenth-century novelistic manner: in certain passages he simply states what it seems we are to take as hard facts concerning the dispositions, characteristics, and motives of individuals.[12] At the other extreme, his figures are presented through the mediums of soliloquy and extended monologues of the Marmeladov type,[13] and in the most important of these—at climactic points—the subject is presented as striving to get hold of something within himself, at some moments with seeming success but at other moments flailing, as if there were nothing real that his self-reflection could encounter that would supply it with friction and allow it to hit on determinate truth.[14] The most extreme expression of this condition is the state of delirium which so interests Dostoevsky. Delirium of course takes its most acute and overt form in Raskolnikov, but it is not confined within the boundaries of his mind: it suffuses the world of *Crime and Punishment*, infecting even its narrative and dramatic architecture—the unaccountable doublings and inverted mirror-imagings of characters and motifs which lend so many scenes and events their fantastical, nightmarish quality. Crucially, this second mode of presentation is bound up with the "practical point of view," the stance of a self-conscious agent for whom something, a course of action or adoption of an attitude, is up for decision. Dostoevsky pairs delirium with deliberation, both states involving indeterminacy, the one passive and the other active, and at key points has them coincide, as if it were in delirium that freedom found its most distinct expression. The value of delirium for Dostoevsky is therefore that it derealizes "character" and contradicts the realm of psychological hard fact—it intimates the possibility of human freedom, something which from the standpoint of character must be regarded as illusory.[15]

On a strictly philosophical plane, there are of course different ways in which the trans-psychological, freedom-bestowing dimension of human subjectivity may be theorized. No exploration of these can be undertaken here, but it will help to mention Schelling's proposal in the *Freiheitsschrift*, which resonates with Raskolnikov's striving to grasp a selfhood which lies beyond the reaches of the world and would give reality to the Good. Schelling locates the source of freedom in an original choice of a self, independent of our empirical existence: at the moment of our creation we determine the fundamental character (or "form") of our selfhood, either its would-be independence from God or its alignment with His will, whence derives its moral quality.[16]

IV. IN THE WAKE OF MURDER: RASKOLNIKOV'S PROJECT *AUFGEHOBEN*

The interpretation of Raskolnikov suggested by Schelling's *Freiheitsschrift* sheds light, I have suggested, on the central puzzle of *Crime and Punishment*. This does not mean, however, that it corresponds to Dostoevsky's own view of freedom and the Good or that it encompasses the final meaning of the work: to excogitate the standpoint that sets the novel in motion is not to articulate its conclusion, and everything said thus far pertains only to its first movement, that is, up until the point where Raskolnikov begins to live in the shadow of what he has done. Let me therefore explain how I think the Schellingian construal of Raskolnikov may be extended to an interpretation of the second movement of the novel and help to illuminate the meaning of the work as a whole.

Clearly Raskolnikov does not achieve satisfaction by murdering Alena Ivanovna. But the act has successfully been performed. So wherein lies his failure?

Crime and Punishment exposes Raskolnikov's understanding of his task as a misunderstanding; at best it was a justified first step in the direction that *appeared* necessary, given the position that he occupied at the beginning. Raskolnikov was not wrong to think that freedom is a condition of the Good and that it demands the possibility of a choice of evil and a transcendence of psychology, but the *manner* in which he takes up these issues—the solution he projects in response to the problem they pose—incorporates a misconception. Viewed one way, he is simply in error; in another light, though one not yet available to him, in a state of sin.

The orbit of Raskolnikov's reflections is circumscribed, until the last few pages of the novel, by his own will: it is through *his own act* that the breakthrough is to be made; provision of the proof is *up to him*. This self-assertion and assumption of absolute self-responsibility makes Raskolnikov unmistakably modern. But from the religious standpoint shared by Schelling and Dostoevsky this is exactly where the mistake lies: any conception that leaves it to the unassisted will of the agent to determine axiological reality is misguided. In undertaking to commit murder, Raskolnikov grasps only one side of freedom. The other and more profound side, which he has still to discover—and which can be revealed to him only once he has become, miraculously, receptive to the exemplary virtue of others—consists in recognition of the dependence of freedom on what precedes and cannot be brought within the orbit of individual will and reflection. To repeat, Raskolnikov was right to think at the outset that, if the Good has reality, then its foundation must lie in absolute and unconditioned freedom, but wrong to think that *he* could supply—instantiate, realize, give proof of—this absolute in his own person. That assumption is of a piece with Kant's defective, merely formal conception of freedom. For even when Raskolnikov's personhood is stripped of all its individualizing features, its universality remains that of a mere human individual, a creature, and the unconditioned absoluteness of human freedom cannot stand on its own two feet but must derive from a higher source, from the Good that is God.[17] The fault in Raskolnikov's attempt to prove the reality of freedom, revealed in the course of the novel, was therefore his implicit pretention to combine in himself humanity with divinity. This made it a foregone conclusion that whatever his experiment might succeed in showing regarding the reality of freedom would make impossible the required further movement toward the Good: Raskolnikov's self-assertive route to freedom precludes the submission and receptivity needed in order to relate oneself to the Good.

All this becomes manifest at the moment when Raskolnikov finds resurrection in Sonya (526–527). Instantly his project is overtaken. Raskolnikov no longer needs the knowledge that drove him to murder Alena Ivanovna, not because he now knows the answer to the question that consumed him in the way that the solution to a philosophical problem may be thought to be known, or because his own psychology has become transparent to him, but because the original condition that put him in need of knowledge has been erased: he now possesses knowledge in a form that makes nonsense of the idea that the knowledge he previously lacked could be attained through willful striving.[18] His great experiment in murder was therefore ill-conceived—it could not have yielded what he wanted—but this is something that he could not have known beforehand, for his original condition was one of sinful ignorance, leading him to pose a question the answer to which requires that one not be in need of it and not strain to know it, and the knowing of which strips the question of meaning. At the very end, Raskolnikov has forgotten the question that drove him to where he now finds himself. Yet his present situation, as a convict in Siberia, calls for no explanation, and for the first time, through his relation to the Good, he becomes conscious of the future as *his own*—his business with Eternity now settled, he is free to take up existence in time. The incommensurability of his earlier and later standpoints, which expressed itself previously in his and Sonya's mutual incomprehension, resurfaces in Raskolnikov's relation to his own past, which after the Sonya conversion becomes to him "something external and strange, as if it had not happened to him at all" (526–527). His ignorance of his motive thus spans the full length of the novel, but at the end it is the opposite of what it was at the beginning—what was privation has become fulfilment.[19]

V. WHAT LITERATURE CAN DO THAT PHILOSOPHY (ARGUABLY) CANNOT

The philosophical theory that I have invoked in an attempt to make sense of Raskolnikov's seemingly inchoate motivation, Schelling's conception of freedom as evil-involving and supra-psychological, belongs to that distinctive class of philosophical propositions which exert a distinctive fascination while lying on the cusp of nonsensicality. I noted earlier that Schelling's theory of freedom, insofar as it asserts the positive reality of evil, may be considered incoherent, and the same is true of Schelling's claim that human freedom stems from a choice made by an atemporal "intelligible" self. Perhaps even more obviously, the conception of (objectless, inarticulable) knowledge advanced in the preceding section must seem highly paradoxical.

There is no scope here to embark on a defense of Schelling's philosophy. Instead I want to use the possibility just described to make a suggestion concerning one way in which literature may carry philosophical significance. Suppose that Schelling's thesis concerning freedom does dissolve under philosophical scrutiny. And suppose it resonates in the way I have suggested with Dostoevsky's novel—in other words, that *Crime and Punishment* (to put the point in a deliberately crude way) is "committed to the truth" of Schelling's thesis. What then is the situation? Must we "reject" *Crime and Punishment*? Insofar as its philosophical vision is integral to the work, the strict nonsensicality of its vision must imply the falsity, in some respect, of the experience which it affords. Yet readers of Dostoevsky do not find the work defective (or if they do, it is for other reasons): its resonance, its hold over us, its "truth-content," appear wholly independent of all beliefs concerning the logical difficulties facing post-Kantian metaphysics of freedom. But if we do not "reject" *Crime and Punishment* in accordance with our philosophical consciences, are we not thereby embracing a contradiction?

Let us first rehearse, in greater detail, how matters appear from the philosophical side. Schelling—and others in his tradition, such as Sartre—formulate their strange ideas not from a perverse desire to obscure the daylight of common sense, but because they consider human freedom to be inherently opaque, conceptually elusive by nature. Any would-be perspicuous representation of freedom, they believe, will destroy it. But what, it may be asked, is the alternative? How can a philosophical theory coherently affirm the reality of opacity?

The issue is of a general nature. It may seem that any attempt to assert the cognitive impenetrability of some phenomenon is bound to miscarry. The very assertion seems to create a puzzle. To describe (philosophically) such and such as opaque is, on the face of it, simply to say that it poses a problem. If talk of "inherent" opacity is intended as a positive claim—if it is meant not to raise but to answer a question—then it must be understood to be saying something either about how the phenomenon is in itself or about how it necessarily presents itself to us. If the former, then we are claiming to know how it is constituted, and this grasp of the constitution-in-itself of the phenomenon transforms its "inherent opacity" into perspicuity; if the latter, then we must explicate its resistance to our cognition, in which case we again remove opacity from the object, by resolving it into a joint fact about the character of the object and our limited mode of cognition.

Both options therefore undermine the original assertion. The first appears to gain nothing, but the second may be recommended on its own account as an effective way of tackling certain philosophical problems. It corresponds in fact to Kant's strategy in the Transcendental Dialectic of the *Critique of Pure Reason* and provides the basis for his famous claim that, due to the finitude of our cognition, we cannot grasp the ground of our capacity for rational motivation, and so can only "comprehend . . . the *incomprehensibility*" of human freedom.[20] In the view of Schelling, however, Kant's strategy, consistent though it may be and whatever worth it may have in other contexts, provides a false account of human freedom, for Kant has simply broken it up into two disconnected components, one of which is in fact entirely comprehensible (freedom = pure practical reason) and the other of which (its ground or inner constitution) is expelled into the problematic noumenal realm. Kant's claim to have made incomprehensibility comprehensible is therefore disingenuous: on the one side freedom is fully comprehended, by dint of its reduction to rationality, and on the other lies nothing whatever.

Now Schelling may also be viewed as attempting to forge a compromise between the demands of explanation and freedom's resistance to it, but his theory is of a different order from Kant's: he is attempting, whether or not successfully, to construct a new mode of sense-making which exhibits rather than disguises the opacity of freedom; his metaphysics are strange because, in his view, human freedom itself is strange. If, however, his proposal fails the test of coherence—this being, recall, the supposition under which we are currently working—then we are back to square one.

With the acuteness of the philosophical difficulty now in sharper focus, let us consider how a literary work might be held to provide a response to it, and perhaps even to take over at the point where philosophy (we are supposing) grinds to a halt.

I suggested that Raskolnikov aims at knowledge. This, in the official terminology of post-Kantian philosophy, makes his project "theoretical" or "speculative." Raskolnikov's drive to knowledge has its motivational source in his desire for the Good, which to be sure is not a theoretical matter, but his concern is with its sheer *possibility*, the existence or non-existence of a *ground* of the Good, and as such it contrasts with non-theoretical, "practical" interest, which aims at acting, at *doing* the right thing. Formally speaking, Raskolnikov's inquiry therefore subordinates the practical standpoint to the theoretical: his concern is not to do the right thing (indeed he knowingly does the wrong thing) but to *know whether or not he is* a free agent; the reality of freedom and the Good is his would-be object of knowledge.

In our reading of the novel, we too adopt a theoretical standpoint, insofar as we are spectators of Raskolnikov's attempt to determine the possibility of the Good; the course of his inquiry is an object of our cognition. But our involvement does not of course end there. If the novel presented us merely with an object of theoretical interest, *Crime and Punishment* would be a description of the same logical order as a case history or news report, but with a fictional subject matter. What it does in addition—"by aesthetic means," whatever exactly that means—is allow us as readers to inhabit *at the same time* the practical point of view, insofar as we live through Raskolnikov's movement from doubt to eventual knowledge. And if that is so, then there is something that literature can do that philosophy (arguably) cannot: it allows us to occupy the theoretical and practical standpoints not merely simultaneously but also *as* a single *unitary* standpoint, whereby it can make available to theoretical cognition objects revealed from the practical point of view which philosophical discourse, in consequence of its exclusively theoretical character, finds itself unable to make sense of. In that way literature may be held to provide a more comprehensive medium of human self-reflection.

To return to the original question: What then is our situation? If we qua readers of *Crime and Punishment* must accept what is revealed to Raskolnikov, then there are two possibilities, which we must decide between. Either our acceptance must be relativized to our literary experience of the novel, or *Crime and Punishment* must be regarded as validating a vision of human existence which can be and has been articulated philosophically, yet cannot be *established* by discursive philosophical means. Common sense and philosophical sobriety recommend the first option. The second raises new questions: Should Dostoevsky's novel therefore be regarded as itself a philosophical medium, a supplementary form of philosophical reflection? Or should it be understood as showing that our present conception of "discursive philosophical means" is unduly restricted? If so, what exactly makes it possible for the novel to "show" this? (What are the "aesthetic means" referred to above?) It would be an understatement to say that these questions have no easy answers. But the other option too is not without its problems. What distinguishes "relativizing acceptance to literary experience" from mere forgetting? When Hume quits his study, his perplexity evaporates but the rational force of his skeptical reflections remains intact. Why suppose the situation to be any different, structurally, when we disengage doxastically from a philosophically compelling work of art? Perhaps our return to the daylight of common sense is a loss of knowledge, a veil redescending. Here I am recommending no conclusion, merely trying to show how—under certain conditions, exemplified by *Crime and Punishment* as read through the lens of Schelling's *Freiheitsschrift*—a mutually beneficial alliance may be forged between literature and philosophical reflection.[21]

NOTES

1. In *Crime and Punishment*, Part Three, Chapter 5, Raskolnikov explains to Porfiry that the proto-Nietzschean thesis which Porfiry finds "hinted" at in his article is a misunderstanding, and seems quite clear that he himself does not instantiate the higher, Napoleonic type. Fyodor Dostoevsky, *Crime and Punishment*, trans. Jessie Coulson (Oxford: Oxford University Press, 2008), 249, 255 (all subsequent references to *Crime and Punishment* will be to this edition and given parenthetically in the text). Raskolnikov may of course be mistaken on both counts, equally so when he later avows commitment to the theory (498, 521). Its position fluctuates, such that we come to view it as only a symptom of the motive. It is crucial that Porfiry in his final confrontation with Raskolnikov (Part Six, Chapter 2) is far from reducing his act to the implementation of the higher man theory: the case is "obscure and fantastic" and displays "resolution of a special kind," which he compares with falling from a precipice but does not try to define; some "theory" is involved, but the murderer was "carried along into crime, as it were by some outside force" (437). This accords with the view I will offer of Raskolnikov as carried by an idea of an exceptional, metaphysical kind, which is indeed in a sense "outside" him.
2. Thomas de Quincey, *On Murder*, ed. Robert Morrison (Oxford: Oxford University Press, 2009), 9.
3. *Meno*, 77b–78b, in Plato, *Meno and Other Dialogues*, trans. Robin Waterfield (Oxford: Oxford University Press, 2005), 106–109.
4. That his conscience was never at issue is also evidenced by his reply to Porfiry (254), his last scene with Dunya (498), and the fact that he never comes to feel remorse (520–521). The reason Raskolnikov never suffers from his conscience is that the meaning of his act never lay on the ethical plane: it was conceived metaphysically; that it violates the moral law was already factored in, an essential part of its intended content, so cannot provide its measure (whatever is wrong with willing evil for its own sake cannot be that it wills evil!). Raskolnikov's distinction of higher types from ordinary folk is a distorted articulation of his metaphysical motive: "Napoleon" represents for Raskolnikov human existence *with* freedom; to be a "louse," like Alena Ivanovna, is to exist without it. That he conceptualizes his motive with reference to historical figures who are laws unto themselves betrays what will later emerge as his

fundamental mistake: Raskolnikov is right, metaphorically, when he says, "I wanted to make myself a Napoleon" (397), insofar as he approached the Good as if it were something to be conquered, seized through his will.

5. The canonical statement of this proposition for purposes of the post-Kantian philosophical development is found in Johann Friedrich Jacobi's *Concerning the Doctrine of Spinoza in Letters to Herr Moses Mendelssohn* (1785), in *The Main Philosophical Writings and the Novel "Allwill,"* trans. and ed. George di Giovanni (Montreal: McGill-Queen's University Press, 1994), 189. That this possibility haunts Raskolnikov is clear from his dialogue with Sonya in Part Four, Chapter 4. Also relevant is his negative vision of beauty (108–109). The nihilistic anxiety is finally given shape as a dream or fantasy in his illness in Siberia (523–524).
6. Friedrich Wilhelm Joseph von Schelling, *Philosophical Investigations into the Essence of Human Freedom*, trans. and ed. Jeff Love and Johannes Schmidt (Albany, NY: SUNY Press, 2006), 48–58. For a fuller account see my "The Metaphysics of Human Freedom: From Kant's Transcendental Idealism to Schelling's *Freiheitsschrift*," *British Journal of the History of Philosophy* 25:1 (2017), 133–156.
7. The conception of human existence as interrogative—as implicating a question by virtue of existing in a certain mode, to be answered by an appropriate mode of *doing*—is familiar from Heidegger. The conception of human action as issuing from metaphysical motivation is elaborated explicitly by Sartre. The Schellingian interpretation of Raskolnikov proposed here follows the pattern of, and up to a point parallels, Sartre's interpretation of Jean Genet in *Saint Genet: Actor & Martyr* (1952), trans. Bernard Frechtman (London: Heinemann, 1963), which is similarly occupied with the themes of freedom, evil, and the transcendence of psychological fact. The decisive difference is that Sartre eliminates all theological possibility, leaving Genet caught in tragic absurdity: Raskolnikov makes his way, stumbling and with miraculous assistance, from freedom to the Good, but Genet remains locked in awareness of freedom that cannot be converted into value.
8. Also relevant here, of course, is the question of possible historical influence. Concerning Dostoevsky's exposure to Schelling and other sources in classical German philosophy, see Isiah Berlin, "A Remarkable Decade," in *Russian Thinkers* (Harmondsworth: Penguin, 1994); Jacques Catteau, *Dostoyevsky and the Process of Literary Creation*, trans. Audrey Littlewood (Cambridge: Cambridge University Press, 1989), chap. 4; Malcolm V. Jones, "Dostoevskii and Religion," in W. J. Leatherbarrow, ed., *The Cambridge Companion to Dostoevskii* (Cambridge: Cambridge University Press, 2004); Joseph Frank, *Dostoevsky: The Stir of Liberation, 1860–1865* (Princeton, NJ: Princeton University Press, 1986); and Bruce Ward, *Dostoyevsky's Critique of the West: The Quest for the Earthly Paradise* (Ontario: Wilfrid Laurier, 1986).

That at least something of Schelling's outlook was known to Dostoevsky is certain, but it is impossible to determine exactly which elements of Schelling's thought he had acquaintance with and in what detail; quite possibly Schelling signified for him merely the Romantic spiritualism of an earlier generation of Russian "Westernizers." I am grateful to Sarah Young for information about these matters.

9. Restated later and lucidly by Svidriglayov: "The whole question is: am I a monster or am I myself a victim?" (269).
10. References to psychological theory abound, associated with different characters: with Zosimov (e.g., 198) and (more equivocally and with greater sophistication) with Porfiry (325–266, 428, 438–440). On the contemporary background, see Robert Belknap, "Dostoevskii and Psychology," in W. J. Leatherbarrow, ed., *The Cambridge Companion to Dostoevskii* (Cambridge: Cambridge University Press, 2004), 131–147.
11. This is Svidriglayov's construal (471–472). Dunya immediately notes the alarming implication—that Raskolnikov has no conscience.
12. E.g., 196–197. Raskolnikov himself subscribed to the "hard fact" conception in his article on criminal psychology (248).
13. E.g., Raskolnikov's internal monologue in his first confrontation with Porfiry (244–245), which explicitly sets up the fact/delirium opposition.
14. The entirety of Raskolnikov's self-account in Part Five, Chapter 4—his equivalent of the Marmeladov scene—has this character.
15. Dostoevsky states the double-aspecthood of the psychological: "Consequently, Porfiry had nothing either, nothing but *delirium*, no kind of facts, only his *psychology*, which *cut both ways*, nothing definite" (343).
16. Schelling, *Philosophical Investigations into the Essence of Human Freedom*, 51–53.
17. Schelling's clearest statement of this conception of freedom is in his *System der gesammten Philosophie* (1804), §§301–310, in *Sämmtliche Werke*, ed. Karl Friedrich August Schelling (Stuttgart: Cotta, 1856–1861), Bd. 6, 537–566.
18. Earlier he had no notion of this form of knowledge: hence Sonya's charge that he knows "nothing at all" (305) and his countercharge that, since she is without the knowledge of the reality of the Good, there is nothing to distinguish her self-sacrifice from self-destruction (308–309). In response to Raskolnikov's attempt to induct (or seduce) Sonya into his metaphysical project (390–391), she calls his questions "empty" and, baffled by his question concerning the Good, asks, "How could it depend on my decision?"
19. The Epilogue is controversial. On my account, Dostoevsky does not ask us to find the conclusion "convincing" but to *assent* to it in all of its unconvincingness. If we do not assent spontaneously to the Epilogue—if we experience the conclusion as coercive, mere authorial stipulation—then either we have failed to follow the argument of the novel or its argument is no good and the novel a failure. If the novel succeeds, then we are free to repudiate the miracle of the

Epilogue only in a "formal" sense: the novel has shown what follows from that decision, and readers who make it owe Dostoevsky a solution (a novel) of their own, for they have put themselves in the condition that Raskolnikov occupied at the very beginning.

20. Immanuel Kant, *Groundwork of the Metaphysics of Morals* (1797), trans. Mary Gregor (New York: Cambridge University Press, 1998), 66 (4:463).
21. I am grateful to Robert Guay for helpful comments on an earlier draft.

Chapter 5

The Family in *Crime and Punishment*

Realism and Utopia

SUSANNE FUSSO

Crime and Punishment was conceived and written in an atmosphere of intellectual and social ferment. In the aftermath of Russia's humiliating defeat in the Crimean War in 1855, the new tsar Alexander II began a program of "Great Reforms," the most important of which was the emancipation of the serfs in 1861. National self-examination was the order of the day, and journalism flourished as the arena for discussion and criticism of Russia's institutions. The general program of reform was supported even by conservative figures like Mikhail Katkov, the editor of the *Russian Herald,* in which *Crime and Punishment* was published in 1866. But the age of reform also gave rise to a more prominent and energetic radical movement, which questioned all the bases of Russian society in a way that horrified proponents of more gradual reform, like Katkov. These young thinkers called themselves "the new people" or "critical realists," but they were labeled "nihilists" in Ivan Turgenev's seminal novel *Fathers and Sons,* published in the *Russian Herald* in 1862. After the publication of Turgenev's novel, Katkov popularized the term "nihilist" in his highly influential articles, and it has become the most standard label for the radical generation of the 1860s to this day. Philip Pomper has given a concise description of the "nihilist style": "It included, among other things, condescension in conversation and a casual attitude toward dress and appearance, if not downright eccentricity. The effect was usually one of austerity, especially for nihilist girls, whose short hair, drab clothing, spectacles, and cigarettes were symptoms of the drive for feminine equality that began in Russia during this period. Nihilists denied not only the traditional roles of women but also the family, private property, religion, art—in a word, all of the traditional aspects of culture and society."[1] *Crime and Punishment* embodies Dostoevsky's response to the radical critique of the family, one that draws on the literary mode of realism (a style of representation that is focused on concrete details, plausibility, and accuracy) as well as "realism" (in the sense of a skeptical view of the potential for the transformation of human society) to counter the utopian thinking and utopian literary style of the radical journalist and novelist Nikolai Chernyshevsky. Nevertheless, Dostoevsky does not entirely avoid the temptations of the utopian style, as we shall see.

Dostoevsky himself had been arrested in 1849 and sentenced to Siberian prison and exile for nearly a decade because of his participation in the Petrashevsky Circle, a group of young men who gathered to read forbidden books and discuss the potential transformation of Russian society. After being allowed to return to European Russia and resume his literary career, he was careful to distance himself from political activity that could be perceived as subversive, and by the end of his life in 1881 he had developed extremely conservative views. But in the early 1860s, at the time *Crime and Punishment* was conceived, he was in love with Apollinaria Prokofievna Suslova, a young woman of radical sympathies with whom he had an apparently passionate relationship in 1861–1862. Suslova was present at the inception of Dostoevsky's novel and served as a kind of negative muse.

Any consideration of how radical ideas were reflected in *Crime and Punishment* must begin with her and her own writings.

The first documented evidence of Dostoevsky's conception of *Crime and Punishment,* with its focus on the ruthlessness of the Napoleonic "extraordinary person," appears in Suslova's diary. Dostoevsky had joined her in Paris in July 1863, only to be told, "You have come a little too late": she had fallen in love with a Spanish medical student named Salvador (who soon dropped her).[2] She and Dostoevsky then traveled in Italy, with Dostoevsky constantly frustrated by her refusal to renew their sexual relationship. She notes in her diary on September 17, 1863, that in a restaurant in Turin he looked at a little girl being given a lesson and said, "Well, just imagine, such a little girl with an old man, and suddenly some Napoleon says, 'Destroy the whole town.' It has always been that way in the world."[3] Dostoevsky later told Suslova that it was her refusal of his proposal of marriage in 1865 (after the death of his first wife) that had caused him to "throw himself into his work and begin to write a novel [*Crime and Punishment*]."[4]

Suslova and her sister Nadezhda, who became the first woman doctor in Russia, were seen by contemporaries as the epitome of the nihilist woman. Diarist Elena Andreevna Shtakenshneider describes Apollinaria as "a girl with shorn hair, in an outfit that from a distance looks like a man's, a girl who goes everywhere alone, who goes to lectures at the university, who writes—in a word, an emancipated woman."[5] Suslova published two stories in Dostoevsky's journal *Time* and one in his subsequent journal *Epoch,* all of which deal to some degree with the "woman question," the problem of woman's role in society, a question then being furiously discussed in Russian journalism and fiction. In her diary, Suslova describes herself arguing with Dostoevsky about the emancipation of women in October 1863, during their journeys around Europe.[6] So when we try to understand Dostoevsky's conception of the family in *Crime and Punishment,* it will help to start with the fiction of Suslova. Suslova's fiction in turn betrays the influence of the theories of Mikhail Larionovich Mikhailov and Nikolai Gavrilovich Chernyshevsky, both of whom were concerned with the transformation of the Russian family as the first step in the transformation of Russian society.[7]

According to the radical critic Nikolai Vasilievich Shelgunov, the "woman question" was first given prominence in Russia by Mikhailov's extensive article "Women, Their Education and Significance in the Family and in Society," published in *The Contemporary* in 1860.[8] Richard Stites, author of the definitive work in English on the Russian women's movement, describes Mikhailov's contribution as follows: "Although not an original thinker and not the first to speak publicly on these matters, he was the first to synthesize the separate strands of the problem (work, education, love) into an anthropological argument . . . He was the publicist-apologist of women's emancipation. By the time of his arrest for radical activities in 1862, Mikhailov had transformed the loosely connected ad hoc arguments of the preceding decade into a compact and perennial, though still problematical, feature of Russia's intellectual life."[9]

In his 1860 article, Mikhailov argues that the transformation of society is dependent on the transformation of the family: "The complete rebuilding [*perestroika*] of society is impossible without remaking its basis, the family; this has been realized sometimes vaguely, sometimes clearly, by all social innovators; out of this realization grew ideas about the so-called emancipation of woman."[10] The word in the title of Mikhailov's article that is translated as "education," *vospitanie*, is broader than the more common word for education, *obrazovanie*. The word *vospitanie* also means "upbringing" and encompasses not just school education but also one's rearing in the home. For Mikhailov, all aspects of the treatment of women must be reexamined: "Only a radical transformation of woman's education [*vospitanie*], of the social rights of woman and of family relationships can in my opinion save contemporary society from the moral shakiness with which it is ailing as if from a senile debility."[11]

For Mikhailov, the subordination of women has led to a general degradation of morality that can be remedied only by giving women full and equal rights. Mikhailov does not offer a detailed description of how the transformation of the family is to take place, but he does hint at the rejection of marriage by the "new people" (as the nihilists called themselves). He writes that women who are inadequately educated hinder their husbands' attempts to do socially useful work: "In the motivations of the husband, personal benefit, narrow and myopic, gradually replaces the good of society, on which the good of each of its members directly depends. It is not for nothing that people who are devoted with all their hearts to striving for knowledge or to caring about the happiness of their native land see an obstacle to these strivings and cares in married life, and renounce it."[12] Mikhailov had been doing his part to undermine the institution of marriage by engaging in a *ménage-à-trois* with Shelgunov and his wife, as described by Irina Paperno: "In accordance with the cultural code, the woman played a decisive role in Mikhailov's spiritual rebirth and his subsequent social activity and revolutionary martyrdom."[13]

Suslova's first story, "Meanwhile," appeared in the May 1861 issue of Dostoevsky's journal *Time*. The story is clearly indebted to Mikhailov's diagnosis of the illness infecting Russian society as a result of the dire situation of women. Although narrated by a man, the story centers on a woman, Zinaida, who marries the narrator's brother without love in order to get away from her mother, "a capricious and quarrelsome old lady infected with absurd prejudices." Mikhailov's ideas are evident in the narrator's description of Zinaida's decision. The narrator first sees Zinaida's marriage as "a revolting lie and disgusting immorality," but then resists censuring her, taking into account that "the position of woman is a dead end, that the evil lies in the family, that the lie is her only defense against the despotism of the head of the family." Her education [*vospitanie*] has made her good for nothing but high-society drawing rooms, and in this the narrator sees "the beginning of slavery." A woman gets married in order to be free, but slavery follows her there in different forms.[14] As the marriage inevitably fails, Zinaida characterizes her fate in terms that recall Mikhailov's constant comparisons of women to Negro slaves: "If love can exist along with the desire to acquire the beloved person as one's property, to subordinate her to one's whim, to arrogate to oneself the right to dispose of her fate, to take upon oneself the responsibility for her acts, to interfere in the business of her conscience, then I have been loved. Can one not wish to be rid of such love? But how can I be rid of it?"[15] Zinaida breaks with her husband and dies in a garret. "The position of woman is a dead end"—no hope is offered at the end of this story.

Suslova's second story, "Before the Wedding," published in *Time* in March 1863, is narrated by a woman, Aleksandra Ivanovna (Alya), who hopes not to have to make a "profitable speculation" out of marriage like the young women she sees all around her, but wishes to lead a "sober, rational life."[16] A potential savior appears in the form of her tutor Darov, who tells her "how difficult and boring it is for an intelligent woman to live in the world" and urges her to engage in serious reading.[17] Darov's tutelage contrasts with the poor education she is given in boarding school, where the female teachers strive only to keep the students unaware of "real life" as of something dirty: "their main goal was to stop our development at the level of ignorance of the simplest human relations, and they were rather successful at this."[18] Finally her mother pushes her into a marriage with a man she does not love, in order to save the family fortunes, saying, "Do this for me; after all, I more than anyone wish you well; I am your mother. Just think how much care and suffering you have cost me."[19] Alya runs to Darov, but in her hour of need he fails to save her. He advises her to reconcile with her mother, and she submits to the distasteful marriage. The story ends with no doubt about the unhappiness of the outcome: "I cried a lot that day and did not know how I would survive it. Poor me, I had no idea how much bitterness lay ahead."[20]

Suslova's second story appeared almost simultaneously with a work that had far greater impact than her writings (which were largely ignored, except, perhaps, by Dostoevsky himself): Nikolai Chernyshevsky's novel *What Is to Be Done?* The story of this novel and its far-reaching influence on radical Russian youth of the 1860s has been told in compelling detail by Irina Paperno in her 1988 study *Chernyshevsky and the Age of Realism*. Chernyshevsky's novel, written while he was in solitary confinement in the Peter and Paul Fortress in St. Petersburg before he was exiled to Siberia, was published in *The Contemporary* in the spring of 1863 and became a kind of bible for the nihilists.

Like Mikhailov, Chernyshevsky seeks the restructuring of society via the restructuring of the family. The heroine Vera Pavlovna, like Suslova's heroines, is in danger of being forced into a loveless marriage for the sake of her family's fortunes. Like Alya's mother in "Before the Wedding," Vera Pavlovna's mother dresses her up as if for sale and reproaches her for all she has cost her parents. Like Alya, Vera Pavlovna encounters an enlightened tutor, Lopukhov, one of the "new people." Unlike Suslova's Darov, however, Lopukhov helps Vera Pavlovna escape the "cellar" of the patriarchal family by marrying her. Chernyshevsky stresses the coerciveness of the Russian family structure, upheld by both state and church. Lopukhov's first plan for saving Vera Pavlovna is to get her a position as a governess, but when the potential employer learns that Vera Pavlovna is going against her family's wishes, she balks, saying, "You know about the rights of parents! In this instance they would take full advantage of them. They would initiate a lawsuit and carry it through to the end."[21] When Lopukhov enlists a young priest to marry them secretly, the priest's voice begins to tremble as he reads the service and thinks of the potential consequences of his act. As the editors of a Russian edition of the novel explain, the penalty for "abducting" an unmarried woman for the purposes of marriage was a potential prison sentence of six months to a year; the priest performing the ceremony could be expelled from the clergy.[22]

Chernyshevsky sees Russian family life in the same way Mikhailov and Suslova do, as a stifling, coercive system that reduces women to pieces of property. But rather than simply describing the terrible state of affairs, as Suslova does in her realistic, despairing stories, Chernyshevsky creates a utopian fantasy of a new type of family order. In the mode of literary realism, Suslova describes life as she sees it existing around her. Writing in a utopian, only superficially realistic mode, Chernyshevsky describes an imaginary life that few could recognize as the contemporary norm. Lopukhov and Vera Pavlovna arrange their home life in a way that evokes the amazement of their uneducated landlords, who think (not entirely incorrectly) that they belong to a strange religious sect. Each member of the couple has his or her own room, and there is also a third, "neutral" room in which they come together to drink tea and converse. Neither spouse can enter the other's room without permission, and each makes sure to be fully dressed before entering the neutral room. The arrangement makes for extreme privacy on the part of each individual.[23]

The respect for Vera Pavlovna's autonomy that is expressed in their living arrangements extends to Lopukhov's willingness to "step aside" when he realizes that she has fallen in love with their mutual friend Kirsanov. Lopukhov, realizing that Vera Pavlovna is not advanced enough to bear the social opprobrium that would accompany engaging in a *ménage-à-trois,* fakes his own suicide, while managing to let Vera Pavlovna know about it, so that she and Kirsanov can come together happily. Eventually Lopukhov returns, disguised as the American Charles Beaumont. He falls in love with a young woman, and the novel ends with the two couples living side by side, all fully aware that Lopukhov is still legally married to Vera Pavlovna, although she is conjugally linked to Kirsanov, and Lopukhov lives with Katya Polozova. Mikhailov's worry that a wife might distract the man who needs to work for the good of society is eliminated in Chernyshevsky's version, as Vera Pavlovna herself works actively to transform society, first by starting a sewing workshop organized on rational communal principles and then by becoming a doctor (like Suslova's sister Nadezhda). The new utopian family structure is used by Chernyshevsky to hint at the coming revolution that he could not speak of openly, but the significance of which was clear to his contemporary readers.[24]

Perhaps under the influence of *What Is to Be Done?*, Suslova gives her third story a hopeful ending. In this story, "Going Her Own Way," published in Dostoevsky's journal *Epoch* in June 1864, the heroine Katerina Mikhailovna is seduced and betrayed by an unworthy man, the nephew of the woman whose daughter she is tutoring. But she is sustained by her correspondence with a friend, Konstantin, who combines the calm reasoning power of Lopukhov with the scientific passion of Kirsanov (he writes of "dissecting frogs" and medically treating peasants in the countryside).[25] After her disappointment in love, Konstantin encourages her, writing, "Go to meet life head-on and demand your share; perhaps happiness is near, you have full right to it."[26] As the story ends, Konstantin and Katerina plan to marry and go abroad for him to study, and eventually to return to the country to help the peasantry.[27]

Children do not play a prominent role in the arguments by Mikhailov or the fiction of Suslova and Chernyshevsky. In Mikhailov's article, children appear mainly as the awed witnesses of the future "harmony of rights, obligations, and actions" of the new type of married couple, who will give their offspring "a truly moral education [*vospitanie*] that is concordant with the general good."[28] Suslova's stories do not address the question of children, apart from the spoiled little girl whom the heroine of "Going Her Own Way" ineffectually tutors in French. Suslova told a doctor treating her for a gynecological complaint (probably ovarian cysts) that she did not want to have children because "I do not know how to educate [*vospityvat'*] them."[29] Chernyshevsky's novel devotes scant attention to children. Vera Pavlovna gives birth to a son by Kirsanov, but he is mentioned once and then disappears. In the vision of the future utopian society in Vera Pavlovna's Fourth Dream, children appear as servants: "[Children] do almost all the chores and enjoy their work very much."[30] It is the romantic and sexual relationships of the adults that Chernyshevsky reshapes in his fiction. Like Mikhailov, he seems to imagine that the situation of children will take care of itself once the problem of women's independence and equality is solved.

Dostoevsky was always interested in and to some extent sympathetic with radical thought, even when he did not agree with its analyses or its aims. The "woman question" appears in *Crime and Punishment* in ways that echo Mikhailov and Chernyshevsky but also betray Dostoevsky's painful memories of his relationship with Suslova. His approach in this novel contrasts with the way Turgenev depicted the ideas of the new generation. Despite Turgenev's ambivalent attitude to the young radicals' assault on art and tradition, in *Fathers and Sons* his nihilist hero Bazarov is an idealistic, charismatic man of science, the central and by far the most interesting character in the book. In *Crime and Punishment,* Dostoevsky degrades the ideas of the young radicals by having them voiced by two minor characters, the egoistic businessman Luzhin and the "uninformed obstinate fool" Lebezyatnikov (348–349; *PSS*, 6: 279). The scene in which Chernyshevsky's ideas about the family are most explicitly referenced, and lampooned, comes at the beginning of Part Five. Luzhin, whose betrothal to Raskolnikov's sister Dunya has just been broken off, is conversing with his former ward Lebezyatnikov, who spouts the ideology of *What Is to Be Done?* in a muddled and ridiculous form. The narrator of *What Is to Be Done?* at one point tells the male reader, "Regard your wife as you did your fiancée: recognize that at any moment she has the right to say, 'I'm dissatisfied with you. Get away from me.' "[31] Lebezyatnikov praises a woman who has abandoned her husband and two children to enter a commune, and has left a note that ends, "Do not hope that I shall return to you; you are too late [*vy slishkom opozdali*]" (353; *PSS*, 6: 282).[32] Instead of Chernyshevsky's "I'm dissatisfied with you," Dostoevsky uses a phrase that is very close to the one with which Suslova dismissed him in 1863 and that he was still pained by years later. In a letter of 1865 to Apollinaria's sister Nadezhda, Dostoevsky wrote, "To this day she taunts me for not being worthy of her love, she complains and constantly reproaches me, but she herself met me in 1863 in Paris with the phrase: 'You've arrived a little too late,' that is, she had fallen in love with another, while two weeks before she had still been writing ardently that she loved me. I reproach her not for her love for another, but for those four lines she sent me in the hotel that included the coarse phrase, 'You have arrived a little too late [*Ty nemnozhko opozdal priekhat'*]' " (*PSS*, 28/2: 121).

Chernyshevsky's theory of "rational egoism" holds that a person who acts purely in accord with his own interests as revealed to him by enlightened rational thought will always act for the good of others as well. This theory is mercilessly caricatured in Luzhin, who twists the Gospel to suit his own mercenary ends: "If, for example, in earlier times it was said to me: 'Love your neighbour' and I acted on it, what was the result? [. . .] The result was that I divided my cloak with my neighbour and we were both left half-naked [. . .] Science, however, says: love yourself first of all, for everything in the world is based on personal interest. If you love yourself alone, you will conduct your affairs properly, and your cloak will remain whole" (142; *PSS*, 6: 116). In Lebezyatnikov's version of Chernyshevsky's utopia, the right to individual privacy is not preserved but obliterated: "Recently we have been discussing whether a member of a commune has at all times the right to enter the room of another member, whether man or woman . . . and it was decided that he has . . ." Luzhin replies, "And what if he or she is occupied at that moment with the unavoidable demands of nature, he, he?" (355; *PSS*, 6: 284).[33]

These and other specific references to Chernyshevsky's and Mikhailov's theories are either concentrated in the comic-relief scene between Luzhin and Lebezyatnikov or mentioned briefly, as with Razumikhin's reference to a work entitled *Woman: Is She a Human Being?* (107; *PSS*, 6: 88).[34] But in a more serious and pervasive way, the novel demonstrates that Dostoevsky, like the radicals, recognizes the trap of the family, the family as coercion. Like Suslova and unlike Chernyshevsky, throughout most of the novel Dostoevsky is more focused on how things are in reality than on a fantasy of what they might be like in the future.[35] The "woman question" is most prominently represented in the story of Raskolnikov's sister Dunya. As the novel begins, she has agreed to marry Luzhin, a man she does not love, in an echo of Suslova's doomed heroines. Their stories end in early death or lifelong bitterness. (Dunya's engagement, however, is more a self-sacrifice for the benefit of her brother than a bid for freedom and self-realization.) But instead of focusing narrowly on the "woman question," as Mikhailov, Suslova, and Chernyshevsky do, as if the only problem with the family were the problem of women's independence, Dostoevsky creates a depiction of the family that is entangled, multifarious, and much more focused on the suffering of children.

Crime and Punishment teems with complicated families in which love is far from the only binding force. To offer but a sampling: In a tavern Raskolnikov hears Marmeladov tell the story of his family group: husband and wife, each with a deceased spouse in the past, and his daughter Sonya, who has become a prostitute for the sake of her little stepbrother and stepsisters, because her drunken father cannot support the family. Later, when Raskolnikov listens to Sonya reading him the Gospel story of Lazarus with religious fervor, he envisions her situation vividly: "He understood that those feelings in fact constituted her real long-standing secret, cherished perhaps since her girlhood, when she was still living with her family, with an unhappy father, a stepmother crazed by grief, and hungry children, in an atmosphere of hideous shrieks and reproaches" (313; *PSS*, 6: 250). In another tavern at another time he hears about Lizaveta, whose stepsister, the old pawnbroker, makes her work as an indentured servant and who is "constantly pregnant" (62; *PSS*, 6: 54). The fate of these babies can only be guessed at.[36] Svidrigaylov marries in order to avoid debtor's prison and is forced to agree to an oral contract with his wife spelling out the exact circumstances under which he is allowed to be unfaithful (453–454; *PSS*, 6: 363). After his wife's death (which he may have had a hand in causing), the fifty-year-old Svidrigaylov becomes engaged to a fifteen-year-old girl, taking advantage of her family situation: "There is [. . .] an invalid father, a retired official, who is in a wheelchair and has not been able to move his legs for three years. There is [. . .] a mother as well—a very sensible lady, mama. The son is serving somewhere in the provinces, and doesn't help them. The married daughter never goes to see them, and they have two little nephews on their hands (as though their own weren't enough)" (460; *PSS*, 6: 369).

Raskolnikov has tried to free himself of the coercion of the family, cutting himself off from both its obligations and its rights. He has come from his home in Ryazan province (also the home province of Chernyshevsky's Lopukhov) to St. Petersburg, ostensibly in order to get an education but ultimately in order to be alone. A conversation between two workmen sums up the allure of the anonymous city: "The things there are in this here St. Petersburg! [. . .] *Except for mother and father,* everything's here!" "*Except for that,* my boy, everything's here" (166; *PSS*, 6: 133; emphasis added). When we first see Raskolnikov, he is sneaking out of his apartment building trying not to be seen by his landlady, a kind of surrogate mother whose late daughter he had planned to marry: "He had cut himself off from everybody and withdrawn so completely into himself that he now shrank from every kind of contact, not just contact with his landlady" (1; *PSS*, 6: 5). Living alone in his tiny room, far from his mother and sister, Raskolnikov has hatched a theory which holds that people are divided into two categories: "into a lower (of ordinary people), that is, into material serving *only for the reproduction of its own kind*, and into people properly speaking, that is, those who have the gift or talent of saying *something new* in their sphere [. . .] *The first preserve the world and increase and multiply*; the second move the world and guide it to its goal" (250–251; *PSS*, 6: 200–201; emphasis added). In other words, the ordinary people procreate; the extraordinary man must be alone, like Chernyshevsky's Rakhmetov, the superman of the future, who says, "I must suppress any love in myself: to love you would mean to bind my hands."[37]

The visible signs of Raskolnikov's aloneness as the novel begins are his rags, his hunger, and his squalid hole of an apartment. The realist details of the novel's texture convey the weight of what it means to be taken care of by one's family and what it means to lose that care. Family care involves clothing and the washing of clothing. Significantly, we see Katerina Ivanovna Marmeladova staying up all night to wash her children's clothes, since they have no spare clothing to change into.[38] Raskolnikov immediately realizes that a young girl he encounters on the street has been sexually assaulted, because her dress has been clumsily refastened: she was dressed "by unskilful hands, masculine hands" (45; *PSS*, 6: 41). Family care involves feeding. Raskolnikov eats only when the maid Nastasya takes pity on him and brings him some soup. He later recalls to Sonya, "For days on end I didn't go out; I didn't want to work, I didn't even want to eat; I just lay there. If Nastasya brought me food, I ate it; if not, I let the day go by without asking, on purpose, out of spite!" (400; *PSS*, 6: 320). Family care involves interior decoration. Late in the novel, after Raskolnikov has been sent to Siberia, his mother, who earlier had been shocked by his "coffin" of an apartment (222; *PSS*, 6: 178), begins in her mental confusion to prepare for his return by refurbishing her home, "arranging the room she intended for him (her own), cleaning the furniture, washing curtains and hanging up new ones, and so on" (517; *PSS*, 6: 414). The perversion of this kind of material care is the prostitute's "special cleanness," the gaudy clothing Sonya must maintain in order to attract clients (20; *PSS*, 6: 20), or the gleaming cleanliness of the pawnbroker's apartment, which, as the reader knows, has been achieved by the unpaid labor of her downtrodden stepsister, who is about to be murdered along with her.

Raskolnikov has cut himself off from family care, but also from his own obligations toward his mother and sister. As a result, he loses his rights over them as well. After reading his mother's letter telling him of the sacrifice Dunya is making in marrying Luzhin, Raskolnikov thinks, "It shall not be, while I live, it shall not, it shall not! I will not accept it!" But he immediately realizes that he does not have the kind of power that this implies: "It shall not be? What are you going to do to prevent it? Will you forbid it? But what right have you to do so? What can you offer that will give you the right? To consecrate your destiny, your whole future, to them, *when you have finished your studies and obtained a situation*?" (42; *PSS*, 6: 38). As it turns out, Dunya's marriage is derailed, at least in part, by yet another lapse in the fulfillment of family obligations, as Luzhin fails to provide adequate transportation and housing for his fiancée and her mother when they come to St. Petersburg to join him. This abdication of responsibility helps to open Dunya's eyes to the mistake she is about to make. Neither Raskolnikov nor Luzhin earns the right to play a role in Dunya's decision-making, because neither has fulfilled his responsibilities toward her.

Dostoevsky had directly confronted Chernyshevsky's model of "rational egoism" in his 1864 novella *Notes from Underground*. James Scanlan has astutely described the ways in which Dostoevsky contrasts Chernyshevsky's psychologically unrealistic characters with a more believable variety of egoism, the kind that can be witnessed every day: "Chernyshevsky's principal characters see themselves as complete egoists, claiming to be guided in their behavior by nothing but informed calculations of their own interests; at the same time, however, they bring great benefit to others and in general behave like paragons of virtue, thus exhibiting the magically benign effects of an 'enlightened' or 'rational' egoism [. . .] Dostoevsky set out in *Notes from Underground* to create, in contrast to Chernyshevsky's sham egoists with their contrived goodness, the figure of a genuine, believable Russian egoist—an authentic, nonaltruistic, morally repugnant egoist."[39] In Dostoevsky's 1865 letter to Nadezhda Suslova, mentioned above, he describes his former lover Apollinaria Suslova as this latter kind of egoist, one who while demanding equality for herself insists on submission and subordination from her partner. He predicts that she will never find happiness precisely because of her unwillingness to recognize her obligations to those she loves. He writes, "Her egoism and selfish pride are colossal. She demands *everything* from people, all the perfections, does not forgive even a single imperfection in view of other good features, but she relieves herself of the slightest obligations toward other people [. . .] I am sorry for her because I foresee that she will be eternally unhappy. She will never find a friend and happiness for herself. Whoever demands everything of another but relieves herself of all obligations will never find happiness" (*PSS*, 28/2: 121, 122). The problem of what Scanlan calls the "authentic, nonaltruistic egoist," who relieves himself of obligations toward other people, is brought to the fore in *Crime and Punishment* through the figures of Svidrigaylov and of Raskolnikov himself.

Unlike Chernyshevsky, who in writing *What Is to Be Done?* was concerned to promote a revolutionary solution to the problems of society, Dostoevsky does not shape his novel as a tract promoting a particular political program. He does, however, depict a noncoercive, voluntary, and love-based model of the family. Whether coincidentally or not, it exists almost completely outside of biological familial connection. Razumikhin has no family of his own, other than an uncle he sees at rare intervals: "He was very poor, and he supported himself absolutely by himself alone, getting money by doing all sorts of odd jobs" (49; *PSS*, 6: 44). But Razumikhin, unsupported by family himself, voluntarily takes on the responsibility of caring for Raskolnikov, offering him translation work, buying him clothes, and feeding him like a baby as he recovers from the illness that strikes him after he commits the murders, constantly addressing him as "brother" (116; *PSS*, 6: 95–96).[40] We learn at Raskolnikov's trial that he too once knew how to extend such voluntary familial care to people outside his biological family: he had supported a fellow student for six months as he died of consumption and then "looked after the old and ailing father who survived him (and whom the son had maintained by his own efforts almost since his fourteenth year), eventually found a place for him in the hospital, and, when he too died, buried him" (514; *PSS*, 6: 412). Although Raskolnikov feels totally alienated from his mother and sister after the murders, he voluntarily enters the Marmeladov family, caring for the dying Marmeladov "as though it were a question of his own father" (170; *PSS*, 6: 138). Later he tells Sonya, "Today I deserted my family, my mother and sister. I shall not go to them now. I have made a complete break [. . .] Now I have only you" (315; *PSS*, 6: 252).

There is a contradiction in Raskolnikov's vision of "aloneness." On the one hand, his theory implies that he freed himself of family ties in order not to be one of the "ordinary" people who only reproduce themselves and that it was his aloneness that drove him to kill, to demonstrate his Napoleonic ruthlessness and extraordinary nature. On the other hand, he tells Sonya just before his confession, "Oh, if only I were alone and nobody loved me, and if I had never loved anyone! *All this would never have happened!*" (500; *PSS*, 6: 401). *Crime and Punishment* remains novelistic in its refusal to offer full and unambiguous explanations or solutions. Just as the question of Raskolnikov's motive for the murders is never definitively resolved, the question of his aloneness is left open: Did he kill because he had renounced his family, or did his worries about his family drive him to kill? Whichever is true, Raskolnikov is unable to maintain his aloneness. After cutting himself off from his biological family and cutting himself off from the human family by committing two murders, he voluntarily seeks a new family in the Marmeladovs, and especially in Sonya.

Of all the things we learn about Raskolnikov's biological family over the course of the novel, one of the most surprising is the way his mother reacts when she reads the article he published long before committing murder, the article in which he expounded his theory of the extraordinary man. She is captivated by the article, and during his trial "she was incessantly reading the article, sometimes even aloud; she all but slept with it" (515; *PSS*, 6: 413). She herself seems to subscribe to the theory of the "two categories" of people, placing herself and her son in the superior category: "I can tell that in a very short time you will be one of the first, if not the very first, among our men of learning. And people dared to think you were mad! Ha, ha, ha! You don't know, but they really did think that. *Wretched crawling worms, how can they understand what true intellect is*?" (493; PSS, 6: 396; emphasis added). In her descent into madness, Raskolnikov's mother reveals a side of her personality that may hold the seeds of her son's destructive arrogance.

Crime and Punishment was conceived and written in an atmosphere of journalistic theory-construction, by a man who had tried to make a career as a journalist as well as a writer, but it stubbornly remains a story, not a philosophical theory. In choosing Sonya over his biological family, Raskolnikov is in a sense choosing to reject theory, the "questions" that young educated people like him, and Lebezyatnikov, and Mikhailov, Suslova, and Chernyshevsky, spend their time contemplating. Unlike his mother, Sonya reacts to his Napoleonic theory with incomprehension and horror. When Raskolnikov confronts Sonya with the abstract "question," who should be allowed to live, Luzhin with his foul deeds or the innocent Katerina Ivanovna?, Sonya replies, "But I can't know God's Providence . . . *And why do you ask what should not be asked?* Where is the point of such empty questions? How could it depend on my decision? Who made me a judge of who shall live and who shall not?" (391; *PSS*, 6: 313; emphasis added). Soon after this conversation, Raskolnikov shows the beginnings of an awareness of the limitations of theory. Lebezyatnikov bursts in with the news that Katerina Ivanovna has gone mad and run into the street with her children. Lebezyatnikov reports that he had tried to console Katerina Ivanovna by explaining to her that her madness had a physiological cause in her tuberculosis. He tells Raskolnikov, in a kind of parody of Chernyshevsky's faith in reason, "If you convince a person logically that in reality he has nothing to cry for, he will stop crying. That's clear. Or don't you think he will stop?" Raskolnikov replies, "That would make it too easy to live" (406; *PSS*, 6: 325). At this point Raskolnikov realizes that logic cannot overcome the hard truths of life.

We see Sonya as a writer at the end of the novel, as she sends letters to Dunya and Razumikhin from the Siberian prison camp. Her style is resolutely non-theoretical: "Sonya's letters were full of the most prosaic actuality, the simplest and clearest description of every circumstance of Raskolnikov's life as a convict. They contained neither statements of her own hopes, nor speculations about the future, nor descriptions of her feelings. Instead of attempts to explain his psychological condition and his inner life generally, there were only facts, his own words, that is, and detailed reports of his health, of what he expressed a wish for at their interviews, the questions he asked her or the commissions he entrusted to her. All this she communicated with extraordinary minuteness. In the end, the image of their unhappy brother emerged of its own accord, exactly and clearly drawn; there could be nothing misleading about it, because it consisted wholly of reliable facts" (518; *PSS*, 6: 415). Sonya's style, based on the observation of what she sees before her rather than the imagination of what might be in some theoretical future, is more like the detailed realism of Dostoevsky than the schematic, theory-driven plot of Chernyshevsky, which relies more on wishful thinking than on plausible human behavior.

Family care involves teaching, especially teaching the word of God, as even the wretched Marmeladov taught scripture to his stepchildren (181; *PSS*, 6: 146). Raskolnikov recalls reading the story of Lazarus "when [he] was at school," but no longer remembers where to find it in the Gospel (312; *PSS*, 6: 249). At the end of the novel, Sonya has given Raskolnikov the copy of the Gospel from which she read him the story of Lazarus. The end of *Crime and Punishment* is often criticized for giving Raskolnikov a too easy religious conversion. But in fact he does not find God: "There was a New Testament under his pillow . . . He himself had asked her for it not long before his illness and she had brought it to him without a word. He had not yet opened it. *He did not open it even now*" (527; *PSS*, 6: 422; emphasis added). Instead of reading the word of God, he thinks of Sonya: "Could not her beliefs become my beliefs now? Her feelings, her aspirations, at least" (527; *PSS*, 6: 422). This is not religious conversion but an aspiration to human familial connection. Raskolnikov has realized *again* that he must voluntarily, with love, assume the responsibilities and obligations of family. Theory has been displaced: "Life had taken the place of dialectics and something quite different must be worked out in his mind" (527; *PSS*, 6: 422).

What Is to Be Done? is full of references to the utopian future, when life and family relations will be completely transformed. One vision, however, is not of the future but of an alternative present. In Vera Pavlovna's Second Dream, she has a vision of what her life might have been like if her mother had not been "a nasty, vile woman" but good and weak, unable to fight for her family in the cruel contemporary world. That alternative life involves a drunken father, an emaciated, worn-out mother, and a daughter who has given herself to an officer. In other words, the vision reveals something like Sonya's life, with her good but weak father Marmeladov.[41] In Vera Pavlovna's dream, the "Bride of Her Bridegrooms," the spirit of the utopian future, tells her, "It won't be like this later. When the good are strong, I won't need the wicked."[42] Raskolnikov tells Svidrigaylov, "I do not believe in the future life" (277; *PSS*, 6: 221). In context this refers to life beyond the grave, but it can just as well be applied to the radicals' future rational utopia.[43] In that sense, when Raskolnikov says, "I do not believe in the future life," he is speaking for Dostoevsky as well. For most of *Crime and Punishment*, Raskolnikov and his creator remain in the present, when the good are weak and strength must be shown through violence.

In the Epilogue, Dostoevsky, like Chernyshevsky, turns his gaze to a "future life," and the accent is on the utopian rather than the realistic. The novel ends, "But that is the beginning of a new story, the story of the gradual renewal of a man, of his gradual regeneration, of his slow progress from one world to another, of how he learned to know a hitherto undreamed-of reality. All that might be the subject of a new tale, but our present one is ended" (527; *PSS*, 6: 422). In Suslova's stories, the Dunyas of the world have no way out. In the Epilogue of *Crime and Punishment*, Dunya, having saved herself from loveless marriage to Luzhin and rape by Svidrigaylov, marries Razumikhin, who combines goodness and strength. Raskolnikov enters into a "hitherto undreamed-of reality" with Sonya, whose strength and goodness have also been proved. Their new family unit is as unconventional in its way as that of the Lopukhovs and Kirsanovs: the "new story" is built on the union of the "murderer and the harlot" (315; *PSS*, 6: 251–252).

At the conclusion of the novel, children have receded from the scene. After Svidrigaylov's suicide, the fate of his fifteen-year-old fiancée is not narrated. Sonya's stepsiblings have been sent, with Svidrigaylov's financial assistance, to a high-class orphanage (421; *PSS*, 6: 336).[44] Sonya has followed Raskolnikov to Siberia, so it is not clear who will visit the Marmeladov children or who is going to help them get over losing both their parents. No mention is made of whether Raskolnikov intends to join those who merely "increase and multiply," by having children with Sonya. This may be because Dostoevsky has moved out of literary realism into Chernyshevsky's utopian mode, and children are a real problem for utopia. As Lebezyatnikov says to Luzhin, "Children are a social question, and one of the first importance, I agree; but the problem of children will be solved in another way. Some people even negate children altogether, like every other hint at the family" (360–361; *PSS*, 6: 289). In his most underrated novel, *A Raw Youth* (1875), Dostoevsky gives a vivid first-person account by his hero Arkady Dolgoruky of what life is like for a child growing up in the kind of "respectable" institution to which the Marmeladov orphans have been sent. Arkady suffers not material deprivation but a soul-crushing loneliness, humiliation, and premature sexual initiation that have a lasting crippling effect. In *Crime and Punishment*, Dostoevsky had the imagination to explore family relations in all their multifariousness, transcending the "woman question." But like Suslova and Chernyshevsky, he ultimately failed to fully confront the problem of children. In his later novels, *The Devils, A Raw Youth*, and *The Brothers Karamazov*, Dostoevsky would not "negate children" but make neglected children the main actors in his narratives.[45]

In *Crime and Punishment,* Dostoevsky was not writing a theoretical treatise in the guise of literature, as Chernyshevsky did in *What Is to Be Done?* Chernyshevsky began with a theory and shaped his characters and plot to advance that theory, with the goal of changing the world. But Dostoevsky did engage the contemporary debate to some extent, offering a vision of the family that was an alternative to the nihilist view of it as outmoded. In the world of *Crime and Punishment* the family, especially when founded on love, still functions in multiple ways as the necessary support for individual well-being. Dostoevsky's vision of the family, particularly in his own version of the utopian, comes with the recognition that authority has to be balanced with reciprocity, power with obligation. Dostoevsky's critique of the nihilist utopia was rooted in observed experience, and his fictional transformation of that experience transcended contemporary discourse.

NOTES

1. Philip Pomper, *The Russian Revolutionary Intelligentsia* (New York: Thomas Y. Crowell, 1970), 67. For more on Katkov's role in the publication of *Crime and Punishment,* see my article, "Dostoevsky and Mikhail Katkov: Their Literary Partnership (*Crime and Punishment* and *The Devils*)," in *New Studies in Russian Literature and Culture: Essays in Honor of Stanley J. Rabinowitz,* 2 vols., ed. Catherine Ciepiela and Lazar Fleishman, Stanford Slavic Studies, vols. 45–46 (Oakland, CA: Berkeley Slavic Specialties, 2014), part 1 [vol. 45]), pp. 35–69; and my book, *Editing Turgenev, Dostoevsky, and Tolstoy: Mikhail Katkov and the Great Russian Novel* (DeKalb: Northern Illinois University Press, 2017). I would like to thank Robert Guay for his editorial suggestions on this essay.
2. Liudmila Saraskina, *Vozliublennaia Dostoevskogo. Apollinariia Suslova: Biografiia v dokumentakh, pis'makh, materialakh* (Moscow: Soglasie, 1994), 97. This book is a fascinating compendium of documents about Suslova, including Suslova's letters, diary, and fiction as well as accounts by contemporaries and scholars. All translations are mine unless otherwise indicated. For discussions of Suslova as a model for Polina in Dostoevsky's 1866 novella *The Gambler,* see Nina Pelikan Straus, *Dostoevsky and the Woman Question: Rereadings at the End of a Century* (New York: St. Martin's Press, 1994), 37–44; and Carol Apollonio, *Dostoevsky's Secrets: Reading Against the Grain* (Evanston, IL: Northwestern University Press, 2009), 44–47.

3. Saraskina, *Vozliublennaia,* 117.
4. Letter from Dostoevsky to Suslova, April 23 (May 5), 1867, in F. M. Dostoevskii, *Polnoe sobranie sochinenii,* ed. V. G. Bazanov et al., 30 vols. (Leningrad: Nauka, 1972–1990), 28/2: 183. Subsequent references to this edition will be given in parentheses in the text as *PSS,* vol.: page.
5. Saraskina, *Vozliublennaia,* 59. For a discussion of Nadezhda Suslova and her fiction, see Peter C. Pozefsky, "Love, Science, and Politics in the Fiction of *Shestidesiatnitsy* N. P. Suslova and S. V. Kovalevskaia," *Russian Review* 58 (July 1999): 361–379.
6. Saraskina, *Vozliublennaia,* 138.
7. Mikhailov's patronymic is sometimes given as Illarionovich. The authoritative source on Chernyshevsky and his theories of family and gender relationships is Irina Paperno, *Chernyshevsky and the Age of Realism: A Study in the Semiotics of Behavior* (Stanford, CA: Stanford University Press, 1988).
8. M. L. Mikhailov, *Sochineniia,* ed. B. P. Koz'min, 3 vols. (Moscow: Khudozhestvennaia literatura, 1958), 3: 679. In a letter to the actress Aleksandra Ivanovna Shubert, Dostoevsky writes, "We will talk about Mikhailov's article later," thus demonstrating that he was familiar with it (Letter of June 12, 1860, *PSS,* 28/2: 15). For more on Mikhailov, see T. A. Bogdanovich, *Liubov' liudei shestidesiatykh godov* (Leningrad: Academia, 1929); and G. A. Tishkin, *Zhenskii vopros v Rossii, 50-60-e gody XIX v.* (Leningrad: Leningradskii universitet, 1984), especially 78–88.
9. Richard Stites, *The Women's Liberation Movement in Russia: Feminism, Nihilism, and Bolshevism, 1860–1930* (Princeton, NJ: Princeton University Press, 1978), 38.
10. Mikhailov, *Sochineniia,* 3: 369.
11. Mikhailov, *Sochineniia,* 3: 375.
12. Mikhailov, *Sochineniia,* 3: 420.
13. Paperno, *Chernyshevsky,* 148. See also Stites, *Women's Liberation Movement,* 41–42. Stites describes how Mikhailov's ideas were shaped by his sojourn in France with the Shelgunovs, during which he had serious discussions with the feminist Eugénie (Jenny) d'Héricourt (41–42).
14. Saraskina, *Vozliublennaia,* 43.
15. Saraskina, *Vozliublennaia,* 50. Stites points out that "the slave–slaveowner analogy was popular among feminists all over the western world in these years" (*Women's Liberation Movement,* 43n).
16. Saraskina, *Vozliublennaia,* 63.
17. Saraskina, *Vozliublennaia,* 70.
18. Saraskina, *Vozliublennaia,* 67.
19. Saraskina, *Vozliublennaia,* 83.
20. Saraskina, *Vozliublennaia,* 85.

21. Nikolai Chernyshevsky, *What Is to Be Done?*, trans. Michael R. Katz, annotated William G. Wagner (Ithaca, NY: Cornell University Press, 1989), 133. Hereafter cited as *WITBD*.
22. The wedding ceremony is described in Chernyshevsky, *WITBD*, 158. The legal consequences are described in N. G. Chernyshevskii, *Chto delat'? Iz rasskazov o novykh liudiakh*, ed. T. I. Ornatskaia and S. A. Reiser (Leningrad: Nauka, 1975), 841.
23. Chernyshevsky, *WITBD*, 170–172.
24. In addition to Paperno, see the introduction to *WITBD* by Michael R. Katz and William G. Wagner, 1–36, for a lucid discussion of Chernyshevsky's intellectual sources and impact.
25. Saraskina, *Vozliublennaia*, 184.
26. Saraskina, *Vozliublennaia*, 193.
27. Suslova wrote another story, "Strangers and One's Own People," which is unpublished and undated (Saraskina, *Vozliublennaia*, 334–350). Saraskina surmises that it was written in 1863, before "Going Her Own Way" (*Vozliublennaia*, 325–326). This story is based closely on Suslova's experiences with Dostoevsky. Like her first two stories, it has an unhappy ending, as the heroine commits suicide.
28. Mikhailov, *Sochineniia*, 3: 429–430.
29. Saraskina, *Vozliublennaia*, 245.
30. Chernyshevsky, *WITBD*, 371.
31. Chernyshevsky, *WITBD*, 354. I have changed the translation slightly, since I believe *nevesta* should be translated as "fiancée" rather than "bride," which would imply an already contracted marriage.
32. Page references given first in parentheses are to the Oxford edition of *Crime and Punishment* (trans. Jessie Coulson, Oxford: Oxford University Press, 2008), but I have occasionally altered the translation to bring it closer to the Russian text.
33. Dostoevsky's reversal of the valorization given to privacy by Chernyshevsky is noted by Boris Tikhomirov, *"Lazar'! griadi von": Roman F. M. Dostoevskogo 'Prestuplenie i nakazanie' v sovremennom prochtenii. Kniga-kommentarii* (St. Petersburg: Serebrianyi vek, 2005), 324.
34. The editors of Dostoevsky's complete works identify this as a reference to a feuilleton by G. Z. Eliseev that includes the ironic subtitle "Various Opinions on the Question: Are Women People?," which appeared in *The Contemporary*, May 1861 (*PSS*, 7: 371). It may also reflect Mikhailov's 1860 article, in which he writes, "Once we acknowledge woman to be a person (or has that become doubtful in our time?), even if we acknowledge that she has comparatively weaker moral, intellectual, and physical capabilities than man, let us at least be consistent enough to consider vice to be vice, in whomever it appears" (*Sochineniia*, 3: 403).

35. Paperno describes Chernyshevsky's propensity for constructing elaborate fantasies about his own life (*Chernyshevsky*, 93, 98, 100). Anna A. Berman analyzes family relationships, primarily sibling relationships, in *Crime and Punishment*. Berman's emphasis on the ways in which characters in Dostoevsky form spiritual, nonbiological familial connections is consonant with my reading here. Anna A. Berman, *Siblings in Tolstoy and Dostoevsky: The Path to Universal Brotherhood* (Evanston, IL: Northwestern University Press, 2015), 62–78.
36. See the discussion of Lizaveta and her pregnancies by S. V. Berezkina, "'Zhivet zhe na kvartire u portnogo Kapernaumova . . .' (Iz kommentariia k 'Prestupleniiu i nakazaniiu' Dostoevskogo)," *Russkaia literatura*, no. 4, 2013: 169–179, 172–174. Berezkina centers her discussion of the "woman question" on Sonya's fate.
37. Chernyshevsky, *WITBD*, 290.
38. For a detailed analysis of clothing in *Crime and Punishment*, see Janet Tucker, "The Religious Symbolism of Clothing in Dostoevsky's *Crime and Punishment*," *Slavic and East European Journal* 44, no. 2 (2000): 253–265.
39. James Scanlan, *Dostoevsky the Thinker* (Ithaca, NY: Cornell University Press, 2002), 61–62.
40. See Berman, *Siblings in Tolstoy and Dostoevsky*, 69–70.
41. Chernyshevsky, *WITBD*, 184–185.
42. Chernyshevsky, *WITBD*, 187.
43. On Chernyshevsky's attitude toward life after death, see Paperno, *Chernyshevsky*, 199.
44. For an interpretation of Svidrigaylov that places a positive accent on his activities, see Apollonio, *Dostoevsky's Secrets*, 75–86.
45. See Susanne Fusso, *Discovering Sexuality in Dostoevsky* (Evanston, IL: Northwestern University Press, 2006).

Chapter 6

Raskolnikov Beyond Good and Evil

RANDALL HAVAS

I. NIHILISM OR ALIENATION

Joseph Frank contends that Dostoevsky intended the character of Raskolnikov to "portray the inescapable contradictions in [the] radical ideology of Russian Nihilism."[1] According to that ideology, the good of the many is to be secured by an elite, rational few who know what is required to achieve it and who are capable of doing what has to be done along the way—even where what, in their estimation, has to be done violates precisely the altruistic moral impulses with which they supposedly began. Thus, Raskolnikov's ostensible motivation for his murder and robbery of the old pawnbroker, Alyona Ivanovna, is to alleviate the misery of the denizens of Petersburg languishing around him. The point of Raskolnikov's travails is not, however, simply that utilitarianism is at odds with altruism. Rather—and more deeply—Dostoevsky contends that Raskolnikov's commitment to utilitarian thinking is an expression of a kind of "egomania."[2] At bottom, Raskolnikov thinks of the murder as a kind of test of himself, to see if he is "strong enough to have the right to kill."[3] The supposed utilitarian motivation drops out; in the end, the murders are a symptom of something deeper. Raskolnikov's pathological egoism is Dostoevsky's real target.

Frank's contention that the real drama of *Crime and Punishment* is that of Raskolnikov's always unsteady recognition of his real motivation for the murders seems to me correct, as does his claim that Raskolnikov himself comes only gradually in the course of the novel to recognize what the reader already knows: namely, that the pawnbroker's murder had in fact nothing to do with an altruistic wish to help others and everything to do with an egoistic fantasy of self-affirmation. Yet Frank does not make clear in what Raskolnikov's egoism or "monomania"[4] consists. He says only that Raskolnikov is meant to embody what Dostoevsky condemned as the Russian nihilists' recommendation of what he calls the "proto-Nietzschean egoism among an elite of superior individuals to whom the hopes for the future were to be entrusted."[5]

My aim in this chapter is to have another look at the question of Raskolnikov's motivation for his murder of the pawnbroker to try to discern a bit more closely in what the ostensibly "Nietzschean" aspects of his character really consist. The differences between Raskolnikov's self-conception and Nietzsche's own views on at least one plausible interpretation are striking and instructive. Raskolnikov's sense of himself presupposes precisely what Nietzsche questions: namely, that those around him have a coherent moral outlook and that individuality demands the creation of an entirely new and unprecedented moral vocabulary of one's own.

Nevertheless, there at least *seems* to be something recognizably Nietzschean about him, even if only as a kind of caricature or stereotype, but the significance of the caricature is not immediately obvious. On the surface, Raskolnikov does appear to think of himself as trying (and ultimately failing) to live, as Nietzsche says, beyond good and evil. More specifically, *he* seems convinced that thinking of himself in terms of the vocabulary that applies to everyone else represents some kind of threat to the very possibility of individuality, and he seeks what he believes "men are most afraid of... Any new departure and especially *a new word*—that is what they fear most of all" (2).[6] I think that we can best understand Raskolnikov's experience of himself, however, if we see him most basically as *alienated* from human community in some profound but quite general way, rather than simply as trying in the name of some perceived "higher" goal to step beyond or over the demands of morality. In the end, *Crime and Punishment* as a whole is an exploration of this sort of alienation and of Raskolnikov's evolving understanding of its precise dimensions. Raskolnikov, in other words, is not simply evil; and *Crime and Punishment* is not a cautionary tale defending morality in the face of evil. Rather he represents a kind of existential apotheosis of adolescence: like the mid-nineteenth-century Russian culture Dostoevsky is trying to understand more generally, he is stuck, so to speak, halfway between the (feudal) old and the (modern) new, unable to go backward, but also unable or unwilling to grow up and move forward. In this sense, then, *Crime and Punishment* is a long meditation on the nature of human agency in modernity, and as we will see, one of Dostoevsky's principal aims is to try to undo certain confusions about what self-determination demands.

The significance of Raskolnikov's alienation *from the law* becomes clearer in the course of his three conversations with the police inspector Porfiry Petrovich before his final confession in the police station at the end of Part Six. We miss Dostoevsky's point here if we think—as Raskolnikov himself often does—of Porfiry only as playing cat to Raskolnikov's mouse, trying by what he calls "psychological" means to extract a confession from him, perhaps because he lacks enough actual material evidence to secure a conviction. Porfiry's aim is instead to erode any *theoretical* account Raskolnikov might have thought he had of his existential position relative to those around him. Porfiry leaves him in the end with no coherent story to tell himself about his motivations for the murders he commits. He wanted to prove to himself that he was different from everyone else; this is what he thinks originality or individuality demands. The effect of his exchanges with Porfiry, however, is to show him that he has no account of what his difference from them might be. As Porfiry puts it toward the very end of their conversations, "*You can't get on without us*" (442). Indeed, far from being a threat to his individuality, the law provides the only vocabulary in which Raskolnikov can enact his existence, and these are the same terms that bind everyone else. As Porfiry sees it, there *is* no other vocabulary. Yet the very possibility of a crime like Raskolnikov's shows that, as it were, no vocabulary applies itself. In the end, Raskolnikov is revealed to be a kind of frustrated Platonist: he believes, in effect, that only a vocabulary that *does* apply itself has any authority for him. Finding no such vocabulary, however, he feels free to try to invent one of his own. But speech—what Raskolnikov calls "a new word"—requires the speaker's *consent* to the vocabulary on hand, not the creation of a different moral code. This is what Porfiry has to teach him about the law.

Raskolnikov, then, experiences himself as utterly estranged from human community and in search of what he calls "a new word." As I just suggested, however, a large part of the point of his conversations with Porfiry is to make clear the real character of Raskolnikov's difficulty here: contrary to what he appears to think, individuality does not require wholesale rejection of one's community's vocabulary, but only one's consent to take up that vocabulary—the only one available in the end. Porfiry's word for this is "confession." As Dostoevsky sees it, Porfiry is right about that much. But Raskolnikov's alienation is ultimately not such that either he or Porfiry can heal it. In the end, overcoming this kind of alienation demands repentance, and nothing Porfiry (and therefore nothing the law generally) can do or say can guarantee *that*. On Dostoevsky's way of conceiving it, then,

Raskolnikov's problem is religious, not moral, and the "drama" of *Crime and Punishment*, such as it is, consists in revealing Raskolnikov's wish for a wholly original, self-interpreting ethical code as stemming from fallenness rather than individuality.

Making all this clear will allow us to understand better what is and what isn't properly "Nietzschean" in Raskolnikov's experience of himself. Like Raskolnikov, the Nietzschean individual condemns the speech of those around him as mere babble or chatter and seeks a "new word" of his own. Unlike Raskolnikov, however, such an individual conceives such a word as the achievement of a kind of community or mutuality with others—those he considers his equals. If it should happen that the would-be individual has no equals, then he remains a mere exception to a general rule of babble, both more and less than Raskolnikov hopes to be.

II. AUTHORITY AND THE LAW

Since we know from the start of the book *who* did it, *Crime and Punishment* is hardly a whodunit. The real question is, *why* did he do it? Or perhaps better, *what* did he do in doing it? This is something Raskolnikov tries to work out for himself in relation to pretty much everyone around him. In different ways his action has, he believes, irrevocably ruptured his relationship with his family, his friends, Sonya, and the world around him quite generally. Indeed, this rupture appears to be what he thinks the murder is meant as much to *establish* as to confirm, despite his apparent compulsion subsequently to give himself away at nearly every turn.[7] Nowhere is this peculiar dialectic displayed as clearly, however, as in his relationship to Porfiry Petrovich, the police inspector in charge of the investigation of the murder and robbery of the pawnbroker and her sister.

Like everyone else who meets him, Porfiry is *fascinated* by Raskolnikov; he is no ordinary murderer. And Porfiry, as we will see in more detail below, is no ordinary police investigator. He is, of course, a man of the law. He is, in fact, a lawyer. However, his relationship to the law is far more reflective than what we have any reason to believe is that of his colleagues on the police force—nearly as reflective, in fact, as that of the former law student Raskolnikov himself. Indeed, there seems to be room to wonder whether in the end Porfiry is not *himself* in some way alienated from the very law he defends. The possibility that Raskolnikov represents—namely, of not finding the law to be authoritative for one—makes him more than a little uneasy. Indeed, Raskolnikov's feeling are, he says, "familiar" (433, modified) to him.

Porfiry undertakes to instruct Raskolnikov on the nature of the law, and his "instruction" takes place in the course of three separate conversations. The first one, in Porfiry's apartment, is largely taken up with a discussion of Raskolnikov's article on crime, in which he articulates what Frank calls his "proto-Nietzschean" challenge to the law. Their exchanges begin at a high altitude of abstraction and descend over the course of several days to the rough ground of direct confrontation at the end, thereby mirroring what is, in Porfiry's mind, the process by which a general legal rule is applied to a particular case: the criminal coming to apply it to himself, consenting to it. Though nothing can compel such consent, Porfiry is convinced that certain obstacles to it can be removed. In the end, however, he cannot remove what Dostoevsky considers to be the most basic obstacle, which is more than merely intellectual.

Their second conversation takes place the next day in Porfiry's office in the police station itself, a location of comically Kafkaesque anonymity. The law as represented by this institutional setting is something truly abstract and general. So conceived, what indeed could the law have to do with Raskolnikov specifically? In this way, the character of Porfiry's office functions as a kind of counterpart to the "philosophical" conception of the law Raskolnikov defends in his article. Ironically enough, however, despite the ostensible abstractness of the place where it unfolds, their second exchange affords Porfiry a more direct confrontation with Raskolnikov than was possible in their first conversation. He aims in particular to remove a central intellectual obstacle to Raskolnikov's consenting to the law: confusion about the relationship between the particular case and the general rule. Contrary to what Raskolnikov seems to believe, the absence of a vocabulary other than that of morality to characterize what he has done does *not* mean that he is condemned to use terms that somehow deprive him of his individuality. Rather that fact makes it clear that there is an aspect of intelligibility that involves taking responsibility for using what terms are available, a responsibility that falls to the individual alone. Indeed, this seems to be what, in Porfiry's view, individuality ultimately consists in: one makes old words "new" by applying them to oneself. This is in the end for him the significance of confession; it is not simply something onto which he must as a police inspector fall back in the absence of sufficiently incriminating evidence of wrongdoing.

Their third and last conversation takes place—after his confession to Sonya—in Raskolnikov's own tiny room. Here Porfiry tells Raskolnikov directly that he should confess to the murders. By now the intended effect of this "direct and open invitation" (439) is to place before Raskolnikov the fact of his guilt without leaving him any means of evading the demand that he own up to it. That putting him in this position is not enough, however, to get him actually to *repent* of his crime indicates what Porfiry's unprecedented references to God's will suggests: namely, that Raskolnikov's alienation is *religious* in character and so requires both a religious diagnosis and a religious response.

III. CONVERSATION 1: PHILOSOPHY

Concerned to learn more precisely what Porfiry may suspect about his connection with the murders, Raskolnikov arrives at his apartment with his friend Razumikhin in tow and pretends to inquire about the various pledges he left with the pawnbroker. At this stage of the narrative, the evidence against Raskolnikov is suggestive but less than compelling: his suspicious fainting fit at the police station, the pledges found in the pawnbroker's apartment, his "confession" to Zametov in the Crystal Palace, and his article "On Crime," which Porfiry claims to have read with interest some two months earlier. All this is certainly enough to make him a suspect, but not enough to convict him. Yet the reader senses that Porfiry feels he has found his killer. Nevertheless, the bulk of their first meeting centers on an exploration of Raskolnikov's article, and their discussion remains "philosophical" almost to the end.

What interests Porfiry about Raskolnikov's article is above all the suggestion he tosses in at the end that there are those who "have every right, to commit any wrong or crime, and that laws, so to say, are not made for them" (248). What matters both to Porfiry and to Raskolnikov here is what he calls "the main principle of my idea" (250): namely, the division of human beings into two types, the ordinary and the extraordinary. This is the properly "proto-Nietzschean" aspect of Raskolnikov's theory. A note in *The Will to Power* articulates an ostensibly similar idea this way: "My philosophy aims at an ordering of rank: not at an individualistic morality. The ideas of the herd should rule in the herd—but not reach out beyond it: the leaders of the herd require a fundamentally different valuation for their own actions, as do the independent, or the 'beasts of prey', etc."[8] As we will see presently, however, the deeper significance of Raskolnikov's own version of this claim is difficult to locate with any precision.

Raskolnikov accepts Porfiry's invitation—scoffing or not—to elaborate on the theme of the exceptional person who is not bound by the normal rules of morality. His elaboration has three parts. He begins, unpromisingly, by defending a version of the principle that "the ends justify the means." "The 'extraordinary' man," he says, "has the right [. . .] to permit his conscience . . . to overstep . . . certain obstacles . . . in the event that his ideas [. . .] require it for their fulfillment" (249). Raskolnikov is none too clear, however, about *which* ends—which "ideas"—he has in mind here, even though the presence of such ideas seems intended to be *some* sort of check on the activity of the extraordinary man, who does not, he insists, "have the right to kill any Tom, Dick, or Harry he fancied, or go out stealing from market-stalls every day" (249). Clearly, the actual ends of the extraordinary individual matter to Raskolnikov. But the most he says at this juncture is that an idea that permits such a person to step over "certain obstacles" (e.g., common morality) "*may sometimes be* salutary for all mankind" (249, emphasis added).

This second version of his main idea might boil down to nothing more than noting that any truly new outlook or practice will *seem* "criminal" from the perspective of the outlook or practice it supplants. Artistic innovation is sometimes greeted this way. Or it might be only a further iteration of his earlier suggestion that a rigorous application of a utilitarian calculus will demand ruthlessness on the part of the agent. Neither claim seems to be what captures Porfiry's interest. Instead, what really fascinates him about Raskolnikov's article becomes clear only with the third and final part of his elaboration of his main idea: the distinction he draws between ordinary and extraordinary people.

Raskolnikov's articulation of his version of this idea remains extraordinarily abstract throughout his first exchange with Porfiry, despite the latter's dogged attempts to bring him down to earth, and as their second conversation shows he doesn't really understand it himself. Ultimately, though, Raskolnikov's real concern, like Nietzsche's, seems to be with the possibility of *originality*, and there is for both of them little that is less abstract than that. It is, in other words, to the possibility of his own *individuality* that Raskolnikov feels morality to be a threat, and it is the confusion behind *this* worry that Porfiry will try to lay bare for him in their second conversation.

So much, then, for Raskolnikov's own presentation of his proto-Nietzschean view; I turn now to Porfiry's interrogation of it. His tone throughout is almost parodically Socratic. Indeed, the comedy of his personal appearance is matched only by the irony of his questions and that in turn only by the irony of his asking ironical questions. Nowhere does he say directly that there are no extraordinary people in Raskolnikov's sense, and nowhere does he defend the suggestion that there are in fact no goals that permit one to ignore the demands of morality. Porfiry asks whether there is a way to distinguish an extraordinary person from someone who merely imagines himself to be extraordinary. How, that is, does Raskolnikov propose to deal with "mistaken confusion between the two categories" (253)? How does one know if in fact one has something truly "new" to say? Can't one think one has something of one's own to say when one hasn't, something that, on Raskolnikov's view, would not in fact permit him to ignore the demands of ordinary morality? Raskolnikov allows that such mistakes are possible, but only on the part of an ordinary person mistakenly taking himself to be extraordinary; and such people "never go far" (252). In fact, such people often scorn "*new people*" (252). In any case, they do not constitute a real threat, since either they will be caught right away and punished or they will punish themselves.

In response, Porfiry shifts the discussion from questions in the abstract about how one can tell a truly extraordinary person from a merely apparent one and from concerns about the dangers such people might pose to everyone else to the case of the man like the one before him: what if "somebody, some young man, fancies he is a Lycurgus or a Mahomet—a future one, of course—and . . . he is to remove all obstacles to that end?" (253). Porfiry says he's been "greatly reassured [. . .] about mistaken confusion between the two categories" (253), but now he wants to know about "various practical cases" (253). He goes further: Could it be, he asks Raskolnikov, that "when you were composing your article—surely it could not be, he he, that you did not consider yourself . . . just a tiny bit . . . to be also an 'extraordinary' man, one who was saying a *new word*—in your sense, that is . . .?" (254) Raskolnikov replies, "Very likely" (255). In that case, Porfiry asks—in, he says, only "a purely literary respect"—whether Raskolnikov could himself rob and kill. At which point, Raskolnikov breaks off the discussion, assuring Porfiry, "If I had indeed done so, then of course I should not tell you" (255). But of course Porfiry has not asked *any* of these questions in a merely "literary respect." His aim has been to prevent their exchange from devolving into philosophy. It is philosophy—Raskolnikov's attempt to turn his real problem into a merely intellectual one—that stands in the way of confession.

The specifically *philosophical* part of their first conversation is now finished. Porfiry asks Raskolnikov to come by his office the next day to answer a few questions about his last visit to the pawnbroker's apartment. Only in the course of this new conversation does Porfiry's real interest in the character of Raskolnikov's alienation begin to take proper shape as he tries more directly to undermine his suspect's conception of what individuality demands. To this end Porfiry elaborates his own theory of the law as a response to the one Raskolnikov defends in his article. In a sense, he and Raskolnikov agree: one can be, as it were, singled out by the law without thereby being forced to recognize the law's *authority*.[9] Raskolnikov misunderstands the upshot of this fact, however. To put the point in quasi-Kantian terms, what Raskolnikov wants in effect is a "deduction" of the law, a demonstration that it applies to *him* in particular. That is to say, he draws a distinction between "the letter of the law" and what we might call "the law per se" (its application to him), and he wants proof that the latter idea is not empty. It is important, however, that Porfiry does *not* provide such a deduction. He aims instead to deprive Raskolnikov of the intellectual tools by means of which he hopes to express his doubts about the matter.

IV. CONVERSATION 2: ETHICS.

As was the case the day before in Porfiry's apartment, the conversation in his office at the police station begins at a high level of abstraction before coming back to earth to confront Raskolnikov with the fact of his own case in a way intended to make it increasingly difficult for him to evade his responsibility for it. The structure of their second conversation mirrors in this fashion the overall structure of the three conversations as a whole. Thus, in response to Raskolnikov's insistence that he be interrogated "in the proper form" (322), Porfiry tutors him on the relationship between the general rule and what he twice calls the "*particular case*" (328, modified; Porfiry's emphasis). It is precisely this relationship that, in Porfiry's estimation, Raskolnikov fails to understand correctly, where correctly understanding it cannot, he insists, be neatly carved off from the activity of confession itself in the way in which Raskolnikov wishes it could be.

Porfiry directs the conversation to legal techniques, procedures, and rules. Thus commences their conversation on the nature of the law, the proper subject of this second conversation. Porfiry offers here what we might think of as his first reflection on the "limitations" of form: it—the law—doesn't apply *mechanically* to cases at hand. He explains, "But why bother about formalities?—in many cases, you know, they mean nothing. Sometimes just a friendly talk is much more use" (324). Indeed, Porfiry stresses that the interrogator's "business is [. . .] some sort of an art, in its own way" (324). But this is not the main point on which Porfiry insists. As I have emphasized, he seeks confession, not just conviction, and confession, for him, does not simply fill in the gaps in the available evidence of a suspect's guilt. It indicates instead that the suspect *consents* to the law he has violated, sees it as binding on him in particular. As such, confession must be freely given and *cannot* be something one may be tricked into giving. Porfiry's first point, then, is that application of the law to the particular demands an exercise of judgment. His second and deeper point, however, is that, in a further sense, the individual must apply the rule to himself, something that demands an exercise of judgment of a different sort.

In his dealings with Porfiry, Raskolnikov himself *never* arrives at a clear understanding of the difference between arrest, on the one hand, and his further incrimination, on the other. He sees that Porfiry is intent on drawing *some* such distinction, but he doesn't understand it. "It is no longer a case of cat and mouse, as it was yesterday. He is not showing me his strength and . . . hinting for nothing: he is much too clever for that! . . . He has some other motive, but what?" (327). Presumably, Dostoevsky's point here is that Raskolnikov, in effect, *confuses* proof, in Porfiry's special sense, with evidence. This is why, unlike the reader presumably, he cannot ultimately see what else Porfiry might be trying to do but trap him.

Porfiry claims, then, that a certain kind of person—Raskolnikov, in particular—can in a sense escape the law even if he's eventually clapped into jail. This is the outcome Porfiry considers it his "bounden duty" (431) to avoid. To this end, he asks Raskolnikov to reflect briefly on the nature of rules generally. He says that "the average case, the case for which all the legal forms and rules are devised, and which they are calculated to deal with, when they are written down in the textbooks, does not exist at all, because every case, every crime, for example, as soon as it really occurs, at once becomes a quite special case, and sometimes it is quite unlike anything that has ever happened before." (325–326). In saying that every case turns immediately into a particular one, Porfiry means to challenge the conception of general and particular that underwrites Raskolnikov's own version of the distinction on which they both insist between ordinary and extraordinary people. Raskolnikov thinks that the general or universal can never capture the individual case. Or rather all it *can* do is, so to speak, to capture it; it can't *comprehend* it. Raskolnikov understands the difference on which his article "On Crime" insists between being a copy/reproduction and being original as that between general and particular. Porfiry's deeper point is that true originality in fact demands that the would-be individual acknowledge the authority of the general rule. There is no *other* vocabulary available, no further perspective that could either *compel* the individual's allegiance to it or *entitle* him to ignore it. Porfiry's point in saying that each case is particular is to challenge the inherent Platonism of the thought that there might be such a vocabulary. As Raskolnikov sees it, in other words, rules have authority only for "ordinary" people who lack the imagination to think or say something "new." What makes this conception of rules broadly Platonist is its confusion of authority with force. Raskolnikov would accept as authoritative for him only a rule that, in his view, *compelled* his obedience. Finding no such rule, he figures it is up to him to invent one for himself. This would be his "new word." Of course, the idea that one can in *this* way give oneself the law is of doubtful intelligibility: I cannot will into existence the authority of my own way of looking at things. I answer to it, not it to me.

Nevertheless, Raskolnikov's feeling that any rule that in this way *requires* consent has no authority locates his confusion fairly precisely. As Porfiry sees it, however, a rule that did not in this sense require consent would not be a rule in the first place. A rule that, *per impossibile*, compelled obedience could not function as a reason for doing or avoiding something, but only as a cause of the associated behavior. This is, of course, precisely how Raskolnikov thinks rules *do* function for run-of-the-mill people, and it is why, for him, their obedience to such rules functions only "for the reproduction of [their] own kind" (260). But the point of saying that each case is particular is that this is in fact *not* how rules function. It is in the nature of things that obedience to authority *cannot* be compelled. Or to put the point another way, what can be compelled will, in this sense, always be something other than obedience. Thus, what Raskolnikov conceives as the weakness of rules is, from Porfiry's perspective, their special power.

On the surface, then, Porfiry seems to be saying exactly what Raskolnikov himself had said in his article: namely, that the law cannot *compel* obedience. But Porfiry understands this point, as it were, grammatically, whereas Raskolnikov thinks it points to a limitation of the law, and he uses that perceived limitation as an excuse for trying to evade it. This is the deeper point behind Porfiry's saying that to arrest Raskolnikov too soon would allow him "to retreat from me into his shell" (325). Because the law cannot compel obedience, Raskolnikov concludes that it doesn't apply to him, hence that obedience[10] to it can be only a poor external substitute for originality (for a new word). But this is a non sequitur. In effect, Porfiry wants Raskolnikov to appreciate both that he has no terms to describe what he has done *except* those of the law and that, from his perspective, the responsibility for applying those terms falls—*by the very nature of those terms (indeed of any terms)*—to him alone.

Once Porfiry has made clear the confusion of authority with force on which Raskolnikov's conception of the law rests, he turns—though still obliquely—to the "particular case" before them both. Even here, however, Porfiry's approach is oblique. He says, "He, let us suppose, will lie, I mean our man, this particular case, sir, Mr. X—and lie extremely well, in the most marvelously clever fashion (328, modified), and goes on to list all the ways in which Raskolnikov has revealed himself to be the murderer. All of this is presented to

Raskolnikov as the "clearest of mirrors" (329) in which to recognize himself; recognition of himself as guilty of a crime is recognition of the authority of the law, and for the reasons we've explored, it cannot be compelled. He has to see himself in that mirror; but he cannot see himself seeing himself there. Confession is, in this sense, a performative act. Thus, Porfiry remains true to his principle that he cannot actually do more than deprive Raskolnikov of his means of evasion. The decision rests with the culprit alone, having been deprived of the intellectual means whereby he has tried to keep that anxiety at bay.

With this Porfiry senses he's making progress: "So you don't trust me? But I tell you that you trust me half-way already, I'll make you trust me all the way yet, because I sincerely like you and wish you well" (333). The "half-way," of course, is the rejection of Raskolnikov's theory. The "all the way" is the entire distance to be covered on the way to confession. The sincerity of his repeated declarations of friendship should not be doubted, but as we've seen, that friendship is expressed as denying Raskolnikov any intellectual means of evading the matter of his guilt. This is part of the function of Porfiry's quasi-Socratic irony: where Socrates declares his ignorance in part at least to derail his interlocutor's wish to be spared the trouble of thinking for himself, Porfiry does everything he can to bring Raskolnikov to the point of confession without pretending—impossibly—to push him over the edge and without providing the psychological comfort of arresting him outright.[11]

V. CONVERSATION 3: RELIGION

The third conversation unfolds at the boundary between ethical and religious discourse. With this shift, Porfiry has come to the end of his ethical tether, so to speak: from the point of view of ethics, he has essentially nothing to add to his earlier point that rules do not apply themselves. He thinks of Raskolnikov's resistance to the authority of the law in the non-ethical terms of what he calls "psychology." But he can conceive such pathology only as "darkening." Like Raskolnikov, then, but from, so to speak, the opposite direction, he has "in one leap reached the farthest extremity" (441) of ethics. And although he will soon characterize at least the *solution* to Raskolnikov's dilemma in broadly religious terms, *as a police investigator anyway,* he has at his own disposal no terms other than those we've explored so far to characterize those limits. Consequently, he himself has no way more deeply to understand Raskolnikov's real *problem.*

As I have emphasized, the overall drift of each conversation is from general to particular. The first conversation passes from Raskolnikov's abstract *theory* of crime in general to the practical application of that theory to his own case. The second conversation passes from Raskolnikov's conception of the law as something that cannot comprehend the particular to Porfiry's conception of the particular person as someone who must consent to the law. The third and last conversation passes now from Porfiry's specifically ethical approach to a quasi-religious appeal to Raskolnikov's future. *As a whole,* then, their conversations pass not just from general to particular, but more specifically from philosophy to ethics to religion. At the religious level, however, Porfiry's particular spade, as we will see, is turned. His own life does not provide the model for Raskolnikov that Sonya's will, and as a result Raskolnikov continues to elude him. Let us now examine more closely the course of their third conversation.

Porfiry tells Raskolnikov the story of Mikolka and explains the circumstances of his false confession at the police station—which explanation makes room, finally, for a more specifically *religious* interpretation of Raskolnikov's own situation. Mikolka is, Porfiry recounts, a youthful religious enthusiast who fell afoul of the law in contemporary Petersburg. Once in prison, he found religion again and conceived a "need for suffering" (436, modified), on the basis of which conception he later confesses falsely to the murders of the pawnbroker and her sister. Porfiry does not elaborate on the nature of Mikolka's need to embrace suffering, but it is presumably an expression of a specifically Christian goal of selflessness, what Kierkegaard calls a self-annihilation before God.[12] Porfiry's willingness to speak in this way signals as clearly as anything else he says that he no longer thinks of himself as representing the authority of the law. He acknowledges that a wish to embrace suffering in this way is indeed "fantastic" (436). And as we've seen, he considers Raskolnikov's own case to be similarly "an obscure and fantastic case" (437). Indeed, suffering of a specifically religious sort is something he soon recommends to Raskolnikov himself. In other words, while in prison Raskolnikov would not, in Porfiry's view, simply be repaying his debt to society. This suggests that he thinks neither of Raskolnikov's crime nor of his punishment in entirely ethical terms: "You see I am convinced that you will 'resolve to accept your suffering'; you don't believe my word now, but you will come to the same conclusion yourself. Because suffering, Rodion Romanovich, is a great thing; don't look at the fact that I am fat myself, that doesn't matter; I still know, and don't laugh at this, that there is an idea in suffering. Mikolka is right" (442). The idea in suffering is clearly religious, however, not ethical.

The advantages *to* Raskolnikov, as Porfiry sees them, of his not simply arresting him now become clear with what he calls his "direct and open invitation—to [Raskolnikov] to come forward with a confession" (439). Some invitation, one might think! But let us look more closely. So far, Porfiry's approach has been primarily negative: he considers Raskolnikov's resistance to the law to be rooted in the pathology of a "psychological" confusion about the nature of authority itself. Once this confusion has been cleared up, an *intellectual* obstacle to the law has been removed. But Porfiry now tries to make a *positive* case on behalf of confession. He says that confessing will be "infinitely better for [Raskolnikov] and better for [Porfiry himself] too" (458) than Porfiry's arresting him without a confession. But what is the "infinite" advantage he sees? In what sense is the opportunity to confess before Porfiry arrests him an "invitation"?

As usual, matters appear on the surface relatively straightforward: if Raskolnikov confesses, Porfiry will be able to close his investigation, and Raskolnikov will get a lighter sentence. As usual, however, such matters are "double-ended." True, Porfiry says that if Raskolnikov confesses, "it will be a weight off [his] mind" (458), but the "it" here is ambiguous between Raskolnikov's case considered, on the one hand, as a purely legal matter and, on the other, as an existential or spiritual matter. Porfiry has clearly had both in mind throughout their conversations. As before, the thought that Porfiry is seeking only a conviction collapses the important distinction between two kinds of crime he draws in the course of their second conversation. Nothing in the text compels us to take the "it" here to refer only to the matter of Raskolnikov's conviction for the crime of murder; it could just as easily refer to the confession Porfiry seeks and the "infinite advantage" he believes it will afford Raskolnikov: by means of confession, he will have access to "the life God destines" (441) for him. And he will thereby have what Porfiry curiously says he himself lacks: namely, a future.

With his mention of the "infinite" advantage of confession, then, Porfiry has come to the end of his role in *Crime and Punishment.* He has destroyed Raskolnikov's philosophical theory. But he has seen that more needs to be done if Raskolnikov is to be, so to speak, brought back within the fold. If Raskolnikov can somehow reinscribe himself into the law, he will have a *particular* life, and in *that* sense he will have possibilities of his own. In their second conversation, Porfiry had expressed the difference between them as that between "an old man" and someone "still a young man [. . .] in [his] first youth, so to speak" (341), underscoring thereby Raskolnikov's position as an adolescent. By and large, as Porfiry presents the matter in his office, Raskolnikov's *second* youth—his having a future—is to be achieved by means of confession alone. As I have tried to show here, their third conversation represents a shift in register, but the closest he gets to a specifically religious version of his thought about the significance of confession is his talk of "an idea" in suffering. He now seems to acknowledge that suffering of this sort—not just confession to but punishment *for* his crime—is required for his having possibilities of his own. In the end, however, Porfiry's problem is that as a representative of the law, he has no more than that by which to distinguish confession from repentance. And this fact seems to help Raskolnikov to continue well into the Epilogue to evade the law even after he has confessed to the murders and been sentenced to hard labor. Repentance is what is required for the possibility of possibility, but eliciting *that* from Raskolnikov is, so to speak, beyond Porfiry's pay grade. He's a lawyer, not a saint, and Raskolnikov needs a saint.

VI. NIETZSCHE

I offer, by way of conclusion, the following points of contrast between Raskolnikov's exceptionalism and Nietzsche's particular brand of elitism.

1. To Raskolnikov's distinction between ordinary and extraordinary people, we can contrast Nietzsche's distinction between herd and individual. Nietzsche's distinction is not burdened with the Platonist conception of rules that seems to plague Raskolnikov's. The Platonist is someone who thinks that laws or rules should take care of themselves. From Raskolnikov's point of view, a law that fails to do that is a law in name alone. His Platonism is expressed as disappointment with the laws around him, because, as he sees, they do not *compel*

obedience. But this conception of the law's authority, we saw, rests on confusing it with force. Authority demands obedience, a fact that both the Platonist and the herd member fail correctly to appreciate. The herd thinks in a different sense that laws should take care of themselves: if a question of justification arises, it is settled by an appeal to convention: "This is just what we do." But the Nietzschean individual is no Platonist: questions of justification are settled with a presentation of reasons, for which presentation the individual alone bears ultimate responsibility.

2. To Raskolnikov's conviction that an extraordinary individual lives alone and apart from others, we can contrast Nietzsche's insistence that individuality be understood as mutuality. It is the *achievement* of community with the individual's peers, where who that is, is determined, in the present age, by one's willingness to take responsibility for the commitments speech and action inevitably entail. On Nietzsche's account someone living apart is a mere "exception" to a rule of general lawlessness.
3. To Raskolnikov's insistence that either one's own lack of resolve or the ordinary moral conventions of the society in which one finds oneself (or both) are obstacles to becoming an extraordinary individual, we can contrast Nietzsche's claim that mediocrity—one's own or that of others—stands in the way of individuality. The anonymity of the herd permits one to ignore the demands of commitment and deny one, what Nietzsche calls, "the right to make promises."[13]
4. Finally, it is worth comparing, even from this very high altitude, Dostoevsky's and Nietzsche's respective strategies relative to their readers. The aim in each case is to draw the reader away from a tempting but ultimately empty understanding of his existential situation in modernity. Dostoevsky creates in

> Raskolnikov a character who is in equal measures appealing and appalling, but with whom a certain kind of reader can anyway easily identify. Dostoevsky is not simply portraying a confused modern Russian nihilist; his goal is instead to understand and undermine that position from within. What tempts Raskolnikov tempts that sort of reader. And for that sort of reader, the collapse of Raskolnikov's various means of evasion will, Dostoevsky supposes, confront him with the same dilemma Raskolnikov must confront. No mere theory of the shortcomings of nihilism could do as much.

Thus, Raskolnikov looks to great individuals of the past—for example, Napoleon—as role models or moral exemplars of extraordinariness; but the way he does so indicates that his conception of their greatness is confused in the ways I have indicated. Imaginative identification with Raskolnikov allows the reader to uncover similar confusion in himself and thereby to free him from it. By contrast, Nietzsche offers his own example both as someone who has overcome his mediocrity and as someone capable of entering into community with his readers. The closest parallel to this sort of relationship in *Crime and Punishment* is *Porfiry's* offer of friendship to Raskolnikov.

This last point of contrast permits us to begin to articulate a final question about Nietzsche and Dostoevsky. How does each of them conceive *obstacles* or *resistance* to mutuality? Like many of Dostoevsky's most famous characters, Raskolnikov suffers from a form of self-hatred that Dostoevsky conceives in religious terms at the deeper significance of which the text of *Crime and Punishment* seems only to hint. It is already clear enough there, however, that he requires a model of repentance that only Sonya can provide. Yet even so it is not obvious from the text what it will take for Raskolnikov to see her model—that is, to feel the need to emulate her life—clearly.[14] The Epilogue makes only the vaguest of gestures in this direction, and one has to look to other works by Dostoevsky—primarily *The Brothers Karamazov*—for further elaboration.

Nietzsche's own view, as I have sketched it here, is structurally Kantian: according to the *Genealogy of Morals*, only what is done out of respect for one's commitments has the Nietzschean equivalent of moral worth. Like Porfiry and unlike Kant, however, Nietzsche thinks a felt need for a justification or deduction of one's perspective reflects confusion about the nature of the authority of that perspective. And unlike Kant, Nietzsche suggests that a form of self-hatred lies at the root of the demand for justification. In the end, what makes our commitments hard to honor is, in this sense, precisely that they are *ours*. Only something with more authority than what we can muster on our own seems to us as though it could truly merit obedience. One cannot, in other words, see how one could oneself be responsible for the meaning of what one says and does. One dreams in one way or another that the problem of being an animal with the right to make promises has or will have taken care of itself. Nietzsche's objection to the Platonist is much the same as Porfiry's: authority cannot *compel* obedience. And the thought that it should do so expresses the Platonist's wish to be told what to do.

NOTES

1. Joseph Frank, "The World of Raskolnikov," in Feodor Dostoevsky, *Crime and Punishment*, Norton Critical Edition, ed. George Gibian, trans. Jessie Senior Coulson (New York: Norton, 1989), 573.
2. Frank, "The World of Raskolnikov," 577.
3. Frank, "The World of Raskolnikov," 577.
4. Joseph Frank, *Dostoevsky: A Writer in His Time* (Princeton, NJ: Princeton University Press, 2010), 492.
5. Frank, *Dostoevsky: A Writer in His Time*, 484.
6. Fyodor Dostoevsky, *Crime and Punishment*, trans. Jessie Coulson (Oxford: Oxford University Press, 2008). All references to *Crime and Punishment* will be to this edition and given by page number parenthetically in the text.

7. I count *at least* the following confessions or all-but-confessions from Raskolnikov in the course of *Crime and Punishment*: to Nikodim Fomich before fainting in the police station, to Zametov in the Crystal Palace, to the workmen cleaning up the pawnbroker's apartment, to Razumikhin after the break with Luzhin, to Porfiry during the course of their first conversation, to Sonya during his first visit to her, to Sonya again later, to Porfiry during their second conversation, to Svidrigaylov after that, and to Dunya, his sister, before finally turning himself in to Ilya Petrovich in the police station itself.
8. Friedrich Nietzsche, *The Will to Power*, trans. Walter Kaufmann and R. J. Hollingdale (New York: Vintage 1968), §287, 162.
9. That is to say, one can understand that if one kills someone in such-and-such circumstances, one will by convention be *counted* a murderer, but only by convention.
10. Indeed, "obedience" and "consent" are precisely the terms Raskolnikov applies to the "material" category of person in his discussion of his article, "On Crime." Such people are "by nature staid and conservative, they live in obedience and like it. In my opinion they ought to obey because that is their destiny, and there is nothing at all degrading to them in it" (250). By contrast, the higher, extraordinary sort of person, "cannot, of course consent to remain in the rut [. . .] and in my opinion they ought not to consent" (250).
11. In quasi-psychoanalytic fashion, Porfiry tries not to rush to give his "patient" the correct interpretation of his behavior before he is, so to speak, ready to stumble onto it himself. Indeed, Freud insists that an all too typical form of resistance to an analytic interpretation consists in assenting to it too soon or too easily. Such assent as resistance is analogous to arrest without confession. The analogy is limited, however, because Dostoevsky does think that Raskolnikov's problem is in the end religious, not purely psychological. He needs more and other help than a therapist can provide.
12. See Søren Kierkegaard, *Concluding Unscientific Postscript*, trans. Alastair Hannay (New York: Cambridge University Press, 2009), 405–412. A version of this vision of things is elaborated by Father Zossima in Fyodor Dostoevsky, *The Brothers Karamozov*, trans. Richard Pevear and Larissa Volokhonsky (New York: Farrar, Straus and Giroux, 1990).
13. Friedrich Nietzsche, *On the Genealogy of Morals*, trans. Walter Kaufmann and R. J. Hollingdale (New York: Vintage Books, 1989), 57 (II:1).
14. To see her as such a model necessarily involves seeing her as someone to be emulated. The absence of the latter indicates an obscured vision of the former.

Chapter 7

Bakhtin's Radiant Polyphonic Novel, Raskolnikov's Perverse Dialogic World

CARYL EMERSON

In grateful memory of my first mentor in both Dostoevsky and Bakhtin: Michael Holquist (December 20, 1935–June 26, 2016)

I. INTRODUCTION

Dostoevsky was not favored by the Bolsheviks or their Stalinist successors. Reading him was discouraged. His fictional characters were too unhealthy, too hysterical and ideologically unreliable to serve the disciplined aims of either revolution or scientific socialism. Work on Dostoevsky by the Soviet academic establishment was timid in its methodology and hemmed in by party guidelines. Unsurprisingly, of all twentieth-century Russian scholarship on this great novelist, Mikhail Bakhtin's *Problems of Dostoevsky's Poetics* (1929, rev. 1963) quickly conquered global Dostoevsky Studies during communism's twilight years.[1] It was the most original and sophisticated study of Dostoevsky to emerge from the 1920s.

Parallels abound between the researcher and his research subject. Like Dostoevsky, Bakhtin was poor, chronically ill, exiled to Siberia, a political miscreant in a vigilantly censored culture, and for most of his adult life an outsider to the mainstream institutions of his time. When Bakhtin's book appeared in Leningrad in 1929, its author had been under arrest for half a year, on obscure charges of "philosophical idealism."[2] Alongside many intellectuals of his generation, Bakhtin saw no conflict between science and faith, or between socialism and Christianity. (Materialist Marxism was a challenge of another order, but not insurmountable: during his interrogation, Bakhtin identified himself as a "Marxist-revolutionary, loyal to Soviet power, religious.") Hospitalized in the summer of 1929 for a worsening of his bone disease (osteomyelitis), Bakhtin was sentenced in absentia to five years in Solovki, a labor camp in the Arctic Far North. Nevertheless, his Dostoevsky monograph, the first serious publication of an almost unknown scholar, received trenchant, not wholly negative reviews from several prominent intellectuals. Largely because of their support, Bakhtin's sure-death prison sentence was commuted to internal exile—and in 1930, he and his wife disappeared into Kazakhstan for a five-year term. Bakhtin had been silenced, but within a small circle of philosophically inclined literary critics his Dostoevsky study became an underground classic.

Given his flawed physical body and the politics of his era, Bakhtin considered his fate "carnivalized," that is, unexpectedly fortunate, productive, and graced. The amputation of his right leg in 1938 so improved his health that he could at last hold down a full-time job, at a provincial teacher's college in Saransk, 600 kilometers east of Moscow. (His "minus" status as a political exile prohibited him from settling legally in any major cities.) Among his survivor skills was the ability to cast his most beloved ideas in the currency of shifting realms: now faintly Marxist, now with a hint of populism or even Christianity, at times indebted to cutting-edge science (Einstein's relativity) but never losing sight of the archaic virtues of the Russian folk collective and the communal body.

On the far side of the Stalinist night, Bakhtin, by then a retired professor of world literature, was persuaded to revise his Dostoevsky book for a second edition. That revision included a huge new chapter on Menippean satire, purportedly Dostoevsky's genre of choice but more likely motivated by Bakhtin's still unpublished dissertation on François Rabelais and cultures of laughter. To the Western academy's decentering poststructuralist mind, weary of pious master narratives and monologic system-mongering, this combination of a pagan carnival impulse with the pluralizing polyphonic word was irresistible. A key legitimizing moment for Bakhtin was the 1970 French translation of the Dostoevsky book, prefaced by Julia Kristeva. Under the title "Une poetique ruinée" (The ruin of a poetics), Kristeva identified dialogism with the spirit of rebellious politics and declared Bakhtin's thought to be anti-totalitarian and anti-theological.[3] Dialogism, polyphony, heteroglossia, and carnival were all packaged together into one positive, secular, open-ended, and freedom-bearing good thing. Outside Russia, Bakhtin was canonized as Dostoevsky's most authoritative Russian interpreter.

By the sheer weight and complexity of Bakhtin's thought, this triumph is well deserved. But it has tended to obscure the unconventional pan-Christian way that Bakhtin integrates Word, body, and spirit (that is, the transcendence of matter through the utterance), as well as to muffle the many voices, from 1930 on, that have questioned the sufficiency of a Bakhtinian lens on Dostoevsky. For Dostoevsky is both more ecstatic and transfigurational, and meaner, darker, and more desperate, than Bakhtin's polyphonic method seems to allow. The task of the present essay is to address this apparent disconnect by examining novelistic polyphony, pro and contra, and then measuring it against two key episodes in *Crime and Punishment*. The first episode occurs early in the novel (Part One, Chapter 3): Raskolnikov's internalization of the letter he receives from his mother informing him of Dunya's humiliation by Svidrigaylov and her engagement to Luzhin. While Raskolnikov reads this letter, his helplessness and family love are turned to hate. The process picks up momentum in what Bakhtin calls a "microdialogue": multiple outside voices are internalized, distilled, hyperbolized into fixed types, and then projected out into the real world—all, of course, within a single consciousness, the feverish interior of Raskolnikov's head. This initial episode is claustrophobic, full of defiant talk that radiates uncontrollably outward from an obsessive center. The second episode, the moment of rapture between Raskolnikov and Sonya at the end of the Epilogue, is expansive and largely silent. Vistas open up, storylines breathe in the air of the Siberian steppe, and what is unfinalized, untellable, and unknown becomes more authoritative than what is fixed and known.

Through these two bookended scenes, I hope to bring together the "spiritual" Bakhtin (the man who identified himself as religious and partial to a divine order) with the materialist, liberationist profile that Kristeva offered the world in the wake of revolutionary Paris, 1968.[4] The second liberationist pole is modern, secular, scientific; the first is medieval and sacred. Both, I believe, are true. For Bakhtin resembled his research subject in this particular also: like Dostoevsky, he saw the stubborn material world of poverty, illness, and caprice of power as a reality compatible with, and conducive to, the transfiguring moods of love and faith. Undeserved suffering was not fatal to this dynamic, but any form of predetermination most certainly was. To create narratives in this realm, Bakhtin argued, a novelist must learn to incorporate open time. Literary structure must accommodate itself to a more fluid sense of plot.[5] Dostoevsky's creative solution would be the "polyphonic hero"—a fictive consciousness assembled out of polyphonic words. Before we sample the insightful depths of a Bakhtinian reading (as well as the blind, or deaf, dead ends), let us recall what verbal polyphony is expected to do.

II. POLYPHONY, THE ENERGY THAT OPENS UP THE WORLD

Bakhtin opens his preface to the Dostoevsky book with a politically prudent disclaimer. His concern will not be with the value system or content of a Dostoevskian novel (its messianic theology, Great Russian imperialism, irrational or disintegrating psyches) but solely with the technical question of *how its words work*.[6] They work, Bakhtin insists, "polyphonically," that is, without a finalized authorial center or a predetermined plan. Words are owned by the fictive persons who speak them. These multiple voices sound in a continual present-tense time, full of potentials that are constantly being realized (or discarded). Polyphony—a "plurality of independent and unmerged voices and consciousnesses," each speaking with equal validity out of its own world (*PDP* 6)—is thus a texture both spatial and temporal, woven together out of emergent subjects.

To illustrate this polyphonic texture, Bakhtin engages in close readings of select Dostoevskian scenes. He rarely speculates on the meaning or shape of an entire novel; that would touch upon those taboo matters of content and value. But one could argue that the methodology itself generates a normative ethics. Working on a local scale with discrete units of direct and indirect discourse, polyphonic analysis is designed to prod out latent dialogic resources: double-voiced intonation, loopholes, provisional penultimate utterances (as opposed to tragically ultimate ones). Uncannily often, such analysis turns on-the-ground desperation into metaphysical hope, chaos into existential freedom, demonic laughter into carnival ambivalence, and indisputably bad infinity into infinite open dialogue. Whether from caution or professional scruples (Bakhtin later hinted that it was cowardly caution), all grand-scale generalization about good and evil, freedom and necessity, or the fallen state of humanity is heavily muted.[7] Not only Marxist watchdogs but even ordinary reviewers noticed that crucial aspects of Dostoevsky had disappeared.[8]

With this muting of the unredeemable and dark—for Bakhtin's Dostoevsky is overall more radiant than tragic—a tough-minded new task for the word is foregrounded, one related to the hard work and counterintuitive faith attending any bestowal or receiving of grace. At the base of polyphony lies an ambitious philosophy of creativity. The polyphonic (as opposed to monologic) novelist creates not "types," not fictive agents who serve some ready-made plot, but characters who can themselves create. (This aspect of Bakhtin's polyphony has prompted some scholars to connect it fruitfully with Kierkegaard's authorship.)[9] What these characters create, by and large, are more words, that is, more of the material out of which they themselves are made. Since words are primary carriers of knowledge, an utterance is an event—and characters who have been designed to know as much as their creators know will inevitably open up event-potentials, which always exceed life's actuals. Bakhtin was much taken by the analogy between novels and real life: a dialogic novel cannot, and should not, appear whole to itself, just as my life cannot appear whole to me as long as I am alive.[10] What matters at any moment are options in the present and immediate future. This is why polyphonic heroes have so little history—and so little need of it. The cultural theorist Ken Hirschkop has called this maiden exposition of dialogism in Bakhtin's first book the "last gasp of the 'pure voice' ": by reducing personality to its embodiment in language, it "made possible the absolute indeterminacy which Bakhtin extracted from Dostoevsky's form."[11]

Through its ability to quicken consciousness, dialogic form is by nature fertile. This is its connection with carnival. Among Bakhtin scholars, Michael Holquist has argued most persuasively that Bakhtin is above all an organicist, a thinker not in principle opposed to systematicity (living things, after all, are fantastically subtle and disciplined systems), but for whom a system was never dead or fixed: it is always in flux, aging, adjusting, preparing to reproduce or mutate.[12] Polyphony needs the presumption of living bodies—but not necessarily the closed integrity of a life span. Thus Bakhtin opens the door to other, potentially non-materialist worlds. By the same logic he insists on the simultaneity of all times and the reciprocity (or dialogic energy) at the core of all being: "The fundamental category in Dostoevsky's mode of artistic visualizing was not evolution, but *coexistence* and *interaction*" (*PDP* 28).

How is the Dostoevskian novel a fertile and organic site, according to Bakhtin? To prioritize simultaneity and coexistence over the individual mortal trajectory, Dostoevsky peopled his novels with *idea-heroes*. These are "fully-weighted" signifiers, not mere pawns or plot functions. But polyphonic design does not imply the absence, abdication, or indifference of the author. Authors must constantly shape—by listening in to—their own "creating creatures," so as to foster in their thoughts and conversations a maximal sense of autonomy and indeterminacy. Because of this persistent but low-visibility authorial work, we the readers are drawn in to the texture of the novel as its primary interlocutors. The energy is well invested, for Dostoevsky's idea-heroes have lots of time to talk with one another while we eavesdrop. They are free from fixed duties and deadening routine. They don't go out daily to work or sit down regularly to meals (though they may have a cognac, perhaps, or a jug of ale in a tavern, but that's largely to loosen the tongue); if babies are born they are low-maintenance for the narrator, usually dying in a few weeks. Idea-heroes have lives we care about, but mostly they are points of view on the world that exist to test the potential of a word or idea. Privileging ideas over everyday events (even over the event of death) puts a huge premium on talk. Although Dostoevsky's heroes are often dysfunctional, they rarely fail in verbal expression. No matter how hungry, angry, or hallucinatory Raskolnikov might be, he continues to think through his idea—his right to kill that worthless pawnbroker—in the most forceful and articulate way. Razumikhin, drunk, lectures a stunned Dunya and her mother on the virtues of living off one's own lies rather than off another's truth. Even the miserable clerk Semyon Marmeladov, tipsy in a pub after days of hard drinking, delivers an inspired oration on sin and forgiveness that leaves the reader spellbound. For this reason did Leo Tolstoy complain that Dostoevsky's characters, colorful as they are, all sounded the same: eloquent.

But polyphonic method promises more than eloquence. If words are empowered to create alternative futures, then through words we can resurrect the dead, converse with them, shape new utterances that can in turn forge new persons. As Bakhtin wrote about the Elder Zosima in his notes for revising the Dostoevsky book, "Personality does not die. Death is a departure . . . The person has departed, having spoken his word, but the word itself remains in the open-ended dialogue" (*PDP* 300). The implications of such a philosophy of language are nothing less than a guarantee of everlasting life. In this philosophy of creativity through the uttered word, we see a defiance of death and an insistence on transcendence that has deep roots in the Russian tradition, both materialist and idealist.[13]

III. THE CASE AGAINST POLYPHONIC DESIGN

Skepticism about polyphony has rested on three major reservations. First is the commonsensical objection that created characters in a novel are not alive and not free. They are words pinned to the page and they do what their authors require them to do. Plato makes this argument in the *Phaedrus*: words fixed in writing are dead, helpless to defend themselves in the face of future audiences. Although these graphic representations "seem to talk to you as if they were intelligent," they will always more resemble an image painted on the wall than they will a live conversation.[14] Fictive people do not and cannot develop independently. The same reservation in harsher form was lodged by Bakhtin's most principled Russian opponent over thirty years, the late, great philologist and verse scholar Mikhail Gasparov (1935–2005).[15] As the Bakhtin Boom became an epidemic, Gasparov's irritation increased. All talk of dialogue and polyphony in a work of art, he argued repeatedly, is worse than delusionary: it is lazy, solipsistic, egocentric, the assertion of the aggressive modern reader (here Bakhtin was exemplary) against a helpless historical trace. Dialogue with a past culture is difficult and delicate; Bakhtin makes it seem easy and pleasant. It takes scholarly modesty to admit that past cultural artifacts were created *not for us*. We do not speak their language. We are fortunate if we can recuperate them even within their own distant, faint contexts. Every day—Gasparov reminds us—we fail to understand our own children, our closest intimates, and Bakhtin would have us talk with Pindar, Pushkin, Dostoevsky! When scholars refuse to respect historical distance and radical cultural difference, texts from the past become mirrors reflecting our own needy, lonely, changing face. To hear the voice of a "living other" on the page, says Gasparov, is nothing other than our endearing but wholly unprofessional desire that all consciousness live forever, and on our terms.

Gasparov's complaint was revisited in 2016 in an exasperated monograph on Shakespeare, Bakhtin, and Dostoevsky by Karen Stepanyan, co-founder in 1991 of the Russian Dostoevsky Society.[16] Gasparov had harshly criticized Menippean satire and Bakhtin's unpersuasive attempt to make this quasi-fabricated tradition central to Chapter 4 of his revised Dostoevsky book. Stepanyan, an avowed Christian believer as Gasparov was not, was outraged by Bakhtin's tolerant carnivalesque side applied to spiritually sophisticated literary texts. Carnival is cruel, pagan, materialistic, relativistic. Not all incarnated matter deserves our reverence, just as not all dialogic complexity merits our respect. Dialogue can be authentically corrupt and perverse. Stepanyan reads Raskolnikov not as some elevated "idea-person" but as tyrannical and self-obsessed, similar to that other law student from an earlier era, Prince Hamlet, for whom killing was also a metaphysical passion. Stepanyan's concern, then, is not the familiar one that so agitated Bakhtinians during the Boom—is Bakhtin's thought Marxist or Christian? Stepanyan wonders, rather, whether Bakhtin is Christian enough in his worldview to make deeds answerable before God and thus to do justice to Dostoevsky at all.

Stepanyan's critique leads us to a second reservation more specific to the poetics of Dostoevsky's novels. It is not true that all the voices in a Dostoevskian novel are "equally weighted." They cannot be within a structured work of art. Dostoevsky's master biographer in English, Joseph Frank, was reluctant to take seriously the term "polyphonic novel" in the strong sense, because Bakhtin "is unable to explain how the absolute independence of fictional character can combine with the unity of a work of art."[17] Artistic unity must be constructed, stable, and value-laden. How can one doubt that *Crime and Punishment* contains a hierarchy of ethical life-ideas, with Sonya Marmeladova and Razumikhin at the virtuous top (representing respectively divine love, *caritas* or *agape*, and love-as-friendship, *philia*) and the shallow, greedy Luzhin at the bottom? Dostoevsky builds dialogues, yes, but within artistic and ethical wholes. That the novelist strove toward an integrated, ultimate higher value, Bakhtin admitted freely. But how this sense of culmination is made compatible with open structure is unclear, since Bakhtin came to suspect that artistic finalization itself was "a variety of violence" (*PDP* 292).[18] Robert Louis Jackson has suggested that Bakhtin's book accommodates both a horizontal and a vertical axis, the horizontal answering to the "jostling truths" of dialogue, the vertical supplied by the author.[19]

We will return to this possible parallel structure and expand on it, for it answers to a third reservation about polyphony: that it ignores the communicative value of silence and undervalues the transformational power of mute unspeaking space.

These reservations about polyphonic design are worth keeping in mind, for Bakhtin had not always understood Dostoevsky in this atomized, talk-oriented, militantly life-bearing way. His earlier reading of the novelist was darker, more in accord with the party line, highlighting a punitive moral structure that at times seems almost Girardian. Between 1922 and 1927, before he had developed his master ideas of dialogism and polyphony, Bakhtin, ailing and hoping to supplement his meager income by group tutoring, delivered lectures on Russian literature in a "home course" to high school students in Vitebsk and later in Leningrad.[20] According to notes taken by one teenaged attendee, Bakhtin's lectures on Dostoevsky (1925) emphasized not the potentials of the fictive hero but rather the discomfort and unfreedom in which Dostoevsky routinely placed his readers, strapped as they were to the hero's back. "We do not observe the hero, we co-experience with him . . . We jump from soul to soul, and the object begins to ripple, become illusory, deprived of its stability . . . there is no place for us in Dostoevsky's works. We must either be inside the hero, or close the book" (*MMB:Ss* 2, 266–267). To be "inside a hero" like Raskolnikov is not to be in a friendly or hopeful place. These lecture notes do contain the germ of character-centered polyphony, to be sure, but it is given to us grimly, not in order to celebrate human agency but to paralyze it. Since we know characters solely from their own inside perspective, we see exclusively what they see, and the "theatrical effect of all this is a dark stage with voices, nothing more" (*MMB:Ss* 2, 267). Such morbid insidedness might be sustainable in first-person narratives (like the pathological *Notes from Underground*), but not when the novelist jumps from soul to soul, body to body. The outside world, abandoned by the author, becomes a chaotic wilderness—and inside the heroes, worlds, and worldviews will bifurcate.

One good example of such bifurcation is the plot of *Crime and Punishment*. A pure "philosophical-psychological novel," it breaks into two planes: the Romantic-rebellious-nihilist and the "inner religious law, conscience" (*MMB:Ss* 2, 273). Dostoevsky's attacks against the former are mounted not in some neutral space (no such space exists in the novel) but from within the suffering heroes themselves. This creates chaos for the reader. "Dostoevsky wanted to kill two hares at once: both Romantics and nihilists. Neither one nor the other acknowledged a higher religious authority and thus both killed the true meaning of life" (*MMB:Ss* 2, 273). Seeking his new word, Raskolnikov "overstepped" the external law, but his body rebelled. He could not overstep the law of conscience. He hovered helplessly around the threshold, along with the anguished reader, until "Sonya helped him to unite organic feeling with conscience" (*MMB:Ss* 2, 274). In these rather conventional lectures from his pre-polyphonic period, Bakhtin takes seriously the linear fate of the hero and allots a vital ideological role to the Epilogue. "In Siberia Raskolnikov becomes a different person . . . earlier he had thought that his own conscience was a better judge of him than were other people; in matters of repentance, he was an individualist. And only now he understood that no matter what, whether in crime or repentance, a person cannot be alone" (*MMB:Ss* 2, 275). Here too we discern germs of the later, other-oriented Bakhtin: salvation and eternal life reside in the communal; survival comes from outside.

By 1929 and the turn toward the polyphonic word, *Crime and Punishment* is mined for entirely other wisdoms. In the Dostoevsky book, the silent, transcendent Epilogue is hardly mentioned. And Raskolnikov's feverish "dialogized inner monologue," far from being a hallucinatory torment between two extremes, is now showcased. Let us consider Bakhtin's treatment of these two scenes.

IV. THE CRAMPED LETTER AND THE UNBOUNDED STEPPE

Bakhtin wishes to document in his *Problems of Dostoevsky's Poetics* an expanding universe of speaking voices, such as would impart to readers a sense of infinite dialogue in Great Time.[21] Such time does not march us toward death, because potentials are kept open by the medium of language itself. Bakhtin illustrates this dynamic at the end of Chapter 2, with the dialogization of Raskolnikov's "first great interior monologue," triggered by his mother's letter (*PDP* 73–74).[22] The author retains for himself in this scene no essential "surplus of meaning," nothing that might finalize or objectify the hero, only enough perspective and authorial muscle to move the story forward. Every possible point of view is packed into Raskolnikov's creaturely consciousness. "From the very beginning he already knows everything, takes everything into account, anticipates everything" (*PDP* 74). Bakhtin calls this "dialogized interior monologue"—the ironic and indignant debate Raskolnikov carries on with himself—"a splendid model of the *microdialogue*," in which "dialogue has penetrated inside every word, provoking in it a battle and the interruption of one word by another" (*PDP* 75). Such word wars testify to the fact that the hero has "already entered into dialogic contact with the whole of life surrounding him" (*PDP* 74). Microdialogue is said to have a good effect on readers (unlike the misery experienced by the novel's readers in Bakhtin's earlier lecture notes), weaning us from our monologic habits and stimulating us to sympathize with new, multiple points of view. "Every true reader of Dostoevsky," Bakhtin concludes, "can sense a peculiar active broadening of his or her consciousness, not so much in the assimilation of new objects . . . as in the sense of a special dialogic mode of communication with the autonomous consciousnesses of others, something never before experienced, an active dialogic permeation into the unfinalizable depths of the human person" (*PDP* 68, translation adjusted). If so, this is the revelatory good news. But is this in fact what happens?

Perhaps it is when compared, say, with the authoritarian Tolstoyan narrator. Tolstoy, while also in the business of broadening consciousness, is known to preach at his readers, making us feel at times pinched, humorless, finalized, whereas Dostoevsky, a great master at redemptive laughter, rarely preaches to us from a pulpit. Within Raskolnikov's own fictive story space, however, microdialogue hardly serves to broaden sympathies—and at no point should the procedure be confused with communication. Dostoevsky (but not Bakhtin) is at pains to present his hero as oblivious to the living words, deeds, and needs of others, including their need to extend love. Part of Raskolnikov's illness, surely, is his delusion that he can "know and anticipate everything" about a loved one through voices he extracts from a letter. Microdialogue is intensely isolating and distortive. In no way does it enable "dialogic contact with the whole of life," for no corrective from the outside world can break into it. Bakhtin would seem to make a dialogizing virtue out of a situation that Dostoevsky considers pathological. *Crime and Punishment* began as a first-person confession. Its self-obsessed hero grows out of the Underground Man—only Raskolnikov is better looking, more resilient, more loved, and less timid. As Gasparov noted about Bakhtin's fantastical equation of human personality with the uttered word, the "dialogue" inside such a hero's head more resembles replicating mirrors or egoistical echo chambers than open-ended expanding worlds.

How does consciousness actually work in this opening scene? Raskolnikov hears a story from a drunken stranger in a tavern, then receives a letter from his beloved mother. The inner voices that crowd his mind come into "a peculiar sort of contact [. . .] impossible among voices in an actual dialogue" (*PDP* 239). Impossible, because real inter-human dialogue will not tolerate contact on those terms.

For it is simply not true, as Bakhtin claims earlier in the chapter, that "to think about [other people] means to *talk with them*" (*PDP* 68). Self-generated talk inside one's own head is dialogic only in a superficial way; by its genesis and structure, microdialogue is a soliloquy of the narcissistic self. Its interior chatter (as Raskolnikov freely admits) is a means of keeping real others out, not of inviting them in. For this reason the eminent Tolstoy scholar Lidia Ginzburg (1902–1990) was unimpressed with Bakhtin's book on Dostoevsky and with Bakhtin's desire to see the idea-hero as altruistic and "unselfish" in pursuit of that idea (*PDP*, 87). It was Tolstoy, in her view, who took the real dialogic risks, designing characters who stand for no idea at all (what idea does Anna Karenina represent? or Pierre Bezukhov?), heroes whose bumbling, often humiliating efforts at outer communication eventually guarantee their inner moral growth. Tolstoy's characters at least try to listen to other people. They must, because they are needy; they crave the actual presence and love of others, not only the chance to assimilate the others' words. To be sure, Ginzburg averred, a character "might find it more *interesting* to conceive of himself in Dostoevskian terms, since doing so would allow him to focus attention on himself."[23]

This tension between Bakhtin's theoretical ideal and Dostoevsky's intent as novelist is not trivial. For it is not the words or voices of living people that impel Raskolnikov toward his double-murder, but fatal timings and coincidences among *things*: sightings, intersections, the unexpected glint of a physical object. Fueled by superstition and a fixed idea, the murder is further propelled by the need of a trapped organism to break out of the mental word chain, to quit the word habit altogether. This was Tolstoy's view of Raskolnikov. And Tolstoy's distrust of words, his unwillingness to grant words any necessary moral potency, is in part why Bakhtin finds that great rival Russian novelist so uncongenial—and why, perhaps, Bakhtin's analysis of the microdialogue triggered by the letter is preceded by his exposure of Tolstoy's hopeless "monologism" (*PDP* 69–73). Tolstoy is Bakhtin's favorite negative example, and with good reason. Tolstoy insisted that the whole structure of verbally driven consciousness is false, because we human beings (whether fictive or flesh-and-blood) don't live by ideas. We *justify* ourselves by ideas, perhaps, but we live by feelings, cravings, habits—and mostly by bad, intoxicating habits. Tolstoy does not forgive addiction and would strike at its root. In his 1889 essay "Why Do Men Stupefy Themselves?," Tolstoy had this to say on *Crime and Punishment*: "Raskolnikov did not live his true life when he murdered the old woman or her sister . . . [then] he acted like a machine, doing what he could not help doing—discharging the cartridge with which he had long been loaded. [. . .] He lived his true life when he was lying on the sofa in his room, deliberating not at all about the old woman [. . .]; when he was doing nothing and was only thinking, when only his consciousness was active: and in that consciousness tiny, tiny alterations were taking place."[24] Those alterations were narrowing, not broadening. Raskolnikov's crime began with a habit of thinking (that is, talking through his idea to himself), tempted perhaps (Tolstoy surmises) by "one glass of beer, or one cigarette" to ease the thinking along, thus further deforming his organism and stifling the impulses of conscience. And yet in Bakhtin's polyphonic readings of Dostoevsky, feverishly proliferating inner "microdialogues" are the essence of an active self-consciousness. They testify to an idea-hero's aliveness and guarantee a complex learning curve in readers. Tolstoy was suspicious of words and ideas. Both, he believed, obfuscate the truth and are easily recruited to serve our lower animal natures. As writer and moral teacher, Tolstoy targeted our pleasure-seeking bodily habits. Bakhtin—whose body hurt all the time, who would chain-smoke and drug himself with strong tea in place of unavailable painkillers—was less punitive. In contrast to Tolstoy, he worshipped the potential of words to make what is painfully mortal both grace-bearing and immortal.

Before leaving the cramped letter scene for the spacious Epilogue, we might note two recent attempts to rethink Raskolnikov's logos-centric terrain. The sociologist of literature Dina Khapaeva has suggested that perhaps Dostoevsky was not attempting to portray dialogic consciousness at all, but—following his great forebear Nikolai Gogol—the preconscious condition of nightmare.[25] How does the transcript of a nightmare differ from narratives built in more benevolent dream space? Khapaeva identifies several markers: frantic and fruitless pursuit with no hope of arrival, the panic of no-exit, a pervasive sense of shame, unfinalizability (the inability to wake up and put an end to it), and a shift from description to experience—because the author of a nightmare does not merely recount a frightening event, but induces the experience of that event in the reader. Like Gasparov and Stepanyan but for other reasons, Khapaeva is bothered by Bakhtin's attribution of the fantastic element in Dostoevsky to the benign energies of the menippea (a comedic literary genre). Menippean satire fails to account for moments of terror, violence, irreversible dead-endedness, and a fantasized escape of the body through the vertical or spectral dimension. In Dostoevsky, she argues, what Bakhtin identifies as the bright laughing grotesque of carnival is in fact the metaphysical grotesque of the gothic, based not on enlightenment but on a darkening.

The second corrective, by the philosopher of literature Alina Wyman, is less pessimistic but equally sobering. In her pioneering book on Dostoevsky, Bakhtin, and Max Scheler, Wyman draws on the early pre-polyphonic Bakhtin to distinguish between passive and active empathy.[26] Passive empathy—those duplicating acts of pity that so appalled Nietzsche and Scheler, the fusion of suffering souls in "emotional infection"—is also, Wyman shows, contrary to Bakhtin's understanding of true communion. The healthy alternative, *active* empathy, requires agency, differentiation, each party briefly "living in" to the other but then returning to one's self and acting out of its own sense of an enriched whole. Here Wyman notes an important difference between Scheler and Bakhtin. Scheler acknowledges a person's right to privacy, positive self-evaluation, and self-regard. Within a Bakhtinian framework, however, one cannot love oneself (one cannot even see or hear oneself; everything inside is in flux); thus all affirmation must come from the outside, from a loving other. Although Wyman focuses on *The Idiot*, her distinctions help us to see what is at stake in this early scene in *Crime and Punishment*. For the letter episode is, among much else, a testing ground for divine grace—which always insists, as its very condition of possibility, that we accept a gift we do not deserve. An Other loves us and we cannot repay the debt. Raskolnikov—proud, generous, abject—enters the novel in that humiliated state. His dearest and closest of kin would sacrifice all they have for him. But to accept a freely offered gift has become for Raskolnikov a fatal, not a liberating (graced) move. So when the word-from-within takes over (and this is what the letter episode is all about), real outside others cease to exist. At best, the result of his "dialogue" with their voices is what Wyman would call passive empathy: the depersonalization, reification, and outward projection of borrowed ideas in the interests of preserving a convenient image of the other. Active empathy, which is always two-way between two viable living beings, depends upon a minimal respect for the self. From the start, Raskolnikov lacks that respect. He is distorted by self-loathing. For his "idea" is not only the abstract Napoleonic one. Of equal and prior potency is the idea in his mother's letter: all-encompassing, all-forgiving family love, the love of a mother and a sibling.[27] It is surely Raskolnikov's terminal disgust at himself in the context of his loving, giving family—and not the "active dialogic permeation" of proliferating abstract options in an expanding universe of words—that Dostoevsky asks us to witness in this awful transformation of a mother's and sister's boundless love into motivation for murder. The polyphonic ideal (which, in keeping with Bakhtin's larger ethics, rules out loving oneself) masks this pathological dynamic.

In 1989, the Russian literary scholar Yurii Karyakin published his huge volume *Dostoevsky on the Eve of the Twenty-first Century.* In it he drew up a balance sheet of the achievements of his good friend Mikhail Bakhtin.[28] Polyphony provides only a partial window into Dostoevsky's art, he concluded, because it concentrates solely on verbal dialogue and its current of ideas, ignoring the fully embodied scenes. In every major Dostoevskian scene, Karyakin argues, there are more than "double-voiced words"; there are triple-voiced words, and the third voice is assigned unapologetically to Dostoevsky as author or stage director. Bakhtin is misled if he thinks that self-consciousness is the hero of Dostoevsky's novels. *Self-deception* is the hero—and all that polyphonic vapor and noise, all that compulsive chatter and multiplication of options is designed by the author to darken the texture of the work and prod the hero to look elsewhere, not to words, for access points to realms of durable truth. In the task of self-deception, words play an awful role. They can cloud over and delay what eyes and gestures communicate immediately. This argument is amplified by Olga Meerson in her treatment of taboo in *Crime and Punishment,* where the desperate verbal games that Raskolnikov plays with his conscience are shown over and over to fail.[29] For Meerson's Dostoevsky, taboo disables the word from within, denies a person access to knowledge, and throws the sinner back on his traumatized body, the doer of the deed. Dialogue and its requisite chattering forms (including microdialogue) will do no damage to a healthy person like Razumikhin; his chatter, both when true (which it is, uncannily often) and when full of inspired fibs, suffices for his flourishing. For the spiritually ill Raskolnikov, who soon after the murders realizes his cosmic isolation, an additional axis is required. Whether dialogue for Raskolnikov is a trap, or faked, or a nightmare, or a repressed tabooed truth, Dostoevsky—so these skeptics argue—might have intended the microdialogic maneuvering of this appallingly self-absorbed hero to be perceived by the reader as thoroughly monologic.

If dialogue is often self-deception, then, what about Bakhtin's treatment of those scenes where we see bodies against a backdrop but do not hear many words? Overall, Bakhtin is very perceptive about Dostoevskian space, a matter of eye-to-eye dialogue over thresholds, staircases, and bridges. But spatial encounters are not only horizontal. There are moments when eye contact does not suffice and a vertical address is required, something beyond immediate vision. Many of Dostoevsky's most potent scenes communicate silently and require an illogical "leap." Christ's kiss to the Grand Inquisitor in *The Brothers Karamazov* is one famous instance; another is Prince Myshkin and Parfyon Rogozhin over the murdered body of Nastasya Filippovna in *The Idiot*. Preceding both is Raskolnikov and Sonya in the Epilogue to *Crime and Punishment*, with an unknowable, perhaps untellable story ahead of them that opens up just as the present story comes to an end. What is the role of polyphonic structure at such silent spiritualized moments?

This Epilogue has been much maligned. Critics object that it is inconsistent, unmotivated, sentimental, less satisfactory than Raskolnikov's suicide would have been. Bakhtin too did not like it, but not for the conventional reasons. In one of his drafts for an introduction to his revised Dostoevsky book, he jotted down: "*Crime and Punishment*, where the author almost never departs from his hero . . . only the afterword is constructed on the literary-informational plane (the trial, the fate of secondary characters), and then: the monologism that structures the plane of the epilogue (in Siberia)" (*MMB:Ss* 6, 315). This passing comment pulls us up short. Monologic, then, is Raskolnikov's ghastly dream of global infection, the silent appearance of Sonya on the riverbank, his sudden weeping and hugging her knees, her happiness and understanding beyond any doubt "that he loved her, loved her endlessly, and that the moment had finally come . . . They wanted to talk, but could not."[30] In his 2016 book *Plots*, Robert Belknap makes the intriguing claim that a Bakhtinian interpretation of the Epilogue is possible, but not within polyphonic design: all that hugging and hopeful love on the Siberian riverbank is the tried-and-true canonical finale for two of Bakhtin's originary novel-types, the Greek romance and the novel of ordeal, which to some extent *Crime and Punishment* is.[31] But such "doctrinal closure" to the novel must have bothered Dostoevsky, Belknap avers, and thus he provides an open end, the promise of more, which allows readers both to put down the book and to sense their "participation in an unfinished story."

The most persuasive analysis of this scene, however, is an early study by the honoree of this essay, Michael Holquist. He sees it as a conversion experience in the spirit of Saint Augustine (or Thomas Aquinas), where words stop, time stops, and chronology loses its power to explicate.[32] The detective story becomes the wisdom tale. But discontinuity does not mean illogicality. Holquist insists that the Epilogue is even "the crux of the novel."[33] Working back from the microbe dream, he asks us to consider the workings of "contagion, disease, immunity, and cure" (111) in Dostoevsky's competing theories of salvation, which depend not so much on what faith a person can accept—for the path to faith is ever torturous—as on what temptations can be *resisted*. Holquist divides the major heroes of *Crime and Punishment* into the healthy (Sonya, Razumikhin, Porfiry Petrovich) and the diseased. If the former group is immune (able to resist infection), the latter group is not just ill but *contagious*, able to infect others. Incorporating this binary into our critique of microdialogue, we see that dialogue, in addition to its positive mind-broadening capacities, can function almost like a communicable disease—and silence is testimony to immunity. Is it possible to reconcile these objections to dialogue with Bakhtin's passionate investment in the salvific properties of the word? In the final segment of this essay, such a reconciliation is attempted.

V. EINSTEIN AND ALLEGORY, MODERN SCIENCE AND MEDIEVAL MUSIC

Human consciousness through the word, says Bakhtin, can neither be contained nor put to death. As long as there is language, there are no punitive systems powerful enough—there is no *reality* powerful enough—to carry out those verdicts. For this sublime idea to be realized, however, Bakhtin's real hero must be not an "idea-hero" but generative time itself, that hopeful substance that spreads out for Raskolnikov and Sonya "after the present story is ended." Generative time is not empty or ahistorical. It does not generate random potentials. In the words of Dmitri Nikulin, a subtle philosopher of dialogue (Bakhtin's and others): "Unfinalizability . . . is not to be taken in the sense of openness or an unrestrained ability to endlessly and purposely invent and produce anew; nor is it an infinite questioning. Personal unfinalizability implies neither incompleteness nor deficiency."[34] What, then, does it imply? Nikulin would answer that each of us is unpredictable, but not arbitrary. As a dialogic being I am the product of my acts, finite and complete at any given moment—but I am not thereby finalized. These paradoxes of Bakhtin's unfinalizability (a condition both responsible and open) might be reconciled, I suggest, if we separate dialogue from polyphony. Dialogue, as we have seen, can often be perverse. Polyphony is almost always radiant.

In their discussions of *Crime and Punishment* here cited, neither Holquist nor Belknap draw any principled distinction between the dialogic and the polyphonic. In this they follow common practice in Bakhtin studies, which assumes a continuum between the two, one being perhaps a subset or extreme case of the other. Let us pursue instead the lead of one Russian scholar, the dialectician Genrikh Batishchev (1932–1990), who, like Nikulin, has approached Bakhtin's work on literature as might a philosopher. In his essay "Dialogism or Polyphonism?" Batishchev identifies those two structuring principles as directly antithetical.[35] In part because of the slackness inevitable when any thinker undergoes a global boom, the umbrella term dialogue has come to cover "absolutely contradictory phenomena." Dialogism is earthbound, exchanged horizontally, rather cold and relativistic, characteristic of the atomized self-affirming individual (presumably its energy can be positive, as in Razumikhin, or destructive, as in Raskolnikov), and often resistant to acts of genuine communion. Polyphony (or polyphonic dialogue) is a dynamic of another order. It is multileveled, prepared to prefer others to itself, gazes upward full of participatory wonder, is "true to absolute values, and gravitates toward unobtrusive Harmony" (123). Confusion between these two Bakhtinian "isms" is natural, Batishchev admits; Bakhtin was not consistent. Later thinkers and critics must reconstruct his core idea and sort out robust readings from weak ones. In our attempt to do so here, two models will come to our aid: one from the world of modern science and one, less familiar, from the annals of medieval sacred music.

The science first. Bakhtin, in keeping with his generation, was a synthesizing modernist. All realms of knowledge were obliged to coordinate their respective discoveries. As he wrote in his new conclusion to the revised Dostoevsky book: "Scientific consciousness has long since grown accustomed to the Einsteinian world with its multiplicity of systems of measurement. But in the realm of *artistic* cognition, people sometimes continue to demand a very crude, very primitive definitiveness, which obviously cannot be true" (*PDP*, 272). The implications of Einstein for Bakhtin's artistic cognition have been investigated by Jonathan Stone, who sees in both polyphony and the chronotope an interactive, decentering idea that renders meaningless any spatially fixed external point of observation and manipulation.[36] Although the boundary between polyphony and dialogism is again blurred, Stone clearly senses that for Bakhtin's ideal dynamic to work, *time itself* must become the hero, the primary ground and the major liberating parameter. Support for this intuition comes in a sketch for an essay on Gustav Flaubert that Bakhtin penned in 1944, in which he muses over the strange habit we have of reducing time to space (thus always crippling it): "A different evaluation of what it means to *move forward*. Forward movement [in time] is now thought of as some pure, unending, limitless distancing from all origins, some pure irreversible departure and distancing along a straight line. That's how people used to represent space—absolute straightness [*priamizna*]. The theory of relativity first revealed to us the possibility of another way of thinking about space, one that permits curvature [*krivizna*], a bending back on itself, the possibility of a return to the beginning . . . Possible here is a whole other model of movement [in time] . . . The relativity of all annihilation."[37] Eternal space, for Bakhtin, cannot guarantee life; it will sooner become a graveyard. Only eternal time can underwrite life. With Batishchev's distinctions in mind, let us assume that time-space works differently in dialogic and polyphonic relationships. This requires one final piece of Russian scholarship. We will then return to Raskolnikov, victim of a paralyzing microdialogue at the beginning of the novel and (contrary to Bakhtin's analysis) beneficiary of a liberating polyphony in the Epilogue. I hope to show that dialogic time can trap us down below, but polyphonic time, which embraces the vertical relation, is never a trap. For this we turn to music.

In 2005, in his essay "The 'Music' of the Word: From the History of a Certain Fiction," the Russian musicologist Alexander Makhov undertook a familiar critical exercise: to trace the source of Bakhtin's seemingly casual appropriation of the term "polyphony" for his study of Dostoevsky's art.[38] Although the term *polyphonischer dialog* occurs in nineteenth-century German criticism (largely to explicate Shakespeare), music professionals have been bothered by Bakhtin's move. Polyphonic construction in musical composition is so much more disciplined and rule-bound than anything Bakhtin seemed to intend for the novel. Can one so cavalierly mix the dynamics of silent words and pitched sounds? Is this not a parasitical raid on another artistic medium, ignoring the constraints of the home discipline? Makhov examines the lengthy, two-way tradition of terminological borrowings between music and verbal-art critics to conclude that Bakhtin is less culpable than one might assume. The term "polyphony," like the term "sonata form," originated in Rhetoric and was borrowed by medieval music theorists from literary criticism. Bakhtin, trained as a classicist, might be seen as returning the concept to its origins. And then Makhov picks up on a theme that has served as a leitmotif throughout the present essay. Literary polyphony—revealed contrapuntally through the forward dynamics of utterances in spoken dialogue—is easy to equate with "melody." As such it has often been isolated, wrongly but innocently by a secular readership, from those other more "harmonic" values precious to Bakhtin's Dostoevsky that we have been at pains here to emphasize: simultaneity, hierarchy, eternity. Simultaneity and structured stasis are essential to the feedback loops that sustain organic life. But they are also in some tension with dialogue as most of us feel its flow: linear, this-worldly, responsive one step at a time, contingent, and messy but heading toward cadence, that is, toward closure and death. Neither hierarchical simultaneity nor eternity, however, is in any tension at all with medieval polyphonic music.

In its historical context, Makhov notes, sacred polyphony was a musical equivalent not of melody, but of allegory. The relevant *figura* was the mystical simultaneity of Old Testament events with their New Testament analogues. The purpose of such figural communication was not to generate or celebrate the new—the task of the modern novel—but to enrich and confirm the reality of the old with new iterations. Music, of course, is ideally suited to this project. It tolerates absolute repetition without threat of ironic double-voicedness. Unlike allegorical narrative, which must carry forward a minimum of verbal plot one word at a time, allegorical polyphonic music can express simultaneous vari-voicedness (*raznoglasie*), in which all voices are guaranteed a place without crowding one another out or risking to be lost in the tonality of the whole. Again (recalling Nikulin on philosophical dialogue), to be unfinalizable or open along a vertical axis is not to be arbitrary, chaotic, or relativistic. Hierarchy and structure are central to the whole and no constraint to it. A tiny cross section of time, no more than an instant, can communicate a manifold number of discrete relationships. But because we are in music, a temporal art, and not in the prison-house of space, no chord stands alone for long. The musicologist Simon Morrison has suggested that Makhov's analogues could be made even more relevant to Dostoevsky by invoking modernist (not only medieval) polyphonic models: non-diatonic, non-tonal polyphony, the atonal fugue. Such musical forms "are ultimately less organic than they are crystalline," Morrison notes, "each subject and counter-subject a semi-autonomous experience of growth and change." A crystalline model, which rigorously privileges strict coincidence and even artifice, can do justice to Dostoevsky's often lonely and alogical "reaching for the divine," not from the realm of sustainable organic everyday life but from darkness.[39]

Bakhtin wrote little about musical genres and claimed, with his trademark modesty, to understand them poorly. But music commands resources far beyond the verbal and semantic parameters of the spoken utterance. Medieval polyphony creates not only a multilayered sound-space but also a multilayered meaning-space, where key sacred events are superimposed and compacted with no loss of suspense or dramatic power. (Makhov's example is a Bach passion.) Knowing what must happen—what has already happened—in the St. Matthew Passion (or in any novel with flashbacks), we are still riveted to the linear unfolding of the scenes. There is nothing unfinalizable about the outcome; both space and time in sacred texts are teleological and seemingly static. But time in sacred narratives is never static in the profane understanding of the word. Time is "fulfilled" and thus canceled out.[40] Such polyphonic heightening helps explain those radiant moments in Dostoevsky where eternal questions are simultaneously posed, tested, fail to alter the real course of tragic events, yet are nevertheless harmonized and resolved transcendentally. The final scenes of *Crime and Punishment* and *The Brothers Karamazov* manifest precisely this structure.

To grasp the whole of a Dostoevskian novel, then, polyphony should not be fused with dialogue or defined merely as its extreme instantiation. Dialogue belongs below, in the novel's profane prisons, garrets, and city streets. It issues out of individual mouths, unpredetermined, unstable, vibrant with personality but limited by it, and so always potentially tragic. Polyphonic design, in contrast, is the upper tier: stable, true, eternal, hierarchical, the realm of harmonious joyful reconciliation. There are voices here, but not mouths. This reconciliation, I suggest, is the "unity of a higher order" that Bakhtin identified with the Einsteinian world, claimed was present in polyphonic novels, but declined to define (*PDP* 298). The hint of such a two-tiered scenario can be found at the end of the Dostoevsky book, in both the 1929 and 1963 revisions. "At the level of his religious-utopian worldview," Bakhtin writes, "Dostoevsky carries dialogue into eternity, conceiving of it as eternal co-rejoicing, co-admiration, con-cord. At the level of the novel, it is presented as the unfinalizability of dialogue, although originally as dialogue's bad infinity" (*PDP*, 252). There is nothing naive or sentimental in this formulation. No tragedies have been swept away, no bad profane infinity made good. The blind and sighted parts of the polyphonic novel have simply been forced to coexist, like the contradictions of Raskolnikov's conscience on the morning of his confession.

So finally: can we integrate the prison of microdialogue on a Petersburg street with a silent, polyphonically resonant Siberia? When, at the beginning of Part Three of *Crime and Punishment*, a frightened Pulkheria Alexandrovna asks Razumikhin for some idea of what her son "likes and doesn't like," what he "wishes for" and "dreams about," she receives in response the most multi-voiced portrait possible: "Sullen, gloomy, haughty, proud, paranoid, generous and kind . . . As if two contrasting characters were taking turns inside him . . . never has time for anyone, yet lounges around doing nothing . . ."[41] Razumikhin, the novel's healthy double, can chatter his way to the truth because contradictions, for him, can coexist on the dialogic plane. Modest forward movement—like words on a horizontal line—is within his comfort zone. Generative time will create for him new options and contexts. But the diseased Raskolnikov is differently constructed, more abrupt and impatient. He rises and falls. Before the crime and even more so after it, he is sunk in self-dialogue. Among its agonizing peculiarities is personal responsibility for knowing beginnings and ends. Until the vertical or polyphonic dimension opens up for him, which is not anchored in this world and does not require that we know, Raskolnikov cannot grow; time generates nothing but full stops. Only after his dream in Siberia, on the novel's last day, do the simultaneous, coexistent, deafening alternatives that paralyzed him on the dialogic plane become tolerable, because they resonate as a fulfilled chord—or as Batishchev would put it, as the "unobtrusive Harmony" of the spheres. Before Sonya appears on the riverbank, the "sound of singing just reached him from the other side."[42]

Raskolnikov's task at the end, then, is to embrace himself as a creature, not only as a failed creator. This means learning to accept undeserved love from the outside. In a Bakhtinian metaphysics, what is seen from the outside can be changed, spoken with, listened to, visited by epiphany and grace—but not finalized, because it can never be fully known. The unknowability of human personhood, modeled on the unknowability of God, is the bedrock of Bakhtin's personalism and puts him (alongside his research subject Dostoevsky) at odds with the systemic rationalism, positivism, and materialism of both nineteenth and twentieth centuries.[43] The unknowable is not necessarily irrational or mystical—but it is always needy, intuitive, and individualized.

During the darkest years of the Second World War, Bakhtin jotted down some thoughts on compromised words and debased images that were translated into English only in 2017, as "The Dark and Radiant Bakhtin. Wartime Notes."[44] In one fragment, known by its opening words "Rhetoric, to the extent that it lies . . . ," Bakhtin expands on an idea that he later hoped to include in his revised Dostoevsky book, but failed to do so: on the inherent violence of form. Cognition itself is a sort of violent act, an entry into the realm of necessity; only love (the realm of freedom) can counter it. Non-judgmental love alone can persuade us that "an object can never be absolutely consumed."[45] Bakhtin's meditations on grace and non-possessive, silently attentive love at a time of total war come midway between his two versions of the Dostoevsky book. This apophatic Bakhtin could be made compatible with Kristeva's hopeful, secular liberationist image. Her Parisian existentialism would have to be shorn, of course, of its political agenda as well as its materialism and anti-theism—ideological curiosities that in any case would have caused Bakhtin great wonderment. But it could be done. Raskolnikov and Sonya on the riverbank would be its proper emblem.

NOTES

1. The first edition, M. M. Bakhtin, *Problemy tvorchestva Dostoevskogo* (Leningrad: Priboi, 1929), published in a print run of 2,000, has not been translated into English. The revised second edition appeared in 1963 as *Problemy poetiki Dostoevskogo* [Problems of Dostoevsky's poetics] and is annotated in the collected works: M. M. Bakhtin, *Sobranie sochinenii* [Collected works] (Moscow: Russkie slovari, 2002), 6: 5–300. The English translation

was made without the benefit of this scholarship: Mikhail Bakhtin, *Problems of Dostoevsky's Poetics*, trans. and ed. Caryl Emerson (Minneapolis: University of Minnesota Press, 1984). References to this English edition are cited as *PDP*, adjusted where necessary. Further references to the *Sobranie sochinenii* are cited as *MMB:Ss* with volume and page number.

2. See Ruth Coates, *Christianity in Bakhtin: God and the Exiled Author* (Cambridge: Cambridge University Press, 1998), esp. chap. 1, "Bakhtin's Religious Biography," 2–9; and Katerina Clark and Michael Holquist, *Mikhail Bakhtin* (Cambridge MA: Harvard University Press, 1984), chap. 5, "Religious Activities and the Arrest," 120–45. During an interview in 1973, the seventy-eight-year-old Bakhtin remembered his arrest as follows. It was his lectures on Kant in 1924, he recalled, denounced in an anonymous letter along with other idealists (Hegel and Vladimir Solovyov), that provided the pretext for his arrest in 1929. Although he was tried together with religious activists like Alexander Meier, he "did not share their views. But officially they had to stick something on us, so they stuck on this. Back then, you know, they didn't care much about the truth [. . .] Philosophical idealism, religious obscurantism and so forth, all those ideas no longer had any place in Soviet society." See *M. M. Bakhtin: Besedy s V. D. Duvakinym*, ed. S. G. Bocharov et al. (Moscow: Soglasie, 2002), Conversation no. 2, 101; no. 3, 164, and no. 4, 166–167. The six interviews appear in an annotated English edition as *Mikhail Bakhtin: The Duvakin Interviews, 1973*, ed. Slav N. Gratchev and Margarita Marinova, trans. Margarita Marinova (Lewisburg, PA: Bucknell University Press, 2019). The Christian fervor of Bakhtin's literary executors in the 1960s–1970s, combined with Bakhtin's largely secular (or pagan) profile in the West, has made this issue highly fraught.
3. Julia Kristeva, Preface to Mikhaïl Bakhtine, *La poétique de Dostoïevski, traduit du russe Isabelle Kolitchev* (Paris: Seuil, 1970). Kristeva's preface was translated into Russian in 1994 as "Razrushenie poetiki" and reprinted with commentary in *Mikhail Bakhtin, Pro et Contra: Tvorchestvo i nasledie M. M. Bakhtina v kontekste mirovoi kul'tury*, vol. 2 (St. Petersburg: Izdatel'stvo Russkogo Khristianskogo gumanitarnogo instituta, 2002), 7–32. Treating Kristeva and Paris '68 as part of the history of Bakhtin reception, the Russian editors, from their more conservative post-communist position, dispute her integrations of Bakhtinian thought into thinkers as diverse as Freud and Albert Camus.
4. The oddness of this radical Franco-Anglophone 1970 debut in light of Bakhtin's full corpus of writings (available only decades later) is discussed in Daphna Erdinast-Vulcan, *Between Philosophy and Literature: Bakhtin and the Question of the Subject* (Stanford, CA: Stanford University Press, 2013), part 1, 33–43.
5. For an early and strong statement of this thesis, see Gary Saul Morson, "Strange Synchronies and Surplus Possibilities: Bakhtin on Time," *Slavic Review* 52, no. 3 (Fall 1993): 477–493.

6. See Bakhtin, *PDP*, "From the Author": "The present book is devoted to problems of Dostoevsky's *poetics*, and surveys his work from that viewpoint only. We consider Dostoevsky one of the greatest innovators in the realm of artistic form" (3).
7. Bakhtin remarked to his disciple Sergei Bocharov in June 1970 that in the Dostoevsky book he "could not speak out directly about the main questions . . . philosophical questions that Dostoevsky agonized about all his life—the existence of God . . . I had to hold back constantly. The moment a thought got going, I had to break it off . . . Backward and forward. I was even equivocal about the Church." S. G. Bocharov, "Ob odnom razgovore i vokrug nego," *Novoe literaturno obozrenie* 2 (1993): 70–89, here 71–72. An edited and abridged English translation by Stephen Blackwell and Vadim Liapunov appears as Sergey Bocharov, "Conversations with Bakhtin," *PMLA* 109, no. 5 (October 1994): 1009–1024, here 1012. Translation adjusted.
8. For a survey of domestic reception, see Caryl Emerson, *The First Hundred Years of Mikhail Bakhtin* (Princeton, NJ: Princeton University Press, 1997), chap. 2, "Retrospective: Domestic Reception During Bakhtin's Life," 75–93, and chap. 3, "Polyphony, Dialogism, Dostoevsky," 127–161.
9. See Alex Fryszman, "Kierkegaard and Dostoevsky Seen Through Bakhtin's Prism," *Kierkegaardiana* 18, ed. Joachin Garff et al. (Copenhagen: C. A. Reitzels, 1996), 100–125. Bakhtin discovered Kierkegaard early, read him in German, considered learning Danish to grasp more, and detected a deep compatibility between the Danish philosopher and Dostoevsky (103).
10. For more on polyphony as an unfolding of potentials into actuals ("characters breaking free"), see Gary Saul Morson, *Narrative and Freedom: The Shadows of Time* (New Haven, CT: Yale University Press, 1994), Ch. 3: 91–93.
11. Ken Hirschkop, *Mikhail Bakhtin: An Aesthetic for Democracy* (Oxford: Oxford University Press, 1999), 220, 222.
12. See Michael Holquist, "Dialogism and Aesthetics," in *Late Soviet Culture from Perestroika to Novostroika*, ed. Thomas Lahusen with Gene Kuperman (Durham, NC: Duke University Press, 1993), 155–176, esp. 166–174 on how a body-based systematics and the "situatedness of perception" (169) separate Bakhtin from the Russian formalists.
13. For a discussion of this quasi-religious Russian logos-centrism in which Bakhtin played so active a part, see Thomas Seifrid, *The Word Made Self: Russian Writings on Language, 1860–1930* (Ithaca, NY: Cornell University Press, 2005).
14. *Phaedrus*, in *The Collected Dialogues of Plato*, ed. Edith Hamilton and Huntingdon Cairns (Princeton, NJ: Princeton University Press, 1961), 521. Socrates suggests that writing and reading, marked by phonic silence and bodily absence, can only enfeeble and efface the genuine other.
15. For this story in English, see Caryl Emerson, "In Honor of Mikhail Gasparov's Quarter-Century of Not Liking Bakhtin: Pro and Contra," in *Poetics. Self.*

Place: Essays in Honor of Anna Lisa Crone, ed. Catherine O'Neil, Nichole Boudreau, and Sarah Krive (Bloomington, IN: Slavica, 2007), 26–49, esp. 33–38.

16. Karen Stepanyan, *Shekspir, Bakhtin i Dostoevskii: Geroi i avtory v bol'shom vremeni* (Moscow: Yazyki slavyanskoi kul'tury, 2016). Near the end of his book (274–275), Stepanyan expresses his regret that Bakhtin's discussion of Christian love and the positive rise of non-carnival seriousness in his wartime writings of 1943–1945 "did not get into *Problems of Dostoevsky's Creative Work* [the title of the 1929 original]."
17. Joseph Frank, *Through the Russian Prism: Essays on Literature and Culture* (Princeton, NJ: Princeton University Press, 1990), chap. 2, "The Voices of Mikhail Bakhtin," 18–33, here 29. Frank admits that polyphony "in a weak sense" does exist and can be said to "highlight Dostoevsky's ability to dramatize his themes without intrusive authorial intervention" (29).
18. For translations of three little-known texts by Bakhtin on the violence of the image (from the war years 1943–1944) and interpretive essays, see the forum "The Dark and Radiant Bakhtin," ed. Irina Denischenko and Alexander Spektor, *Slavic and East European Journal* 60, no. 4 (Summer 2017).
19. See Robert Louis Jackson, "Bakhtin's Poetics of Dostoevsky and 'Dostoevsky's Christian Declaration of Faith,'" (1993), repr. in Robert Louis Jackson, *Close Encounters: Essays on Russian Literature* (Boston: Academic Studies Press, 2013), 277–304. Jackson visited the gravely ill Bakhtin in Moscow in February of his final year, 1975, to inform him that Yale University had nominated him for an honorary degree. Jackson's moving photographs of the honoree remain startling proof of the extent to which the word can keep the violence and decay of the body at bay.
20. See "Zapisi lektsii M. M. Bakhtina po istorii russkoi literatury: Zapisi R. M. Mirkinoi," lectures on Dostoevskii, *MMB:Ss* 2, 266–288. Rakhail Mirkina's notes, at least four times recopied by their author and surviving the Siege of Leningrad, are our only testimony to the content of these lectures.
21. "Great Time" is mentioned at the end of Bakhtin's late, editorially reconstructed essay "Toward a Methodology for the Human Sciences," in M. M. Bakhtin, *Speech Genres and Other Late Essays*, trans. Vern W. McGee (Austin: University of Texas Press, 1987), 170. Bakhtin suggests that our personal freedom is guaranteed by the very fact of the verbal utterance: "This personalism is not psychological, but semantic."
22. In the 1929 first edition, *Problemy tvorchestva Dostoevskogo*, discussion of this letter occurs at the beginning of part 2, chap. 3, "The Word of the Hero and the Hero's Narration in Dostoevsky's novels." See *MMB:Ss* 2: 138–141.
23. Lydia Ginzburg, *On Psychological Prose* (1966), trans. Judson Rosengrant (Princeton, NJ: Princeton University Press, 1991), 243. Ginzburg's arch retort seems to be in response to Bakhtin's remark, in *Problems of Dostoevsky's Poetics*,

that "all of Dostoevsky's major characters, as people of an idea, are absolutely unselfish, insofar as the idea has really taken control of the deepest core of their personality" (*PDP*, 87).

24. Leo Tolstoy, "Why Do Men Stupefy Themselves?" (1889), in Leo Tolstoy, *Recollections & Essays*, trans. with an introduction Aylmer Maude (London: Oxford University Press, 1937), 81–82.
25. See the chapter "Experiments on the Writer: Mikhail Bakhtin, *Problems of Dostoevsky's Poetics*," in Dina Khapaeva, *Nightmare: From Literary Experiments to Cultural Projects* (Leiden: Brill, 2013), 156–166.
26. Alina Wyman, *The Gift of Active Empathy: Scheler, Bakhtin, and Dostoevsky* (Evanston, IL: Northwestern University Press, 2016), especially the overview provided in chap. 1, "Bakhtin and Scheler: Toward a Theory of Active Empathy," 14–40.
27. For a bold reading of the letter episode, in which Raskolnikov's love for his sister Dunya is shown to predate and model his attraction to Sonya (in the author's words, "a radically different approach to the novel in which Dunya is the primary figure, with Sonya becoming her stand-in"), see Anna A. Berman, *Siblings in Tolstoy and Dostoevsky: The Path to Universal Brotherhood* (Evanston, IL: Northwestern University Press, 2015), 65–67, esp. 66.
28. Yurii Karyakin, *Dostoevskii i kanun XXI veka* (Moscow: Sovetskii pisatel', 1989). His case for the triple-voiced word is made on pp. 26–30, and the case against consciousness and for self-deception as the "hero" of Dostoevsky's novels discussed on pp. 69–72.
29. Olga Meerson, *Dostoevsky's Taboos*, Studies of the Harriman Institute (Dresden: Dresden University Press, 1998), chap. 1, "The Correlation Between Raskolnikov's Napoleonic Idea and His Main Sore Spot" and "Tabooing in *Crime and Punishment* vs. Other Dostoevskian Taboos," 74–79. In the spirit of Tolstoy, Meerson would replace the idea-hero with "the hero with sore spots"—to which he responds hysterically or with silence when they are touched.
30. I use the brilliant new translation by Oliver Ready, Fyodor Dostoevsky, *Crime and Punishment* (New York: Penguin Classics, 2014), 516.
31. Robert L. Belknap, *Plots* (New York: Columbia University Press: 2016), chap. 20, "The Epilogue of *Crime and Punishment* Crystallizes Its Ideological Plot," esp. 124–125.
32. Michael Holquist, *Dostoevsky and the Novel* (1977) (Evanston, IL: Northwestern University Press, 1986), chap. 3, "Puzzle and Mystery, the Narrative Poles of Knowing: *Crime and Punishment*," esp. 93–95.
33. James M. Holquist, "Disease as Dialectic in *Crime and Punishment*," in *Twentieth Century Interpretations of* Crime and Punishment, ed. Robert Louis Jackson (Englewood Cliffs, NJ: Prentice-Hall, 1974), 109–118.

34. Dmitri Nikulin, *On Dialogue* (Lanham, MD: Lexington Books, 2006), 57. Among the valuable distinctions Nikulin draws are those between "unfinalizability" and (respectively) "unfinishedness," hermeneutic openness, finitude, and historicity (56–62).
35. G. S. Batishchev, "Dialogizm ili polifonizm? (Antitetiki v ideinom nasledii M. M. Bakhtina)," in *M. M. Bakhtin kak filosof*, ed. L. A. Gogotishvili and P. S. Gurevich (Moscow: Nauka, 1992), 123–41.
36. Jonathan Stone, "Polyphony and the Atomic Age: Bakhtin's Assimilation of an Einsteinian Universe," *PMLA* 123, no. 2 (2008): 405–421. "The picture of a universe rife with simultaneous possibilities and choices that emerged after the popularization of relativity found a strong resonance in Bakhtin's exposition of the novel . . . His debt to Einstein resides in the power to reevaluate the known world through subtle yet epiphanic shifts of perspective" (406).
37. M. M. Bakhtin, "<O Flobere>" (1944), in M. M. Bakhtin, *Sobranie sochinenii* (Moscow: Russkie slovari, 1996), 5: 135. Noting the cruel atomization of Flaubertian naturalism, Bakhtin closes this dark sketch with the thought: "Everything gets in the way of a person getting a good look back at his own self" (137).
38. A[leksandr] Makhov, "'Muzyka' slova: Iz istorii odnoi fiktsii," *Voprosy literatury*, no. 5 (September–October 2005): 101–123, especially the subsection "Polifoniia," 119–121.
39. Simon Morrison, personal communication to the author, July 3, 2016. Morrison's examples of "Dostoevskian" polyphony in the modern period are Richard Strauss and Scriabin.
40. I thank Denis Zhernokleyev for this clarification. He continues: "Fulfilled time is never teleological in a purely linear sense but only in the apocalyptic sense, where it is dramatically intensified, not merely sped up along a linear progression. In Dostoevsky's apocalyptic imagination, this is Christian time" (personal communication to the author, July 8, 2016).
41. Fyodor Dostoevsky, *Crime and Punishment*, trans. Oliver Ready (New York: Penguin Classics, 2014), 200.
42. Dostoevsky, *Crime and Punishment*, trans. Ready, 516. On the oral/audible dimensions of the novel as a complement to sacred space (the iconic ladders of Petersburg and Sonia as Orthodox saint), see Janet G. Tucker, *Profane Challenge and Orthodox Response in Dostoevsky's* Crime and Punishment (Amsterdam: Rodopi, 2008), esp. 40–42 and 98–116.
43. For a masterful discussion, see Randall A. Poole, "The Apophatic Bakhtin," in *Bakhtin and Religion: A Feeling for Faith*, ed. Susan M. Felch and Paul J. Contino (Evanston, IL: Northwestern University Press, 2001), 151–175. Poole later glossed his essay: "Bakhtin was committed to the ideal of truth ("unity of a higher order"), and thoughtful open-ended process was the way to it. The most truthful process or dynamic is polyphony . . . Truthful process is one of

spiritual movement, and while spiritual it is also sensual (nothing arid or disembodied here)" (personal communication to the author, July 14, 2016).

44. "Bakhtin Forum, The Dark and Radiant Bakhtin. Wartime Notes," trans. and ed. Irina Denischenko and Alexander Spektor, *Slavic and East European Journal* 61, no. 2 (Summer 2017): 188–310. The forum provides the original Russian with English translations of three fragments: "Rhetoric, to the extent that it lies . . ." (1943), "A Person at the Mirror," and "On Questions of Self-Consciousness and Self-Evaluation," followed by interpretive essays by the two editors, Irina Sandomirskaia, and an afterword by Caryl Emerson.
45. Denischenko and Spektor, "Bakhtin Forum," 207.

BIBLIOGRAPHY

Apollonio, Carol. *Dostoevsky's Secrets: Reading Against the Grain.* Evanston, IL: Northwestern University Press, 2009.

Aristotle. *Nicomachean Ethics.* Trans. Roger Crisp. New York: Cambridge University Press, 2000.

Austin, J. L. *How to Do Things with Words,* 2nd ed. Ed. J. O. Urmson and Marina Sbisa. Cambridge, MA: Harvard University Press, 1962.

Austin, J. L. "Performative Utterances." In *Philosophical Papers,* 2nd ed., 233–252. Oxford: Oxford University Press, 1970.

Bakhtin, M. M. *Besedy s V. D. Duvakinym.* Ed. S. G. Bocharov et al. Moscow: Soglasie, 2002.

Bakhtin, M. M. *Mikhail Bakhtin. The Duvakin Interviews, 1973.* Ed. Slav N. Gratchev and Margarita Marinova. Trans. Margarita Marinova. Lewisburg, PA: Bucknell University Press, 2019.

Bakhtin, M. M. "<O Flobere>" [1944]. In *Sobranie sochinenii,* 5: 130–137. Moscow: Russkie slovari, 1996.

Bakhtin, M. M. *Problems of Dostoevsky's Poetics.* Trans. and ed. Caryl Emerson. Minneapolis: University of Minnesota Press, 1984.

Bakhtin, M. M. *Problemy poetiki Dostoevskogo.* In *Sobranie sochinenii,* 6: 5–300. Moscow: Russkie slovari, 2002.

Bakhtin, M. M. *Problemy tvorchestva Dostoevskogo* Leningrad: Priboi, 1929.

Bakhtin, M. M. "Toward a Methodology for the Human Sciences." In *Speech Genres and Other Late Essays.* Trans. Vern W. McGee. Austin: University of Texas Press, 1987.

Bakhtin, M. M. "Zapisi lektsii M. M. Bakhtina po istorii russkoi literatury. Zapisi R. M. Mirkinoi." In *Sobranie sochinenii*, 2: 266–288. Moscow: Russkie slovari, 2008.

Batishchev, G. S., "Dialogizm ili polifonizm? (Antitetiki v ideinom nasledii M. M. Bakhtina)." In *M. M. Bakhtin kak filosof*, ed. L. A. Gogotishvili and P. S. Gurevich, 123–141. Moscow: Nauka, 1992.

Belknap, Robert L. "Dostoevskii and Psychology." In *The Cambridge Companion to Dostoevskii*, ed. W. J. Leatherbarrow, 131–147. Cambridge: Cambridge University Press, 2004.

Belknap, Robert L. *Plots*. New York: Columbia University Press, 2016.

Berezkina, S. V. "'Zhivet zhe na kvartire u portnogo Kapernaumova . . .' (Iz kommentariia k 'Prestupleniiu i nakazaniiu' Dostoevskogo)." *Russkaia literatura*, no. 4 (2013): 169–179.

Bergmann, Frithjof. *On Being Free*. Notre Dame, IN: University of Notre Dame Press, 1977.

Berlin, Isaiah. "A Remarkable Decade." In *Russian Thinkers*, 114–210. Harmondsworth: Penguin, 1994.

Berman, Anna A. *Siblings in Tolstoy and Dostoevsky: The Path to Universal Brotherhood*. Evanston, IL: Northwestern University Press, 2015.

Blake, Elizabeth. "Sonja, Silent No More: A Response to the Woman Question in Dostoevsky's *Crime and Punishment*." *Slavic and East European Journal* 50 (2006): 252–271.

Blank, Ksana. *Dostoevsky's Dialectics and the Problem of Sin*. Evanston, IL: Northwestern University Press, 2010.

Bocharov, S. G. "Ob odnom razgovore i vokrug nego." *Novoe literaturno obozrenie* 2 (1993): 70–89.

Bocharov, Sergey. "Conversations with Bakhtin." *PMLA* 109, no. 5 (October 1994): 1009–1024.

Bogdanovich, T. A. *Liubov' liudei shestidesiatykh godov*. Leningrad: Academia, 1929.

Bratman, Michael. *Intentions, Plans, and Practical Reason*. Cambridge, MA: Harvard University Press, 1987.

Briggs, Katherine Jane. *How Dostoevsky Portrays Women in His Novels: A Feminist Analysis*. Lewiston, NY: Edwin Mellen Press, 2009.

Broackes, Justin, ed. *Iris Murdoch, Philosopher: A Collection of Essays*. Oxford: Oxford University Press, 2012.

Catteau, Jacques. *Dostoyevsky and the Process of Literary Creation*. Trans. Audrey Littlewood. Cambridge: Cambridge University Press, 1989.

Chernyshevsky, Nikolai. *Chto delat'? Iz rasskazov o novykh liudiakh*. Ed. T. I. Ornatskaia and S. A. Reiser. Leningrad: Nauka, 1975.

Chernyshevsky, Nikolai. *What Is to Be Done?* Trans. Michael R. Katz, annotated William G. Wagner. Ithaca, NY: Cornell University Press, 1989.

Clark, Katerina and Michael Holquist. *Mikhail Bakhtin*. Cambridge MA: Harvard University Press, 1984.

Coates, Ruth. *Christianity in Bakhtin. God and the Exiled Author*. Cambridge: Cambridge University Press, 1998.

Denischenko, Irina and Alexander Spektor, eds. "Bakhtin Forum, The Dark and Radiant Bakhtin." *Slavic and East European Journal* 61, no. 2 (Summer 2017), 188–310.

Dennett, Daniel. *Elbow Room: The Varieties of Free Will Worth Wanting*. Cambridge, MA: MIT Press, 1984.

De Quincey, Thomas. *On Murder*. Ed. Robert Morrison. Oxford: Oxford University Press, 2009.

Dostoevsky, Fyodor. *The Brothers Karamazov*. Trans. Richard Pevear and Larissa Volokhonsky. New York: Farrar, Straus and Giroux, 1990.

Dostoevsky, Fyodor. *Crime and Punishment*. Trans. Jessie Coulson. Oxford: Oxford University Press, 2008.

Dostoevsky, Fyodor. *Crime and Punishment*. Trans. Oliver Ready. New York: Penguin Classics, 2014.

Dostoevsky, Fyodor. "The Dream of a Ridiculous Man." In *A Gentle Creature and Other Stories*, Trans. Alan Myers. Oxford: Oxford University Press, 1995.

Dostoevsky, Fyodor. *Notes from Underground*. Trans. Richard Pevear and Larissa Volokhonsky. New York: Vintage, 1993.

Dostoevsky, Fyodor. *Polnoe sobranie sochinenii*. Ed. V. G. Bazanov et al. 30 vols. Leningrad: Nauka, 1972–1990.

Eliot, T. S. *Four Quartets*. New York: Harcourt Brace Jovanovich, 1943.

Emerson, Caryl. *The First Hundred Years of Mikhail Bakhtin*. Princeton, NJ: Princeton University Press, 1997.

Emerson, Caryl. "In Honor of Mikhail Gasparov's Quarter-Century of Not Liking Bakhtin: Pro and Contra." In *Poetics. Self. Place: Essays in Honor of Anna Lisa Crone*, ed. Catherine O'Neil, Nichole Boudreau, and Sarah Krive, 26–49. Bloomington, IN: Slavica, 2007.

Erdinast-Vulcan, Daphna. *Between Philosophy and Literature: Bakhtin and the Question of the Subject*. Stanford, CA: Stanford University Press, 2013.

Frank, Joseph. *Dostoevsky: The Stir of Liberation, 1860–1865*. Princeton, NJ: Princeton University Press, 1986.

Frank, Joseph. *Dostoevsky: A Writer in His Time*. Princeton, NJ: Princeton University Press, 2010.

Frank, Joseph. *Through the Russian Prism: Essays on Literature and Culture*. Princeton, NJ: Princeton University Press, 1990.

Frank, Joseph. "The World of Raskolnikov." In Feodor Dostoevsky, *Crime and Punishment*, Norton Critical Edition. Trans. Jessie Senior Coulson. Ed. George Gibian. New York: Norton, 1989, 567–578.

Frankfurt, Harry G. *The Importance of What We Care About: Philosophical Essays*. Cambridge: Cambridge University Press, 1988.

Freud, Sigmund. *Writings on Art and Literature*. Ed. Neil Hurtz. Stanford, CA: Stanford University Press, 1997.

Fryszman, Alex. "Kierkegaard and Dostoevsky Seen Through Bakhtin's Prism." *Kierkegaardiana* 18, ed. Joachin Garff et al. (Copenhagen: C. A. Reitzels Forlag, 1996): 100–125.

Furtak, Rick Anthony. *Wisdom in Love*. Notre Dame, IN: University of Notre Dame Press, 2005.

Fusso, Susanne. *Discovering Sexuality in Dostoevsky*. Evanston, IL: Northwestern University Press, 2006.

Fusso, Susanne. "Dostoevsky and Mikhail Katkov: Their Literary Partnership (*Crime and Punishment* and *The Devils*)." In *New Studies in Russian Literature and Culture: Essays in Honor of Stanley J. Rabinowitz*, 2 vols., ed. Catherine Ciepiela and Lazar Fleishman. Stanford Slavic Studies, part 1 [vol. 45], 35–69. Oakland, CA: Berkeley Slavic Specialties, 2014.

Fusso, Susanne. *Editing Turgenev, Dostoevsky, and Tolstoy: Mikhail Katkov and the Great Russian Novel*. DeKalb, IL: Northern Illinois University Press, 2017.

Gardner, Sebastian. "The Metaphysics of Human Freedom: From Kant's Transcendental Idealism to Schelling's *Freiheitsschrift*." *British Journal of the History of Philosophy* 25, no. 1 (2017): 133–156.

Ginzburg, Lydia. *On Psychological Prose* (1966). Trans. Judson Rosengrant. Princeton, NJ: Princeton University Press, 1991.

Grice, H. P. *Studies in the Way of Words*. Cambridge, MA: Harvard University Press, 1989.

Hagberg, Garry L. "Wittgenstein Underground." *Philosophy and Literature* 28, no. 2 (October 2004): 379–392.

Hagberg, Garry L. "Word and Object: Museums and the Matter of Meaning." *Philosophy*, suppl. vol.: *Philosophy and Museums* (2016): 261–293.

Hegel, G. W. F. *Phenomenology of Spirit*. Trans. A. V. Miller. New York: Oxford University Press, 1977.

Hirschkop, Ken. *Mikhail Bakhtin. An Aesthetic for Democracy*. Oxford: Oxford University Press, 1999.

Holquist, James [Michael]. "Disease as Dialectic in *Crime and Punishment*." In *Twentieth Century Interpretations of* Crime and Punishment, ed. Robert Louis Jackson, 109–118. Englewood Cliffs, NJ: Prentice-Hall, 1974.

Holquist, Michael. "Dialogism and Aesthetics." In *Late Soviet Culture from Perestroika to Novostroika*, ed. Thomas Lahusen with Gene Kuperman, 155–176. Durham, NC: Duke University Press, 1993.

Holquist, Michael. *Dostoevsky and the Novel*. Evanston, IL: Northwestern University Press, 1986.

Jackson, Robert Louis. "Bakhtin's Poetics of Dostoevsky and 'Dostoevsky's Christian Declaration of Faith.'" In *Close Encounters: Essays on Russian Literature*, 277–304. Boston: Academic Studies Press, 2013.

Jacobi, Johann Friedrich. *The Main Philosophical Writings and the Novel "Allwill."* Trans. and ed. George di Giovanni. Montreal: McGill-Queen's University Press, 1994.

Jones, Malcolm V. "Dostoevskii and Religion." In *The Cambridge Companion to Dostoevskii*, ed. W. J. Leatherbarrow, 148–174. Cambridge: Cambridge University Press, 2004.

Jones, Malcolm V. *Dostoyevsky after Bakhtin: Readings in Dostoyevsky's Fantastic Realism*. Cambridge: Cambridge University Press, 1990.

Kant, Immanuel. *Groundwork of the Metaphysics of Morals*. Trans. Mary Gregor. New York: Cambridge University Press, 1998.

Karyakin, Yurii. *Dostoevskii i kanun XXI veka*. Moscow: Sovetskii pisatel', 1989.

Khapaeva, Dina. *Nightmare: From Literary Experiments to Cultural Projects*. Leiden: Brill, 2013.

Kierkegaard, Søren. *Concluding Unscientific Postscript*. Trans. Alastair Hannay. New York: Cambridge University Press, 2009.

Kristeva, Julia. Preface to Mikhaïl Bakhtine, *La poétique de Dostoïevski*. Trans. Isabelle Kolitchev. Paris: Seuil, 1970.

Kundera, Milan. *Immortality*. Trans. Peter Kussi. New York: Harper Perennial Classics, 1999.

Locke, John. *An Essay Concerning Human Understanding*. New York: Oxford University Press, 1975.

Makhov, A. "'Muzyka' slova: Iz istorii odnoi fiktsii." *Voprosy literatury* 5 (September–October 2005): 101–123.

Maritain, Jacques. *The Dream of Descartes*. Trans. Mabelle Andison. New York: Philosophical Library, 1944.

Matual, David. "In Defense of the Epilogue of *Crime and Punishment*." In *Fyodor Dostoevsky's Crime and Punishment*, ed. Harold Bloom, 105–114. Philadelphia: Chelsea House, 2004.

Meerson, Olga. *Dostoevsky's Taboos*. Studies of the Harriman Institute. Dresden: Dresden University Press, 1998.

Mele, Alfred. *The Springs of Action*. New York: Oxford University Press, 1992.

Mikhailov, M. L. *Sochineniia*. 3 vols. Ed. B. P. Koz'min. Moscow: Khudozhestvennaia literatura, 1958.

Miller, Robin Feuer. *Dostoevsky's Unfinished Journey*. New Haven, CT: Yale University Press, 2007.

Moran, Richard. *Authority and Estrangement: An Essay on Self-Knowledge*. Cambridge, MA: Harvard University Press, 2001.

Morson, Gary Saul, *Narrative and Freedom: The Shadows of Time*. New Haven, CT: Yale University Press, 1994.

Morson, Gary Saul. "Strange Synchronies and Surplus Possibilities: Bakhtin on Time." *Slavic Review* 52, no. 3 (Fall 1993): 477–493.

Murav, Harriet. *Holy Foolishness: Dostoevsky's Novels & the Poetics of Cultural Critique*. Stanford, CA, Stanford University Press, 1992.

Murav, Harriet. "Reading Women in Dostoevsky." In *A Plot of Her Own*, ed. Sona Stephan Hoisington, 44–57. Evanston, IL: Northwestern University Press, 1995.

Murdoch, Iris. "The Sublime and the Good." *Chicago Review* 13, no. 3 (Autumn 1959): 42–55.

Murdoch, Iris. "Vision and Choice in Morality." *Proceedings of the Aristotelian Society*, suppl. vol. 30 (1956): 32–58.

Nietzsche, Friedrich. *The Antichrist*. Trans. Anthony M. Ludovici. Amherst, NY: Prometheus Books, 2000.

Nietzsche, Friedrich, *On the Genealogy of Morals*. Trans. Walter Kaufmann and R. J. Hollingdale. New York: Vintage Books, 1989.

Nietzsche, Friedrich. *The Will to Power*. Trans. Walter Kaufmann and R. J. Hollingdale. New York: Vintage Books, 1968.

Nikulin, Dmitri. *On Dialogue*. Lanham, MD: Lexington Books, 2006.

Noddings, Nel. *Caring: A Feminine Approach to Ethics and Moral Education*. Berkeley: University of California Press, 1984.

Nussbaum, Martha. *Upheavals of Thought: The Intelligence of Emotions*. Cambridge: Cambridge University Press, 2001.

O'Hear, Anthony. *The Element of Fire: Science, Art and the Human World*. London: Routledge, 1988.

Paperno, Irina. *Chernyshevsky and the Age of Realism: A Study in the Semiotics of Behavior*. Stanford, CA: Stanford University Press, 1988.

Plato. *Meno and Other Dialogues*. Trans. Robin Waterfield. Oxford: Oxford University Press, 2005.

Plato. *Phaedrus*. In *The Collected Dialogues of Plato*, 475–525. Ed. Edith Hamilton and Huntingdon Cairns. Trans. Huntingdon Cairns, Princeton, NJ: Princeton University Press, 1961.

Pomper, Phillip. *The Russian Revolutionary Intelligentsia*. New York: Thomas Y. Crowell, 1970.

Poole, Randall A. "The Apophatic Bakhtin." In *Bakhtin and Religion: A Feeling for Faith*, ed. Susan M. Felch and Paul J. Contino, 151–175. Evanston, IL: Northwestern University Press, 2001.

Pozefsky, Peter C. "Love, Science, and Politics in the Fiction of *Shestidesiatnitsy* N. P. Suslova and S. V. Kovalevskaia." *Russian Review* 58 (July 1999): 361–379.

Reginster, Bernard. *The Affirmation of Life: Nietzsche on Overcoming Nihilism*. Cambridge, MA: Harvard University Press, 2006.

Rhees, Rush. "Gratitude and Ingratitude for Existence." In *Rush Rhees on Religion and Philosophy*, ed. D. Z. Phillips, 159–165. Cambridge: Cambridge University Press, 1997.

Roberts, Robert C. *Emotions*. Cambridge: Cambridge University Press, 2003.

Roberts, Robert C. "What an Emotion Is: A Sketch." *Philosophical Review* 97 (1988): 183–209.

Saraskina, Liudmilla. *Vozliublennaia Dostoevskogo. Apollinariia Suslova: Biografiia v dokumentakh, pis'makh, materialakh*. Moscow: Soglasie, 1994.

Sartre, Jean-Paul. *Saint Genet: Actor & Martyr*. Trans. Bernard Frechtman. London: Heinemann, 1963.

Scanlan, James P. *Dostoevsky the Thinker*. Ithaca, NY: Cornell University Press, 2002.

Schelling, Friedrich Wilhelm Joseph. *Philosophical Investigations into the Essence of Human Freedom*. Trans. and ed. Jeff Love and Johannes Schmidt. Albany, NY: SUNY Press, 2006.

Schelling, Friedrich Wilhelm Joseph. *System der gesammten Philosophie*, In *Sämmtliche Werke*. Ed. Karl Friedrich August Schelling, vol. 6. Stuttgart: Cotta, 1856–1861.

Schopenhauer, Arthur. *The World as Will and Representation*, vol. 2. Trans. E. F. J. Payne. New York: Dover, 1966.

Seifrid, Thomas. *The Word Made Self: Russian Writings on Language, 1860–1930*. Ithaca, NY: Cornell University Press, 2005.

Seneca. *Ad Lucilium Epistulae Morales*. 2 vols. Ed. L. D. Reynolds. New York: Oxford University Press, 1965.

Seneca. *Dialogi*. Ed. L. D. Reynolds. New York: Oxford University Press, 1977.

Stepanyan, Karen. *Shekspir, Bakhtin i Dostoevskii. Geroi i avtory v bol'shom vremeni* Moscow: Yazyki slavyanskoi kul'tury, 2016.

Stites, Richard. *The Women's Liberation Movement in Russia: Feminism, Nihilism, and Bolshevism 1860–1930*. Princeton, NJ: Princeton University Press, 1978.

Stone, Jonathan. "Polyphony and the Atomic Age: Bakhtin's Assimilation of an Einsteinian Universe." *PMLA* 123, no. 2 (2008): 405–421.

Straus, Nina Pelikan. *Dostoevsky and the Woman Question: Rereadings at the End of a Century*. New York: St. Martin's Press, 1994.

Strawson, P. F. *Freedom and Resentment and Other Essays*. New York: Routledge, 2008.

Taylor, Charles. *Hegel*. New York: Cambridge University Press, 1975.

Taylor, Charles. "Hegel and the Philosophy of Action." In *Hegel's Philosophy of Action*, ed. L. S. Stepelevich and D. Lamb, 1–18. Atlantic Highlands, NJ: Humanities Press, 1983.

Taylor, Charles. "What Is Human Agency?" In *Human Agency and Language*, 15–44. New York: Cambridge University Press, 1985.

Tikhomirov, Boris. *"Lazar'! griadi von": Roman F. M. Dostoevskogo 'Prestuplenie i nakazanie' v sovremennom prochtenii. Kniga-kommentarii*. St. Petersburg: Serebrianyi vek, 2005.

Tishkin, G. A. *Zhenskii vopros v Rossii, 50-60-e gody XIX v.* Leningrad: Leningradskii universitet, 1984.

Tolstoy, Leo. "Why Do Men Stupefy Themselves?" (1889). In *Recollections & Essays*, trans. with an introduction Aylmer Maude, 67–89. London: Oxford University Press, 1937.

Tucker, Janet. *Profane Challenge and Orthodox Response in Dostoevsky's* Crime and Punishment. Amsterdam: Rodopi, 2008.

Tucker, Janet. "The Religious Symbolism of Clothing in Dostoevsky's *Crime and Punishment*." *Slavic and East European Journal* 44, no. 2 (2000): 253–265.

Ward, Bruce. *Dostoyevsky's Critique of the West: The Quest for the Earthly Paradise*. Ontario: Wilfrid Laurier, 1986.

Watson, Gary. *Agency and Answerability: Selected Essays*. New York: Oxford University Press, 2008.

Williams, Rowan. *Dostoevsky: Language, Faith, and Fiction*. Waco, TX: Baylor University Press, 2011.

Wittgenstein, Ludwig. *Philosophical Investigations*, 4th ed. Ed. P. M. S. Hacker and Joachim Schulte. Trans. G. E. M. Anscombe, P. M. S. Hacker, and Joachim Schulte. Malden, MA: Wiley-Blackwell, 2009.

Wollheim, Richard. "Art, Interpretation, and Perception." In *The Mind and Its Depths*, 132–143. Cambridge, MA: Harvard University Press, 1993.

Wollheim, Richard. *On the Emotions*. New Haven, CT: Yale University Press, 1999.

Wyman, Alina. *The Gift of Active Empathy: Scheler, Bakhtin, and Dostoevsky*. Evanston, IL: Northwestern University Press, 2016.

INDEX